WRITER'S ACTIVITY BOOK
WITH EXTRA PRACTICE

·5·
WORLD
OF
LANGUAGE

SILVER BURDETT & GINN

MORRISTOWN, NJ • NEEDHAM, MA
Atlanta, GA • Cincinnati, OH • Dallas, TX • Menlo Park, CA • Deerfield, IL

CONTENTS

INTRODUCTORY UNIT

UNIT 1

UNIT 2

UNIT 3

UNIT 4

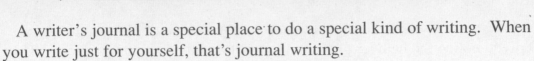

A WRITER'S JOURNAL

A writer's journal is a special place to do a special kind of writing. When you write just for yourself, that's journal writing.

What to Put in a Journal

You can use your journal as a place to
◇ express your thoughts and feelings.
◇ record experiences and events.
◇ save writing ideas that you can draw on later.
◇ practice and experiment with different kinds of writing, such as a story beginning or a conversation.
◇ write your opinions of a book or a movie.
◇ describe sensory observations.
◇ record new impressions of people or places.
◇ think through a difficult problem.
◇ write about something new you learned in math or science.

A Journal Is . . .

Here are some ways to think about what a journal is for:

A journal is an attic. In it you can store thoughts and observations you might use someday.

A journal is a rehearsal stage. It's a place to try out ideas you aren't ready to show an audience.

A journal is a costume. Try it on when you want to see what it feels like to be someone or something else.

A journal is a fountain. Dip into it when you need some refreshment for writing ideas.

How to Make a Journal and a Writing Folder

Did you notice the heavier pages in the front and the back of this book? They are special materials for you. Use the set from the front to make a journal. Use the set from the back to make a writing folder for pages you want to keep from this book.

To make your journal, first remove the special pages at the front of the book. They are punched to hold three-hole looseleaf paper. Place some blank looseleaf paper between the journal covers. Line up the holes of the paper with the holes of the covers. Fasten the covers and inside pages together with ribbon, yarn, or brass fasteners. You can add pages as you need them.

You can make a writing folder the same way you made your journal. Use the two heavy pages at the back of this book for covers. For your writing folder, you will be inserting pages from this activity book.

When you see **SAVE** at the bottom of a page in this book, save that page in your writing folder.

Write your name on the covers of your journal and writing folder and decorate the covers. Have fun!

INTEREST INVENTORY

You may sometimes need help thinking up things to write about. This interest inventory can help you. It can help you discover things you are interested in or would like to know more about. Fill in the interest inventory. After you complete the interest inventory, remove it and place it in your writing folder. Look at it when you need writing ideas.

You can redo the inventory as your interests change.

Name your favorite

game _____

school subject _____

sport to play _____

sport to watch _____

food _____

place to visit _____

thing to do _____

television show _____

animal _____

kind of book _____

hobby _____

singer _____

athlete _____

season _____

holiday _____

Circle everything you'd like to know more about.

puppets	monsters	dolphins
birds	the Solar System	clouds
plants	park rangers	hiking
insects	earthquakes	Eskimos
gymnastics	bats	pioneers
computers	the Olympics	airplanes

INTEREST INVENTORY

Fill in the blanks with wishes.

I wish I could . . .

visit this place _____

play this instrument _____

play this sport _____

meet this person _____

build this thing _____

become an expert on this _____

have this animal for a pet _____

spend more time doing this _____

do this on a vacation _____

explore this place _____

have this job _____

For each subject, use a check (✔) to indicate your level of interest.

	No Interest	Some Interest	Much Interest
history	_____	_____	_____
sports	_____	_____	_____
nature	_____	_____	_____
music	_____	_____	_____
outer space	_____	_____	_____
animals	_____	_____	_____
underwater life	_____	_____	_____
art	_____	_____	_____
video games	_____	_____	_____
inventions	_____	_____	_____
science experiments	_____	_____	_____
movies	_____	_____	_____

◆ WRITING FORMS ◆

Have you ever written an article about how to play your favorite game? Have you ever written a letter to a friend at camp? If so, you are a writer! Articles and friendly letters are two forms of writing.

Here are many more writing forms. Put a check next to the forms you have written and the ones you want to try.

Save this list in your writing folder. You can look at it when you need ideas for writing. Be sure to keep your "Have Written" list up to date.

	Have Written	**Want to Try**
adventure story	_____	_____
advertisement	_____	_____
book review	_____	_____
bulletin	_____	_____
business letter	_____	_____
caption for a picture	_____	_____
character sketch	_____	_____
conversation	_____	_____
description	_____	_____
directions	_____	_____
feature story	_____	_____
folktale	_____	_____
haiku	_____	_____
how-to article	_____	_____
interview	_____	_____
journal entry	_____	_____
legend	_____	_____
limerick	_____	_____
mystery story	_____	_____
news release	_____	_____
opinion poll	_____	_____

WRITING FORMS

	Have Written	Want to Try
personal narrative	_____	_____
persuasive letter	_____	_____
play	_____	_____
poem	_____	_____
record review	_____	_____
research report	_____	_____
short story	_____	_____
speech	_____	_____
sports column	_____	_____
tall tale	_____	_____
tongue twister	_____	_____
want ad	_____	_____

Add other forms you have written or would like to try.

_____	_____	_____
_____	_____	_____

A writer who uses any of the forms in the list has at least one reason, and often more, for writing. Below are some reasons why writers write. For each reason, there is an example of a form that a writer might use.

Reason for Writing	Writing Form
Narrating	personal narrative
Informing	how-to article
Imagining	tall tale
Persuading	persuasive letter
Describing	character sketch
Researching	research report
Creating	poem
Classifying	article that compares

BOOK LOG

You can use the following pages to record information about each book you read. Keep the book log in your writing folder, and review it from time to time. Your teacher can give you additional pages if you need them. A book log can help you

◇ discover what kinds of books you enjoy.
◇ record information for friends who ask for book recommendations.
◇ learn about good writing from the books you read.

Title _____

Author _____

Kind of Book _____

Personal Rating (Circle 1 to 4 stars.) ★   ★★   ★★★   ★★★★

Reading as a Writer

Here's something the book made me think about: _____
_____
_____

I especially liked the way the author _____
_____
_____

Some words or phrases I liked in the book are: _____
_____
_____

The part on page ____ was interesting because _____
_____
_____

I'd like to tell _____ about this book.

He/She would like it because _____
_____

◆ BOOK LOG ◆

You can use the following pages to record information about each book you read. Keep the book log in your writing folder, and review it from time to time. Your teacher can give you additional pages if you need them. A book log can help you

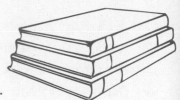

◇ discover what kinds of books you enjoy.
◇ record information for friends who ask for book recommendations.
◇ learn about good writing from the books you read.

Title _____

Author _____

Kind of Book _____

Personal Rating (Circle 1 to 4 stars.) ★   ★★   ★★★   ★★★★

Reading as a Writer

Here's something the book made me think about: _____
_____
_____

I especially liked the way the author _____
_____
_____

Some words or phrases I liked in the book are: _____
_____
_____

The part on page ____ was interesting because _____
_____
_____

I'd like to tell _____ about this book.

He/She would like it because _____
_____

BOOK LOG

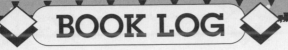

You can use the following pages to record information about each book you read. Keep the book log in your writing folder, and review it from time to time. Your teacher can give you additional pages if you need them. A book log can help you

◇ discover what kinds of books you enjoy.
◇ record information for friends who ask for book recommendations.
◇ learn about good writing from the books you read.

Title _____

Author _____

Kind of Book _____

Personal Rating (Circle 1 to 4 stars.) ★ ★★ ★★★ ★★★★

Reading as a Writer

Here's something the book made me think about: _____
_____
_____

I especially liked the way the author _____
_____
_____

Some words or phrases I liked in the book are: _____
_____
_____

The part on page ____ was interesting because _____
_____
_____

I'd like to tell _____ about this book.

He/She would like it because _____
_____

BOOK LOG

You can use the following pages to record information about each book you read. Keep the book log in your writing folder, and review it from time to time. Your teacher can give you additional pages if you need them. A book log can help you

◇ discover what kinds of books you enjoy.
◇ record information for friends who ask for book recommendations.
◇ learn about good writing from the books you read.

Title _____

Author _____

Kind of Book _____

Personal Rating (Circle 1 to 4 stars.) ★   ★★   ★★★   ★★★★

Reading as a Writer

Here's something the book made me think about: _____
_____
_____

I especially liked the way the author _____
_____
_____

Some words or phrases I liked in the book are: _____
_____
_____

The part on page ____ was interesting because _____
_____
_____

I'd like to tell _____ about this book.

He/She would like it because _____
_____

WRITER'S PROFILE

On this sheet you will complete your writer's profile. The writer's profile will help you discover what kind of writer you are and what usually works best for you as a writer. Remember that everyone writes differently. Your writer's profile will probably be very different from classmates' profiles.

Put a check in the box that best describes you or your writing style. Then keep this sheet in your writing folder so you can refer to it from time to time before you begin writing.

	Sometimes	Always	Never
1. Before I write, I like to talk about my ideas with a friend.	☐	☐	☐
2. I like to list my ideas before I write my first draft.	☐	☐	☐
3. I like to know just what I'm going to say before I begin.	☐	☐	☐
4. I write out my piece quickly from start to finish. Then I make changes.	☐	☐	☐
5. My final version might be very different from my first version.	☐	☐	☐
6. It helps to have readers respond to my writing before I do the final version.	☐	☐	☐
7. I like to inform people through my writing.	☐	☐	☐
8. I enjoy expressing my thoughts and feelings in my writing.	☐	☐	☐
9. I like to entertain others through my writing.	☐	☐	☐
10. I like to know my readers' reactions.	☐	☐	☐

I like to write

_____ quickly   _____ slowly
_____ with noise around   _____ in a quiet place
_____ anytime   _____ at a particular time
_____ anyplace   _____ in a special place
_____ with a pencil or a pen _____ on a word processor

WRITER'S PROFILE

Sometimes you may hear or read language that really interests you. You can use this sheet to list the language you come across. You may want to use some of the language later in your own writing. Use extra pages as your collection grows.

Words and Phrases

_____

_____

_____

_____

_____

_____

_____

_____

_____

_____

_____

Sayings and Expressions

_____

_____

_____

_____

_____

_____

_____

_____

_____

_____

Name_____

Writing Sentences

A. Max sent this postcard to Jamie while he was on vacation. Jamie
was happy to get the postcard from his friend, but he could not
understand it all. Max did not always use complete sentences. Add
words to make complete sentences. Correct any other errors you
find also so that Jamie can understand Max's postcard. Use the
revising and proofreading marks on this page. Some corrections
have been done for you.

1·29.

U.S. POSTAGE

Dear jamie,

This is a ≡great

∧ (grate) vacation. An exciting day yesterday.

Out on a ship. An enormous whale and

her calf. Leaped out of the water. About

fifty feet long. The captain Took lots of

fotos. Hope they tern out so you can see

the whales. At the beech today. Riding the

waves. One wave. Back home next Wenesday.

See you then.

Jamie Wilson

21 Sycamore Road

Greensburg, PA

15601

                    Your freind,

                    Max

B. Pretend you are Max's friend. You are on vacation with your family. Send a postcard to Max. Tell him where you are, what you are doing, and what exciting things you are seeing. You want to make sure Max can understand what you write. Are your sentences complete? Use revising and proofreading marks to show your changes.

_____

_____

_____

_____

_____

_____

_____

Max Anderson
14 Maple Lane
Greensburg, PA
15601

 C. Max sent a postcard to his teacher, but some of his sentences are incomplete. Add words to make complete sentences. The first letters of the complete sentences tell where Max was on his vacation. Write these letters on the lines below to find out the name of the place.

Arrived last night. Friends from home have the next trailer. Fished together. Early in the morning the fish. Lois caught the biggest fish. Others got away. All the kids. Row boats are for rent at the dock. Heavy and hard to row. It's best to take turns. Favorite food from the menu. Dinner at the pool is fun. The boats on the lake. After Labor Day we go home.

___ ___ ___ ___ ___ ___ ___

Four Kinds of Sentences

A.

1-36. Yoko and Mike are actors. They are trying to rehearse their parts for a camping scene. Unfortunately, they do not know where the sentences begin or end. Help Yoko and Mike by adding the capital letters and punctuation marks the script writer forgot. Correct any other errors you find also. Use the revising and proofreading marks on this page.

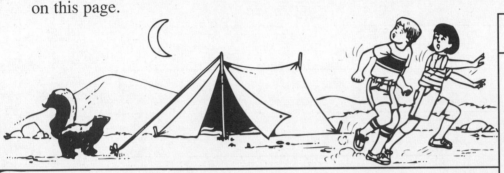

Yoko: did you hear that noise it sounded lik

footsteps (Yoko stiks her head out of the sleeping bag.)

Mike: go back to sleep it's just the wind here in the rockies.

Yoko: what if it's not the wind what if it's a bare or a mountain lion

it doesn't sound like the wind to me

Mike: don't be scared. give me the flashlight I'll investigate

(Yoko hands Mike the flashlight. Mike goes outside the tent.)

Yoko: there's the noise again it is coming from behind that rock

Mike: hey, look at this what a funy-looking cat it is

Yoko: that's not a cat that's a skunk let's get out of here fast

(Both Yoko and Mike run offstage.)

Name_____

 B. Pretend you are a script writer. Here is the situation. The doorbell
rings. Yoko and Mike go to the front door. At the door they find a
gift-wrapped box about the size of a trunk. Write a script that tells
what Yoko and Mike say as they stare at the box and then open it.
Include the four kinds of sentences in your script. Use revising and
proofreading marks to show any changes you make.

Yoko: _____

Mike: _____

Yoko: _____

Mike: _____

Yoko: _____

Mike: _____

 C. Here is the message that was attached to the box. Can you figure
it out? Write the message above the clues. Insert the correct
punctuation and capital letters.

_____

_____

_____

_____

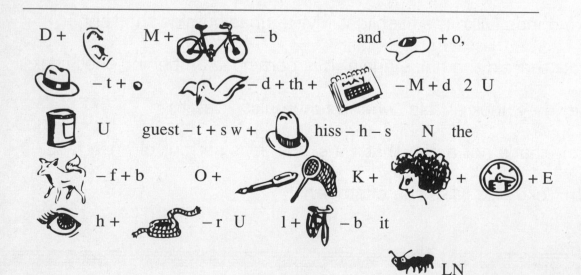

Complete Subjects and Predicates

A. Kids' Korner store is having a back-to-school sale. Alicia wrote
a sale notice for the newspaper. She was in such a hurry that she
1-22. left out some important information. Help Alicia. Add subjects or
predicates to make complete sentences. Correct any other errors you
find also. Use the revising and proofreading marks on this page.

Revising Marks	
cross out	_____
add	∧
move	↶

Proofreading Marks	
capital letter	≡
small letter	/
indent paragraph	¶
check spelling	⬭

Save   Save   Save!

Kid's Korner

The annual back-to-School sale.

What bargains. Our everyday low prices.

Hundreds of items.

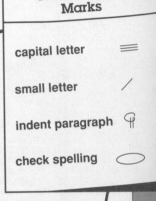

Will continu threw september. All

warm fall clothes.

Shoes 25% less. Will receive a gift.

Will bee a winner?

Our prices are low. Our styles the latest.

Open from 9:00 A.M. too 9:00 P.M.

Monday two Friday.

On Saturdays until 5:30 P.M.

B. Pretend you are having a garage sale. Write a sale notice about the things you will sell. Each sentence must have a subject and a predicate. Check to see that your sentences are complete. Use revising and proofreading marks to show any changes you make.

Garage Sale Today!

_____

_____

_____

_____

_____

_____

_____

_____

_____

_____

C.

23-32. In five minutes write as many sentences as possible using the subject and predicate parts listed below. All the sentence parts in Column A are subjects but not all of the sentence parts in Column B are predicates. Compare your answers with a friend. How many different sentences did you make?

Column A

Many styles of sweaters

Kids' Korner prices

Famous brands of jeans

Our ski jackets

Long-sleeved cotton shirts

Column B

are unbeatable

with patch pockets

have matching tops

come in assorted colors

for boys and girls

18

Simple Subjects

A. Wendy is a reporter. She covered a story about Frank and John Shore. The two brothers spotted and reported a fire in an apartment house. Tomorrow the boys are being honored at City Hall. As Wendy reread her article about the incident, she noticed she had left out some simple subjects. Help Wendy make changes and correct any errors in the article, using the revising and proofreading marks on this page.

1-22.

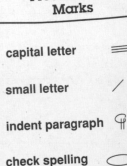

Revising Marks	
cross out	_____
add	∧
move	↪

Proofreading Marks	
capital letter	≡
small letter	/
indent paragraph	¶
check spelling	⬯

The Gazette

Two young smelled smoke on their way to school last week. frank and John Shore noticed flames coming from a building on Maple Street. Immediately alerted the fire department. Then the ran back to ring the doorbells and nock on the windows and doors. Responded within minits and put out the fire. Not one was hurt because of the brothers' quick acshuns.

Tomorrow the will honer the brothers for their good deed. The will receive a special award from the mayor. The will be held in the auditorium at City Hall. Begins at noon. The is invited to attend. Afterward the will meet with the residents of the building. then their whole from Hilltop School will tour the fire station with them.

B. Pretend you are a reporter. Write your own news story about an event that has taken place in your family, neighborhood, or school. Think about these questions as you write your article: Who? What? Where? When? Why? How? Remember to include a simple subject in each of your sentences. Use revising and proofreading marks to show any changes.

_____

_____

_____

_____

_____

_____

 C. Unscramble these sentences to learn what the work of the firefighter is. Underline the simple subject for each. Be sure to use capital letters and end the sentence with the correct punctuation mark.

23. the department of the community members whole the serve fire

_____

24. very is important it

_____

25. firefighter has a job the dangerous

_____

26. these risk brave people their lives

_____

27. help they accident and victims too disaster

_____

28. special in receive aid first firefighters training

_____

29. fire talk they prevention children to about school

_____

30. hard engines their good of take workers these care

_____

Simple Predicates

A. Sergio writes ads for new food products. He wrote this ad for
1-21. Crunchy Oats, the newest cereal on the market. Sergio was
interrupted before he could finish checking over his ad. Some
simple predicates are missing. Show the changes you would make
to improve the ad. Correct any other errors you find also. Use the
revising and proofreading marks on this page.

Kids of all ages Crunchy Oats in the morning.

Americans crunchy oats first. One taste your

sleepy taste buds. One portion you all the

important vitamins and minerals.

I more good news The top of your Crunchy

Oats box very valuable to. Knew customers a gift.

Each box top you for baseball cards. just male your

tops to Crunchy Oats, Box 32, Akron, ohio 07538.

The best news last. The makers of this great cereal

a surprise right in the box. Can you guess the

surprise? Maybe this hint you. You a pencil to

use the surprise.

Name_____

 B. Now you can create your own ad. Think about your favorite cereal or breakfast food. What would you say to persuade someone to try it for the first time? Explain how it tastes and why it is good for you. Remember to include precise action words as simple predicates in your sentences. Use the revising and proofreading marks to show any changes you want to make.

_____

_____

_____

_____

_____

_____

_____

_____

 C. Read the sentences about cereal. How quickly can you find the correct simple predicate hidden in each sentence? Underline the word with the hidden predicate. Write the hidden predicate above. Time yourself. Then compare your answers with those of a classmate.

22. Americans breathe over twenty billion bowls of cereal a year.

23. Most ready-to-eat cereals consistent of wheat and oats.

24. People usually deserved cereal with milk or cream.

25. Companies refuse several different ways to make cereal.

26. They grinder and troll the grains into flakes.

27. Sometimes they sadden sugar.

28. Hot cereals welcome in three forms: regular, quick cooking, and instant.

29. Regular hot cereal mistakes about fifteen minutes to cook.

30. Most cereals shaved vitamins and minerals.

Subjects in Imperative Sentences

A. Lani moved to a town thirty miles away. Her friend Heather is coming to visit next weekend. Lani sent Heather directions and a

1-24. map to show the way to her new house. Lani did not need to use the subject you in each imperative sentence. Help her improve the directions by taking out you in the imperative sentences and correcting any other errors you find. Use the revising and proofreading marks on this page.

Revising Marks	
cross out	_____
add	∧
move	↻

Proofreading Marks	
capital letter	≡
small letter	/
indent paragraph	¶
check spelling	⬭

You take Route 20 west for twenty-five mils. You

turn left at Mountain Avenue. You continue to the end

of the rode where you have to turn either left or right

You go right. That's Route 120. You follow the road

until you get to the top of the hill. Then you make a

left turn at the gas stashun onto West Point Drive. At

the next corner you make a right tern onto Newport

Road. You keep going about ate hundred feet. Our

house is the forth on the left. There is a long driveway.

You drive all the weigh back to the barn. You will

probably find me there with the new kittens.

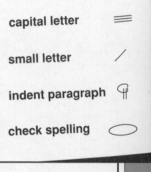

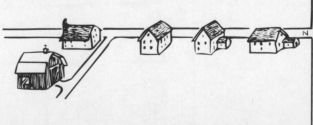

Name_____

B. How do you tie your shoelaces? How do you fold a sheet of paper to make an airplane? How do you make a sandwich? Write a set of directions to tell how to do something. After you finish writing, check to make sure the directions are clear. Are the imperative sentences written correctly? Use revising and proofreading marks to show any changes.

_____

_____

_____

_____

_____

_____

_____

C. Ann has directions to the post office, but some of the important words are missing. Use the map to help you write sentences that tell Ann how to get to the post office. Use imperative sentences.

25. Go east on Park Street.

26. Poplar Place

27. Linden Road

28. Locust Street

29. at Woodland Road

30. on Elm Street

31. Maple Way

32. middle of the block.

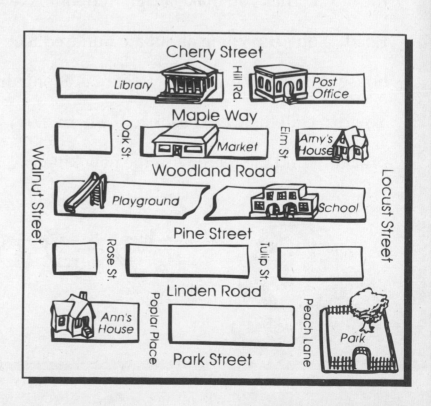

Unit 1, Lesson 6 • Use after page 15.

Name_____

An Observation Chart

You can use these forms to make observation charts for the
Critical Thinking lesson on pages 22–23.

A.

B.

Name_____

An Observation Chart

You can use this form to make an observation chart for the
Writing to Learn activity on page 29.

You can use this form to make an observation chart for the
Writing to Learn activity on page 46.

Name_____

Narrating

You have read a selection from <u>The Midnight Fox</u> by Betsy Byars. Now imagine that you are visiting Aunt Millie's farm. You are sitting on the rock next to the stream pictured below. When you look up, you see something on the other side of the stream that startles you. On the back of this page, tell what you see and what happens.

Writing Tips

◇ Use complete sentences to express your ideas. Use capital letters and punctuation carefully.

◇ Make character, setting, and plot work together in your story.

◇ **Focus:** Remember to use the words <u>I</u> and <u>me</u> to tell your story.

◇ You may wish to reread <u>The Midnight Fox</u> before you begin. Choose one thing that you like about the writer's way of writing, and try to use it in your own narrative.

Name_____

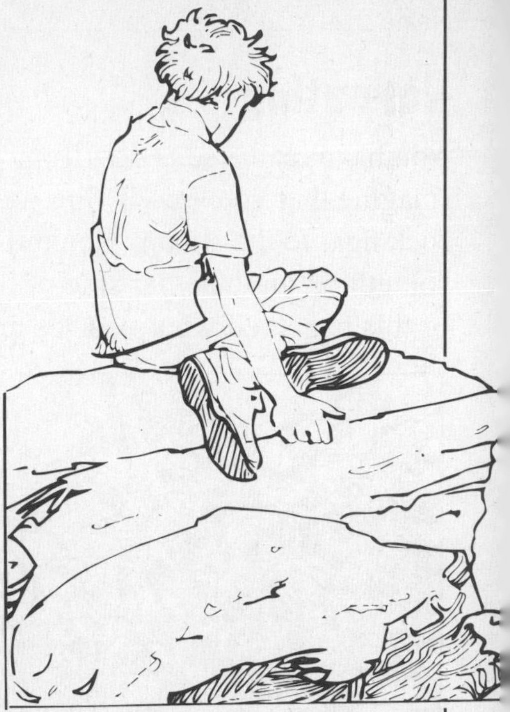

_____

_____

_____

_____

_____

_____

_____

_____

_____

_____

_____

_____

_____

_____

_____

_____

_____

_____

_____

Strategy: A Conversation

Use this page to take notes if you choose a conversation
as a prewriting strategy for your personal narrative.

_____
_____
_____
_____
_____
_____
_____
_____
_____
_____
_____
_____
_____
_____
_____
_____
_____
_____
_____
_____
_____

Strategy: An Observation Chart

Use this page if you choose an observation chart as a prewriting
strategy for your personal narrative.

<table>
<tr><td colspan="2"></td></tr>
<tr><td></td><td></td></tr>
<tr><td></td><td></td></tr>
<tr><td></td><td></td></tr>
</table>

| cross ——— | add ∧ | move ↝ |
| out | | |

A Personal Narrative

Practice your revising on the personal narrative below. Use the revising
tips as a guide. Don't copy the story. Use the revising marks to cross out,
add, or move words and sentences.

Revising Tips

Check to see that the writer has

◇   told about a personal experience.
◇   made the reader understand what has happened and how the writer feels.
◇   used the first person point of view.
◇   used interrogative, imperative, and exclamatory sentences for variety.
◇   used precise words for words such as <u>play</u> and <u>happened</u>.
◇   used quotations to show the exact words of a speaker.

    I have been playing the drums since the third grade. I never thought that
I would play in front of a big group of people though. I played in front of
my whole school

    It all started when three friends wanted me to enter a talent show with
them. Each of us plays a different instrument. We practiced together for
weeks. We were beginning to sound pretty good. Jerry plays the guitar,
Luis plays the bass, and Jolan sings.

    The day of the talent show arrived. Jolan was very nervous. Then a
strange thing happened. We started playing the first song, and Jolan did not
sing. He just stood there. A microphone was next to my drums, so I started
singing. I sang the whole song while playing the drums. I forgot about
being scared. Afterwards I asked Jolan what happened. He said he couldn't
remember the words to the song and thanked me for taking over.

    Now Jolan wants to play drums. He wants me to be the singer. I will
have to think about this!

≡	/	⊓	⬭
capital letter	**small letter**	**indent paragraph**	**check spelling**

A Personal Narrative

Practice your proofreading on the personal narrative below. Use the proofreading tips as a guide. Don't copy the story. Use the proofreading marks to make corrections.

Proofreading Tips

Check to see that the writer has

◇ spelled words correctly.

◇ indented paragraphs.

◇ used capital letters correctly.

◇ used correct marks at the end of sentences.

Yesterday was field day at school. The whole school Spent the day outdoors. We even ate lunch outside on picnic tables. It really was a lot of Fun. My favorite activities were relay racing, climing the rope, and jumping on the trampoline. Have you ever jumped on a trampoline A funny thing happened to me yesterday when I jumped on the trampoline during field day. Our teacher told us to jump very high and then drop to our knees. I started jumping until i was very high in the air. I was jumping so high that my stumach felt funny on the way down. At last I was ready to drop to my knees. When I dropped to my knees, I held my nose. Everyone laffed loudly.

"why did you hold your nose?" my friend Julie asked.

"The reason I held my nose is because when I jump into a pool, I always hold my nose."

This just made them laugh harder. now I have a new nickname. Everyone calls me "the Swimmer."

Writing a Personal Narrative

Use this form as you do the Writing Process lesson beginning on page 38. Put a check next to each item you can answer yes to.

Revising

☐ **Purpose:** Did I write about a personal experience I had with an animal?

☐ **Audience:** Will my classmates understand what happened and how I felt?

☐ **Focus:** Did I use first-person point of view?

☐ **Grammar Check:** Have I used some interrogative, imperative, or exclamatory sentences to make my story more interesting?

☐ **Word Choice:** Have I used precise words?

☐ **Writing♦Quotations:** Have I used quotation marks to show the exact words of a speaker?

Proofreading

☐ Did I spell words correctly?

☐ Did I indent paragraphs?

☐ Did I use capital letters correctly?

☐ Did I use correct marks at the end of sentences?

☐ Did I use my best handwriting?

Publishing

☐ Have I shared my writing with readers or listeners?

☐ Has my audience shared reactions with me?

☐ Have I thought about what I especially liked in this piece of writing?

☐ Have I thought about what I would like to work on the next time?

Use the space on the other side to tell what you liked about your writing and to make notes of your plans for improvement.

Name _____

What I liked about my writing: _____

_____

_____

_____

_____

_____

_____

_____

_____

My plans for improvement: _____

_____

_____

_____

_____

_____

_____

_____

_____

_____

_____

_____

Reader's Name_____

Writer's Name_____

Writing a Personal Narrative

Use the questions below and on the other side of this page to help you review a classmate's personal narrative. Then give this form to the writer to read and save. Your comments can help the classmate improve the personal narrative.

A First Reaction

Here is what I thought in general about your personal narrative:

_____

_____

_____

_____

_____

_____

A Second Reaction

Now I have looked at your personal narrative more closely. I have more specific comments about it.

Here is something you have done well as a writer:

_____

_____

Here is an area that might be improved:

_____

_____

Here is an idea for improvement:

_____

_____

Writing a Personal Narrative

Check Yes or No for each item. If you check No, explain or give a suggestion for improvement.

Yes No   *Revising*

☐ ☐ **Purpose:** Did the writer tell about a personal experience with an animal?

_____

☐ ☐ **Audience:** Did I understand what happened and how the writer felt?

_____

☐ ☐ **Focus:** Did the writer use first-person point of view?

_____

☐ ☐ **Grammar Check:** Are there some interrogative, imperative, or exclamatory sentences to make the story more interesting?

_____

☐ ☐ **Word Choice:** Has the writer used precise words?

_____

☐ ☐ **Writing♦Quotations:** Has the writer used quotation marks to show the exact words of a speaker?

_____

Yes No   *Proofreading*

☐ ☐ Are words spelled correctly?

_____

☐ ☐ Are paragraphs indented?

_____

☐ ☐ Are capital letters used correctly?

_____

☐ ☐ Are there correct marks at the end of sentences?

_____

☐ ☐ Is the handwriting neat and legible?

_____

Writing with Nouns

A. Gayle is preparing some ads for the Yellow Pages of the telephone directory. She does not think they give enough information. Help Gayle change the nouns so that the ads are more specific. Correct any errors you find also. Use the revising and proofreading marks on this page.

1-15.

GLORIA'S GIFT SHOP

Do you need a special thing?

We are the place for you!

examine our lovely things.

Our trained people will help you find exactly what you are looking for.

121 North Avenue 555-1200

TOM'S TV

Honest Dependable

We repare all makes of things.

Our factory-trained people have years of experience.

We are located at a convenient place.

132 South Street 555-1432

BEN'S ART BARN

Come in and luk around.

you'll love our place.

You'll find one-of-a-kind things.

Creative works from people all over the place are sold here.

1549 West Road 555-6766

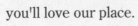

Name_____

B. Imagine that you work for a store. You have been asked to write an ad that will appear in the Yellow Pages. Choose one of the stores below, or make up one of your own.

BART'S BIKES   PETE'S PET PALACE   COMPUTER COTTAGE

Use specific nouns to include as much information as possible in your ad. If you need to make changes, use revising and proofreading marks.

C. Read the following lines from several Yellow Pages ads. Many words have been scrambled. Unscramble them to complete the line from each ad. Then circle the unscrambled words that are nouns.

16. Visit ruo decorating retcen for all your apint and wallpaper.

17. We are the equipment spertex you can trust.

18. Our ellextenc service is the secret of our eccsuss.

19. Come to our warehouse for the seggtib insagrab in nowt.

20. Our manycop has served the tri-state area rof thirty sarey.

21. Beauty si our sesubnis.

22. We serve good ofdo at reasonable scripe.

23. You'll dinf special jelyrew at special savings.

Singular and Plural Nouns

A. Ms. Bennett asked Mark to make a list of all the art supplies in the classroom closet. She needs to see what supplies must be reordered. Mark wants to make sure his list is free of errors. Help Mark by checking his spelling of plural nouns. Correct any other errors you find also. Use the revising and proofreading marks on this page.

1-21.

Art Supplies

12 gum erasers	4 compass
2 dozen brush	9 jar of paste
8 box of crayons	20 pound of clay
15 marker	4 watercolor set
4 paint knife	3 key to supply closet
2 easels	4 pairs of sissors
8 8 x 10 frame	5 bunch of artificial cherry
24 toobs of oil paint	1 can of paint thinner
1 duzzen rulers	2 bottle of blue ink
16 stretched canvas	100 foot of silver foil paper
8 sketch pad	1 pack of battery
1 pack of drawing paper	3 package of colored pencils

B. In the space below, make a list of all the items you can find in one of the following places: school desk, a closet at home, or the classroom. Then check your list to make sure you have spelled the plural nouns correctly. Use revising and proofreading marks if you need to make changes.

_____

_____

_____

_____

_____

_____

_____

_____

_____

C. Think of a related item that you can add to each of the following lists. Be sure to use the plural forms of nouns correctly.

22. forks

spoons

_____

23. brownies

fairies

_____

24. taxis

subways

_____

25. legs

ankles

_____

26. tales

jokes

_____

27. trees

branches

_____

28. infants

newborns

_____

29. articles

features

_____

30. fourths

thirds

_____

31. shoes

sneakers

_____

32. elk

deer

_____

33. apples

oranges

_____

Common and Proper Nouns

A. Jessica interviewed a new girl in her class for the school newspaper and wrote an article about her. Read Jessica's first draft below. Notice that she did not give enough specific information in her article. Help Jessica get her article ready for the newspaper deadline. Replace some of the common nouns with proper nouns. Correct any other errors you find also. Use the revising and proofreading marks on this page.

1-25.

Samantha Lewis is a new student at school. Samantha is in the fith grade She and her famly recently moved to town from a foreign country she lived their for too years. Her father works for the bank. Her mother teaches language. She is teaching at the junior high. Samantha says living in europe was intresting, but she is glad to be back home in this country. Her new home is on the main road near the lake.

Samantha haz lots of hobbies and plans to join the club. She also enjoys sports and will try out for the team this month. You can also here her singing with the school group.

Good luck, Samantha. we are glad you are here

B. Interview one of your classmates, a teacher, or a new student in your school. Then write an article to tell some interesting facts about the person. Use proper nouns to make your article more specific. Use the revising and proofreading marks to improve your work.

_____

_____

_____

_____

_____

_____

_____

_____

_____

_____

C. How are you at breaking codes? Read the clues below and guess the famous person, place, and thing. Then use the alphabet code to check your answers. For the code, write the letters from A to Z. Then number each letter from 1–26, beginning with the letter A.

26. This gift from France greets those entering New York's harbor.

___ ___ ___ ___ ___ ___   ___ ___   ___ ___ ___ ___ ___ ___ ___
19 20 1 20 21 5   15 6   12 9 2 5 18 20 25

27. John Adams was the first to live here. Everyone who followed John Adams has lived here, too.

___ ___ ___   ___ ___ ___ ___ ___   ___ ___ ___ ___ ___
20 8 5   23 8 9 20 5   8 15 21 19 5

28. A child's letter suggested he would look better with a beard. He became the first president to wear one.

___ ___ ___ ___ ___ ___ ___   ___ ___ ___ ___ ___ ___ ___
1 2 18 1 8 1 13   12 9 14 3 15 12 14

Capitalizing Proper Nouns

Revising Marks

cross out	_____
add	∧
move	⟍

A. Willow Valley is having a poster contest for its summer festival.
1-25. The winning poster will be printed and used throughout the valley to advertise the event. Jessie made a poster, but she forgot to capitalize some of the proper nouns. Help Jessie fix the poster. Capitalize all the proper nouns and correct any other errors you find also. Use the revising and proofreading marks on this page.

Proofreading Marks

capital letter	≡
small letter	/
indent paragraph	⁋
check spelling	⬭

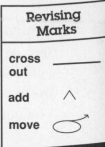

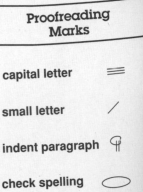

20th Annual willow valley Festival at

entertainment   food   games and rides

Come join in fun!

friday, july 28th throgh saturday, august 4th

mount pleasant fair grounds

route 136 and Scottdale road

adults $2.50   children $1.50   senior citizens $1.00

Profits will be donated to

willow valley children's library.

For additional informashun call:

mary ann zimmer. 555-1900

or peter rivera. 555-9765

B. Design a poster for a real or an imaginary event such as a concert, a fair, or an art contest. The event can be held by your school, the community, or group that you belong to. Make sure to capitalize any proper nouns that you use. Use revising and proofreading marks if you need to make corrections.

 C. Solve the picture clues! Each series of clues leads to a proper noun. Notice that sometimes you must subtract letters from the word represented by the picture. Write the proper nouns correctly.

26. 🧦 - s - k + 🐦 + 🥶 = _____

27. ✏️ + 🌬️ + "yup" - p = _____

28. 🐟 + 🎁 - t 🍼 = _____

29. A + 🦓 - ze + 🍖 🔗 + 🔌 = _____

30. bar - b + 🥫 + 🪚 = _____

Abbreviations

A.

1-27. Harry took these telephone messages for his family. He made several mistakes writing the initials and abbreviations. Help Harry write them correctly. Correct any other errors you find also. Use the revising and proofreading marks on this page.

Time: 9:00 Am

Date: tu, jan 31

To: Dad

From: mr Alexander

Message: you can pick up the part for the car at the shop on 6th av

Message taken by: Harry

Time: 6:30 p.m.

Date: Feb 1

To: Beth

From: ms Warren at libary

Message: The book you reserved is in Pick it up by 8:00 pm fr. night.

Message taken by: Harry

Time: 12:15 P.M.

Date: WED

To: Mom

From: Dr carlson

Message: Appointment has been changed from thu, mar 29, to mon., apl 4.

Message taken by: Harry

Time: 11:30 am

Date: Ap 2

To: Mom

From: Dad

Message: Pick Dad up between 5:45 pm and 6:00 pm at the bus stop on Rt 136

Message taken by: Harry

Name_____

B. Make up a name and title for yourself. Pretend to be that person as you make a telephone call to a partner. Take turns giving and taking messages. Include in the message the time, place, and location of a birthday party you are giving for a friend. Use abbreviations in your message. Use revising and proofreading marks if you need to make changes.

Time: _____	Date: _____

To: _____

From: _____

Message: _____

_____

_____

Message taken by: _____

C. Some words in the following sentences can be abbreviated. Write the abbreviations and the initials that can be used in sentences above the words. Then use the first letter of each abbreviation and each initial to find a hidden message.

28. Mister Oliver Small, Mister Marcus Brown, and my cousin, Michael, met unexpectedly last week.

29. It was at 10:00 in the morning.

30. They were all in Doctor Chu's sports medicine office on Pine Street.

31. There were some magazines from last January and some newer ones too.

32. Edward Fernandez, Junior, the doctor's assistant, greeted us.

33. He told us the doctor was delayed but would see us all by 11:30 in the morning.

34. Mister Small said he would have to come back another time.

35. The nurse gave him an appointment for next Tuesday.

Message: __ __ __   __ __ __ __   __ __ __

Possessive Nouns

A. The Lucky Label Company makes labels for anything. Their artist has just designed some new labels, but he has made mistakes in possessive nouns. Help the artist fix the labels. Correct each possessive noun. Correct any other errors you find also. Use the revising and proofreading marks on this page.

1-15.

Revising Marks	
cross out	___
add	∧
move	⟲

Proofreading Marks	
capital letter	≡
small letter	/
indent paragraph	¶
check spelling	⬯

Uncle Billys Barbecue Sauce

Tessies Tasty Taters

The Joneses Jams & Jellies

McIntoshs Marvelous Corn Muffins

Seven Sisters Spaghetti Sause

The Rosses Raisins

My Dogs Dinner

Silass Spicy Salami

Krauss Crispy Corn

Too Brothers Burgers

Working Womens Waffles

dr. Dukes Cough Syrup

B. The Lucky Label Company needs labels for some new products. Think of a clever name for each item below. Exercise A will give you some ideas. Use a possessive noun in each label. Use revising and proofreading marks if you need to make changes.

16. popcorn _____

17. cereal _____

18. rice _____

19. yogurt _____

20. pet food _____

21. spaghetti sauce _____

22. applesauce _____

23. orange juice _____

C. Look at the picture of the Fun-For-You Pet Shop. Find one or more things belonging to each pet or person on the list. Write what is owned next to the owner. Be sure to form possessive nouns to show ownership.

24. the hamsters _____

25. Polly _____

26. the puppy _____

27. Mr. James _____

28. the mouse _____

29. The rabbit _____

30. the fishes _____

31. Ms. Adams _____

32. The rabbit _____

33. The dog _____

Name_____

An Order Circle

You can use these forms to make order circles for
the Critical Thinking lesson on pages 78–79.

A.

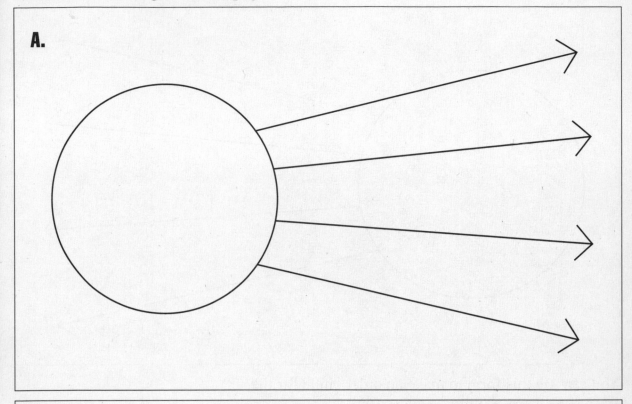

B.

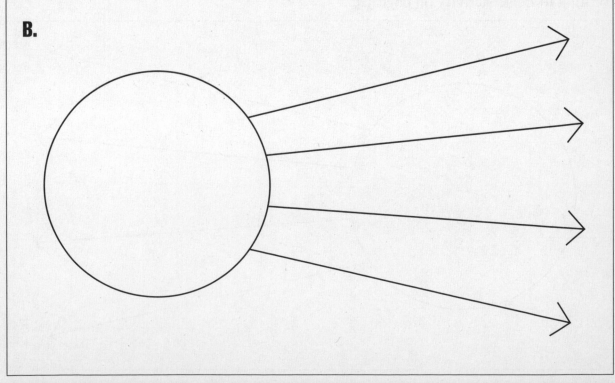

Name

An Order Circle

You can use this form to make an order circle for the
Writing to Learn activity on page 83.

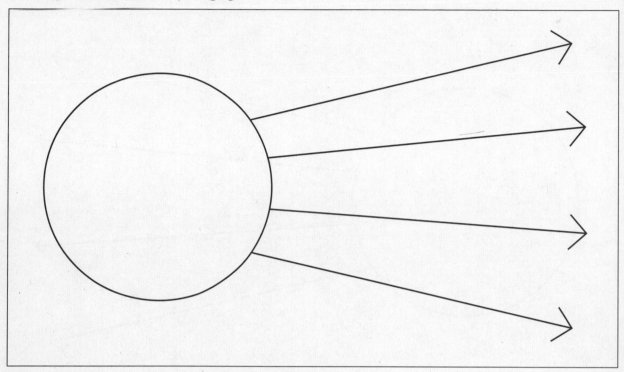

You can use this form to make an order circle for the
Writing to Learn activity on page 102.

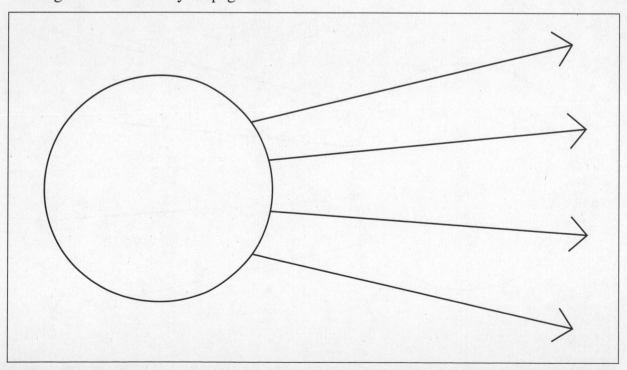

Story Starter

Name_____

Informing

You have read "Handicrafts" by Patricia Fent Ross. Now imagine that you and your classmates are having an international festival with foods from different countries. Think about what dish you would bring. On the back of this page, explain how to prepare the dish.

Writing Tips

◇ Use complete sentences to express your ideas. Use capital letters and punctuation carefully.

◇ State the main idea of your paragraph in a topic sentence. Develop the main idea in your supporting sentences.

◇ **Focus:** Remember to use words like <u>first</u>, <u>next</u>, <u>then</u>, and <u>last</u> to show the order of the steps.

◇ You may wish to reread "Handicrafts" before you begin. Choose one thing that you like about the writer's way of writing, and try to use it in your own writing.

Unit 2 • LITERATURE • Use after the Reading-Writing Connection on pages 92–93.

51

Name_____

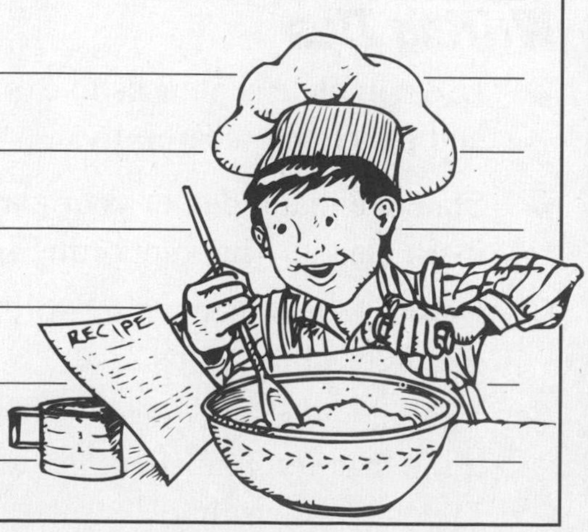

_____

_____

_____

_____

_____

_____

_____

_____

_____

_____

_____

_____

_____

_____

_____

_____

_____

_____

_____

_____

_____

_____

_____

_____

Strategy: An Order Circle

Use this page if you choose an order circle as a prewriting strategy for your how-to article.

Strategy: A Clock Graph

Use this page if you choose a clock graph as a prewriting
strategy for your how-to article.

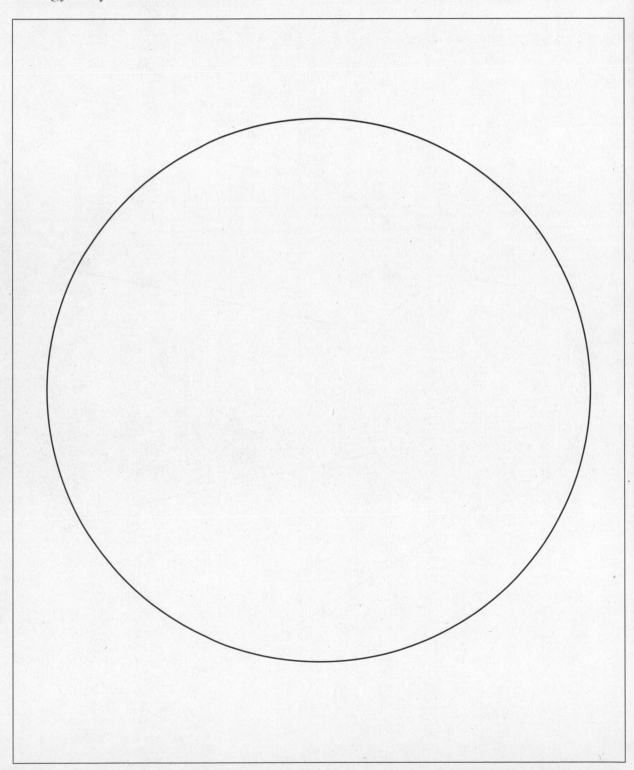

Name_____

cross ——— out	add $\wedge$	move

A How-to Article

Practice your revising on the how-to article below. Use the revising tips as a guide. Don't copy the article. Use the revising marks to cross out, add, or move words and sentences.

Revising Tips

Check to see that the writer has

◇ explained how to do something.

◇ described the steps so that classmates can follow them.

◇ used words like <u>first</u>, <u>next</u>, and <u>last</u> to make the order clear.

◇ used exact nouns to make meaning clearer.

◇ used precise words for words such as <u>get</u>, <u>things</u>, and <u>good</u>.

◇ given complete directions and explained the steps in order.

◆

Granola is my favorite snack. We always used to get granola at the store. The kind at the store is good, but homemade granola is really good. Now I know how to make homemade granola. You can do it, too. It is very easy to make.

You need to buy the things you want to put in your granola. You may be creative with the things. I change my recipe a little every time I make it. You put all the ingredients in a bowl and add 1/4 cup of honey. Then stir the mixture well. Now your homemade granola is done. Store it in an air-tight container to keep it good. I like to use peanuts, raisins, banana chips, cashews, and dried dates.

Maybe you can try to make your own granola sometime. Next you may want to package the granola so that you can take it to school. Put the four corners of the plastic wrap together and twist them around. Then use a piece of ribbon. I usually make about five packages at a time. Sometimes I like to give my granola snacks to friends. They always ask me recipe.

≡	/	∏	⬭
capital letter	small letter	indent paragraph	check spelling

A How-to Article

Practice your proofreading on the how-to article below. Use the proofreading tips as a guide. Don't copy the article. Use the proofreading marks to make corrections.

Proofreading Tips

Check to see that the writer has

◇ spelled words correctly.
◇ indented paragraphs.
◇ used capital letters correctly.
◇ used correct marks at the end of sentences.

Do you know how to give a dog a bath? i will tell you how to bathe a dog the easy way.

First you need to find the dog and bring him outsid. If you don't have a fenced-in yard, you may need to put your dog on a leash. Otherwise he may run away when he knows it's Bath time. Next get a large tub, a hose, some soap, a brush, and some flea powder. Begin by filling the tub with water. Place the dog in the tub and wet his fer. Then Soap him down, beginning with the ears. You must start with the ears because fleas sometimes try to hide in them. Lather his whole body. Next rinse your dog with the hose. Wach out when your dog gets out of the tub He will shake water all over. dry your dog off with a towel. If it is a warm day, allow him to run around the Yard to dry. Finally apply flea powder and brush your dog. After his bath your dog will look beter and feel great.

Writing a How-to Article

Use this form as you do the Writing Process lesson beginning on page 94. Put a check next to each item you can answer yes to.

Revising

☐ **Purpose:** Did my article explain how to do something?

☐ **Audience:** Will my classmates be able to follow the steps?

☐ **Focus:** Have I used words like <u>first</u>, <u>next</u>, and <u>last</u> to make the order clear?

☐ **Grammar Check:** Have I used exact nouns?

☐ **Word Choice:** Have I used precise words?

☐ **Writing◆Topic Sentence and Supporting Sentences:** Have I used topic sentences and supporting sentences to make my writing clear?

Proofreading

☐ Did I spell words correctly?

☐ Did I indent paragraphs?

☐ Did I use capital letters correctly?

☐ Did I use correct marks at the end of sentences?

☐ Did I use my best handwriting?

Publishing

☐ Have I shared my writing with readers or listeners?

☐ Has my audience shared reactions with me?

☐ Have I thought about what I especially liked in this piece of writing?

☐ Have I thought about what I would like to work on the next time?

Use the space on the other side to tell what you liked about your writing and to make notes of your plans for improvement.

Name _____

What I liked about my writing: _____

_____

_____

_____

_____

_____

_____

_____

My plans for improvement: _____

_____

_____

_____

_____

_____

_____

_____

_____

_____

_____

Writing a How-to Article

Use the questions below and on the other side of this page to help you review the writer's how-to article. Then give this form to the writer to read and save. Your comments can help the writer improve the how-to article.

A First Reaction

Here is what I thought in general about your how-to article:

_____

_____

_____

_____

_____

_____

A Second Reaction

Now I have looked at your how-to article more closely. I have more specific comments about it.

Here is something you have done well as a writer:

_____

_____

Here is an area that might be improved:

_____

_____

Here is an idea for improvement:

_____

_____

Reader's Name _____

Writer's Name _____

Writing a How-to Article

Check Yes or No for each item. If you check No, explain or give a suggestion for improvement.

Yes No *Revising*

☐ ☐ **Purpose:** Did the article explain how to do something?

_____

☐ ☐ **Audience:** Was I able to follow the steps?

_____

☐ ☐ **Focus:** Were words like <u>first</u>, <u>next</u>, and <u>last</u> used to make the order clear?

_____

☐ ☐ **Grammar Check:** Did the writer use exact nouns?

_____

☐ ☐ **Word Choice:** Did the writer use precise words?

_____

☐ ☐ **Writing◆Topic Sentence and Supporting Sentences:** Has the writer used topic sentences and supporting sentences to make the writing clear?

_____

Yes No *Proofreading*

☐ ☐ Are words spelled correctly?

_____

☐ ☐ Are paragraphs indented?

_____

☐ ☐ Are capital letters used correctly?

_____

☐ ☐ Are there correct marks at the end of sentences?

_____

☐ ☐ Is the handwriting neat and legible?

_____

Writing with Action Verbs

A. Antonio is filming an important scene for a movie he is directing.
He has written the following script for the actors to follow. After
–18. reading over the script, Antonio decided that the actors needed more
exact directions. Help Antonio make the directions clearer by
changing ordinary verbs to more vivid verbs. Correct any errors that
you find also. Use the revising and proofreading marks on this page.

"Scene I"

Jody closes the door behind her as she walks
into the room. Martin runs toward her,
frowning. he takes Jody's arm and takes her
over to the window Grandfather Jones gets
out of his chare and moves toward Jody
and Martin. Jody looks at Grandfather Jones.
Grandfather Jones opens his mouth to speek
to Jody and Martin. Martin moves slightly,
looking frightened. Jody pulls to Martin's
arm and looks at Grandfather Jones.
Grandfather Jones closes his mouth, turns
quickly away from them, and walks slowly
around the room.

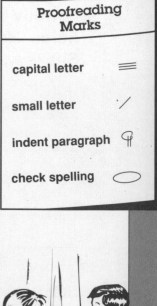

B. Now you try writing some script directions. Read the following description. Then write what you think each actor or actress will be doing for the next few moments of the scene. Be sure to use vivid verbs to make your directions clear. If you need to show changes, use revising and proofreading marks.

The scene takes place at a horse corral. "Tex" is sitting on the coral fence holding a lasso. Betty is wearing jeans, cowboy boots, a plaid shirt, and a hat. She is sitting on a horse. Betty's mother, Mrs. Lane, stands inside the corral. She is watching Betty with a worried look on her face.

_____

_____

_____

_____

_____

_____

 C.

19–25. Help one of Antonio's actors find his way to the treasure. Beside each diamond write a vivid verb that tells what he must do to pass each obstacle.

Linking Verbs

Revising
Marks

cross _____
out

add   ∧

move   ↻

A. Carla is Antonio's casting director. She interviews actors and
actresses for parts in his films. Below are some notes Carla made
1–24. about the people who tried out for the various parts. In her notes,
Carla left out some linking verbs. Help Carla add linking verbs that
connect the subject with a word or words in the predicate. Correct
any other errors that you find also. Use the revising and
proofreading marks on this page.

Proofreading
Marks

capital letter   ≡

small letter   /

indent paragraph   ¶

check spelling   ⬭

Barbara short. Her speaking voice is very

pleasant. Her eyes very expressive. She a

singer. She very graceful.

Earl quite tall. His speaking voice not

plesant. He handsome. He not a good

dancer, but he a good singer.

Kathy right for the leed. She light on her

feet. her singing voice right for the part.

The Sims twins good dancers. They good

for the chorus They right. They happy all

the time.

James a grate dancer. His leaps

spectacular. His singing voice also good.

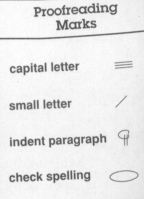

B. Imagine that you are a casting director interviewing student actors and actresses for parts in a film. Write notes about them. Use linking verbs to connect the subject with a word or words in the predicate. If you need to indicate changes, use revising and proofreading marks.

_____

_____

_____

_____

_____

C. Use a linking verb from the box to complete each sentence. Some verbs are used more than once. Then use the numbered letters to spell out a message that tells something about you.

am	is	are	was	were	seem
taste	tastes	feel	feels	felt	seems

25. Tammy __ __ a good dancer.
            1

26. Some actors __ __ __ superstitious.
                      2

27. They __ __ __ __ nervous sometimes.
                  3

28. Fresh corn __ __ __ __ __ __ delicious.
                        4

29. Those fabrics __ __ __ __ soft.
                        5

30. The actors __ __ __ ready for a picnic.
                    6

31. The tables __ __ __ filled with food.
                    7

32. Cal __ __ the cook.
          8

33. The sun __ __ __ __ warm.
                9

34. Pat __ __ smart.   __ __ __ __ __ __ __ __ __ __ c!
          10   1   2   3   4   5   6   7   8   9   10

Name_____

Main Verbs and Helping Verbs

A. Kelly has written a campaign speech to convince her classmates she would make a good class president. As you can see, she has made some mistakes with helping verbs and main verbs. Help Kelly make the helping verbs work with the main verbs. Correct any other errors that you find also. Use the revising and proofreading marks on this page.

1–16.

First I have tell you about my experience. As class secretary I have written the meating notes. I was presented them to the class. as class vice-president, I were presided over meetings. I was worked on many class projects.

I am work hard to make our school better. I have set aside time each week when all of you can speak to me privately You may wants to suggest activities that we have do as a class. I will listens to each suggestion you make. I had make a fare and honest class president. I have hopping you will vote for me.

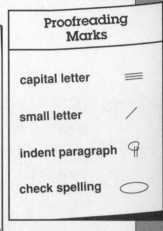

B. Write a campaign speech for yourself. Be sure to use main verbs and helping verbs correctly. If you need to indicate changes, use revising and proofreading marks.

_____

_____

_____

_____

_____

C. Complete each sentence with the correct helping verb or main verb from the box. You may use a verb more than once. To answer the riddle at the end, write the numbered words and letters on the line provided.

are	need	will	am	tried
serve	bat	were	had	tasted

17. Sean _____ read a mystery story to us.
    _1_

18. He will _____ to find his glasses.
    _2_

19. Will Carla __ __ __ the ball?
    _3_

20. Mr. Joseph's students __ __ __ planning to win the game.
    _4_

21. The batter on second has __ __ __ __ __ to steal third.
    _5_

22. Have you __ __ __ __ __ __ maple syrup?
    _6_

23. The players __ __ __ practicing this afternoon.
    _7_

24. The chefs will __ __ __ __ __ a breakfast favorite.
    _9_ _8_

25. What do baseball players and pancakes have in common?

    For both you _____ _____ __ __ __ __ __ __ __ .
              1   2   3 4 5 6 7 8 9

Verbs with Direct Objects

A. Amy has written captions for pictures of last week's baseball game.
She has forgotten to include direct objects after action verbs. Help
1–19. Amy add the direct objects. Use the revising and proofreading
marks on this page. Correct any other errors you find also.

Revising Marks	
cross out	_____
add	∧
move	↺

Proofreading Marks	
capital letter	≡
small letter	/
indent paragraph	¶
check spelling	⬯

Mark stands on the
pitcher's mound   He nods.
He throws. The ball races
towards home plait. The
pitcher kicks.

Melody stands at
home plate. She
grips. She hits. The
ball flys into the air
The ball seems to
touch the clouds.

Gwen runs. Gwen
slides right under
the catcher's arm.
She touches. The
catcher catches.
She is safe?

Kenny waits in right
feild. He raises.
Kenny catches.
Kenny the kangaroo
catcher earns
his nickname again!

John sees. He
raises his. He
catches. This was
the first baseball to
go into the stands
this seson.

Name_____

 B. Now write your own captions for the following pictures. Try to make your captions brief and exact. If you need to indicate changes, use revising and proofreading marks.

_____   _____

_____   _____

_____   _____

_____   _____

 C. To complete each sentence, solve the picture puzzle. Write the missing direct object. Then circle <u>what</u> or <u>whom</u> to show what question the direct object answers.

20. Sheila forgot the . _____ (what, whom)

21. We examined in the science class. _____ (what, whom)

22. We paid the er for her work. _____ (what, whom)

23. Todd hung the up in the tree. _____ (what, whom)

24. We thanked the for saving our lives. _____ (what, whom)

25. The carpenter moved the 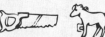 _____ (what, whom)

26. Mom fixed my _____ (what, whom)

27. We hired the  er to work at the circus. _____ (what, whom)

Tenses of Verbs

A.

1–24. Don has written the beginning of a research report on the Abominable Snowman. As you can see, he has made some mistakes with verb tenses. Help Don correct the verbs. Correct any other errors you find also. Use the revising and proofreading marks on this page.

○ According to lejend the Abominable Snowman will live in the himalayan Mountains. It stand over seven feet tall its face resemble a human being's face. The snowman's arms reach its knees. The Abominable Snowman is also called Yeti. This word meaning evil-smelling man of The snows. The monster is said to have a very Strong odor. In 1960 scientists will look for the

○ creture. They explore in the mountains for many cold months They study large footprints in the snow. scientists decide that other animals made the tracks and the sun made the tracks larjer as they will melt. Today some People still believe that the Abominable Snowman exists. have you ever sean the Abominable Snowman? Do you believe it exists

○

Name_____

B. Write a paragraph for a report about one of the topics below or one
you choose. Tell what you know about the topic. Be sure to use
present, past, and future tenses of verbs correctly. If you need to
show changes, use revising and proofreading marks.

     robots   space travel   computers   video games

_____

_____

_____

_____

_____

_____

C. Complete each sentence using the correct tense of the verb in
parentheses. Then write that verb in the crossword puzzle.

Across

1. We _____ to go to the fair
   yesterday. (want)
5. She _____ the box two days ago.(label)
8. I _____ I could go to the movies
   today. (wish)
9. He will soon _____ into the
   large crowd. (disappear)
12. Susan _____ the skirt
    around her waist. (belt)
13. I will _____ the picture
    on my paper. (trace)

Down

2. Last night the fireworks _____
   above the castle. (explode)
3. Sherry and I will _____ the glasses
   to the top. (fill)
4. They _____ every day. (fish)
6. Today we will _____ about the
   future. (dream)
7. He _____ the books in a
   corner. (pile)
10. She _____ very quickly. (paint)
11. It _____ all day long
    yesterday. (rain)

© Silver Burdett & Ginn

70   Unit 3, Lesson 5 • Use after page 125.

Using the Present Tense

A. Lee has written headlines for some stories for the school newspaper.
1–23. The editor of the newspaper has found some mistakes in subject and verb agreement. Help the editor by changing the present-tense verbs so that they agree with their subjects. Correct any other errors you find also. Use the revising and proofreading marks on this page. Remember that each important word in a headline begins with a capital letter.

Revising Marks	
cross out	_____
add	∧
move	↻

Proofreading Marks	
capital letter	≡
small letter	/
indent paragraph	¶
check spelling	⬭

> Teacher Urge Good Studey Habits
>
> Principal Declare Holaday
>
> Runners Competes in State meet
>
> Students Joins Debating team
>
> Sixth Graders Hears Speech
>
> council Members Agrees on Rules
>
> Spring Show Begin Thursday
>
> Softball Team Win Championship
>
> Football Tryouts Begins Next week
>
> Field Day Attract Many Students
>
> Students Are Reading More Than Ever
>
> Field Trip to the Zoo Was a Wild Suces
>
> Bake Sale business Bring Big Profits
>
> New Bike Racks Makes Parking Easier
>
> Mayor Visit School in May
>
> Fifth Graders Writes to Pen Pals in russia

★ **B.** Be a headline writer. Write four headlines about school events or other real or imaginary events. Use the present tense. If you need to indicate changes, use revising and proofreading marks.

_____

_____

_____

_____

★ **C.** Complete each sentence by choosing the correct form of the verb in parentheses. Write the verb on the line and circle the letters as indicated. Then write the letters on the lines below to find Mary's prediction.

24. Mary _____ that something exciting will happen tomorrow. (think, thinks) <u>Circle last letter</u>.

25. Exciting things _____ every day. (happen, happens) <u>Circle third letter</u>.

26. Yes, but Mary _____ that this will be really exciting. (say, says) <u>Circle second letter</u>.

27. They _____ to Mary's house. (race, races) <u>Circle last two letters</u>.

28. I _____ I knew how Mary can predict the future. (wish, wishs) <u>Circle last two letters</u>.

29. Two people _____ on the sidewalk. (trip, trips) <u>Circle last two letters</u>.

30. Some children _____ baseball near Mary's house. (plays, play) <u>Circle second letter</u>.

31. You _____ Mary what the newspaper headlines will be tomorrow. (ask, asks) <u>Circle first letter</u>.

32. Mary _____ that we don't believe in her ability to predict the future. (sense, senses) <u>Circle third letter</u>.

33. He _____ stories about people who can predict the future. (reads, read) <u>Circle the last two letters</u>.

__ __ __ __   __ __ __ __ __   __ __ __ __ __

Using Irregular Verbs

Revising
Marks

cross
out   _____

add   ∧

move   ⤵

A. Tony has written a letter to his friend Jack describing a trip he has
taken. When he read the letter, Tony noticed that he had made some
mistakes with the tenses of irregular verbs. Help him correct the
verbs in the letter. Correct any other errors you find also. Use the
revising and proofreading marks on this page.

1–23.

Proofreading
Marks

capital letter   ≡

small letter   /

indent paragraph   ⌐P

check spelling   ◯

Dear jack,

   I go to the beech last week with my folks. It taked
us almost an Hour to pack the car. My grandparents
also come with us. to get to the beach, we rided
in the car for three hours. We seen a flock of canvas-
back ducks near the beach. They had flew down
from alaska.

   When we got to the beach, the first thing i did
was swim. My dad had gave me lesons last year.
it was so much fun The waves were so high that I
must have fell about tweny times. I actually ridden
one wave right back onto the beach! after that
fierce wave, I run back to my family's beach blanket

   Sorry I haven't wrote sooner. I've been so busy!

                 See you soon,

                 Tony

Name _____

B. Write a description of a trip you have taken. It could be a trip to the local park or mall. Use irregular verbs such as <u>see</u>, <u>eat</u>, <u>grow</u>, <u>run</u>, <u>wear</u>, or <u>write</u> in your description. If you need to indicate changes, use revising and proofreading marks.

_____

_____

_____

_____

_____

_____

_____

C. Use the past and past participles of the verbs given to complete each puzzle.

24.
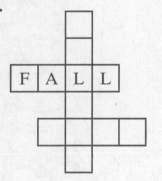

25.

26.
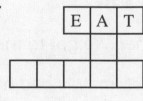

27.
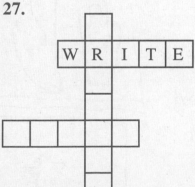

28.
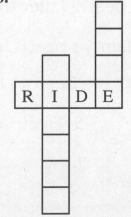

29.
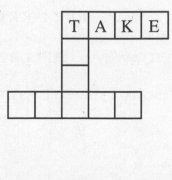

Name_____

Using Irregular Verbs

A.

1–25. Jill has written a newspaper article. Her editor noticed that she used irregular verbs incorrectly. Help the editor correct the irregular vebs in Jill's article. Correct any other errors you find also. Use the revising and proofreading marks on this page.

In an interview earlier today, ace detective Rita sayed, "Farmer Jones can relax I have find the Chicken egg theif." Rita had been trying to catch the egg thief for months. She had almost thinked that the case could not be solved. "At first I think it was a dog," explained Rita. "Then yesterday I choosed to watch the hen house. I bringed a thermos of juice and a sandwhich. I drinked the juice and waited. I catched the fox in the Act. he had broke many eggs." When Farmer Jones was interviewed, he sung rita's praises. He spoke of her patience and cleverness. "Rita breaked this case!" exclaimed Farmer Jones. "She catched that chicken egg thief in a jiffy. I had think that Rita was a very pashent and clever detective. I am glad I goed to her with my problem."

Once again Rita has baffled the experts with Her detective work.

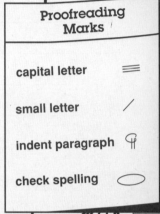

B. Write a newspaper article about school events or other real or imaginary events. Use the past and past participle of irregular verbs such as <u>say</u>, <u>think</u>, <u>find</u>, <u>speak</u>, and <u>choose</u>. If you need to show changes, use revising and proofreading marks.

_____

_____

_____

_____

_____

_____

C. Find and circle the past or past participles of these verbs in the puzzle: <u>break</u>, <u>choose</u>, <u>find</u>, <u>say</u>, <u>freeze</u>, <u>speak</u>, <u>ring</u>, <u>sing</u>, <u>swim</u>, <u>think</u>. Write a sentence for each one.

26. _____

27. _____

28. _____

29. _____

30. _____

31. _____

S I C L A A R B E L W O

W A H N R T F R O Z E N

_____

32. _____

U T L R U C H O S E E T

M R T E V F U K N S P H

_____

33. _____

Q E E S P O K E N M X O

_____

S A N G Z U L N U B R U

34. _____

A R E S T N O R N L U G

_____

35. _____

B U S A I D M N L P N H

_____

D R T B A R M L A A G T

Using Troublesome Verb Pairs

A. Melissa would like to be a greeting card writer. She is practicing writing some verse for cards. After reading her verses Melissa **1–23.** realized that she had used the verb pairs <u>can</u>, <u>may</u> and <u>sit</u>, <u>set</u> incorrectly. Help Melissa correct the verbs. Correct any other errors you find also. Use the revising and proofreading marks on this page.

Revising Marks	
cross out	_____
add	∧
move	⤴

Proofreading Marks	
capital letter	≡
small letter	/
indent paragraph	¶
check spelling	⬭

_ay imagine your exsitement

_s you set and wait

_or the wonderful celebration

That's coming your way today.

there will be candles glowing

and friends who come to play.

Do as you can wish,

It's your tenth birthday!

Though you are not you're self,

And feel a little down,

i know you wont set for long.

You'll soon be up and around.

But if you need a freind

I'll sit aside some time

And try to chear you up at once,

A Project I may not mind!

Can I tell you I like you?

Can I tell you you're my frend?

Will you set beside me,

So this happy time won't end?

although we may be sisters,

You are my best friend too

Can I take this chanse

to tell you?

I will always love You!

Name _____

 B. Write your own greeting card verses. Use the verbs <u>can</u>, <u>may</u>, <u>sit</u>, and <u>set</u>. If you need to show changes, use revising and proofreading marks.

_____

_____

_____

_____

_____

_____

C. Complete each sentence with <u>can</u>, <u>may</u>, <u>sit</u> or <u>set</u>. Then use the numbered letters to answer the riddle at the bottom.

24. __ __ __ I speak to Maria?
     1

25. We will __ __ __ at the table to eat.
          2

26. __ __ __ the tapes on the shelf.

27. We __ __ __ tell that it will rain.
       3

28. If we all __ __ __ down, we will be able to see.
          4

29. You __ __ __ watch TV after dinner.
     5

30. Carol __ __ __ play the clarinet well.

31. Don __ __ __ that book on the table.
      6

32. Would you __ __ __ the package down?
        7

33. Let's __ __ __ near the front of the theater.
     8

34. What is a good name for Tom Thumb's teeny-tiny, sloppy bedroom?

__ __ __ __ __ __ __ __
1 2 3 4   5 6 7 8

Name_____

Answering "What If?"

You can use these forms to make "what-if" charts for the
Creative Thinking lesson on pages 140–141.

A.

B.

Name_____

Answering "What If?"

You can use these forms to make "what-if" charts for the
Writing to Learn activity on page 145.

You can use this form to make a "what-if" chart for the
Writing to Learn activity on page 160.

Name _____

Imagining

You have read a selection from "Sky-Bright Axe" by Adrien
Stoutenberg. Now imagine that you and your friends are visiting the
great northern timber country where Paul Bunyan and Babe the Blue Ox
once logged. You never really believed in these legendary characters, but
something amazing happens to change your mind. On the back of this
page, write a short tale about Paul and Babe. Tell what they do.

Writing Tips

◇ Use complete sentences to express your ideas. Use capital letters
and punctuation carefully.

◇ Use similes and metaphors to make creative comparisons.

◇ **Focus:** Use humorous exaggeration in your tall tale.

◇ You may wish to reread "Sky-Bright Axe" before you begin. Choose
one thing that you like about the writer's way of writing, and try to use
it in your own tall tale.

Unit 3 • LITERATURE • Use after the Reading-Writing Connection on pages 150–151.

81

Strategy: A Comic Strip

Use this page if you choose a comic strip as a prewriting strategy for your tall tale.

Strategy: Answering "What If?"

Use this page if you choose a "what-if" chart as a prewriting strategy for your tall tale.

cross out _____	add ∧	move ⟲

A Tall Tale

Practice your revising on the tall tale below. Use the revising tips as a guide. Don't copy the tall tale. Use the revising marks to cross out, add, or move words and sentences.

Revising Tips

Check to see that the writer has
- ◇ told a tall tale.
- ◇ narrated the tall tale so that classmates will understand it.
- ◇ used humorous exaggerations in the tall tale.
- ◇ used vivid verbs to make the writing more lively and interesting to read.
- ◇ used similes and metaphors to make the writing vivid.

My brother, David, is very strong for a baby. The doctor said that he is the strongest baby he's ever seen. David's muscles are big. His legs are hard. "He's a little powerhouse!" said the doctor.

The first day David was home from the hospital, he lifted his baby crib over his head and moved it by the window. We were all surprised. I guess David wanted to look outside.

One day Dad, David, and I were on our way to the store. We saw a man with his foot under a big rock. We stopped to see if we could help. David moved the rock up off the man's foot. His arm looked like a crane as he held the rock up high. "Thank you!" said the man.

My friends and I were playing baseball yesterday. David wanted to play. He took a tree out of the ground and used it as a bat. He hit the ball so hard it landed far away. We had to take a trip on an airplane to get the ball back. I just don't know what we will do if David gets much stronger!

PROOFREADING PRACTICE

≡	/	ꟼ	⬭
capital letter	small letter	indent paragraph	check spelling

A Tall Tale

Practice your proofreading on the tall tale below. Use the proofreading tips as a guide. Don't copy the tall tale. Use the proofreading marks to make corrections.

Proofreading Tips

Check to see that the writer has

◇ spelled words correctly.
◇ indented paragraphs.
◇ used capital letters correctly.
◇ used correct marks at the end of sentences.

Jeff had wanted a pupy for a long time. At last his mother got him one from the pet store. Mr. Sneed, the pet shop owner, seemed glad to sell the puppy. "This is a cute puppy," said the pet shop owner. "I must warn you though. He has a big apetite."

Mr. sneed was not joking. Jeff's new puppy was always hungry. He was a walking garbage disposal. For brekfast he usually ate three huge bags of dog food. For lunch he ate 75 peanut-butter-and-jelly sandwiches and 4 gallons of milk. For dinner he normally ate a dozen steaks, 3 pounds of Potatoes and 10 cans of gren beans.

Jeff named the puppy Chubby. Chubby was eating Jeff's family out of house and home. in fact, one day while Chubby was waiting for his diner, he took a bite of the house. He liked the flaver so much that he ate the whole thing. after that, Jeff's family had to live in a tent Chubby didn't like the flavor of the tent, so he sarted eating trees. Finally the family got Chubby a job clearing land. The money from this job gave the family Enough money to buy another house.

Name _____

Writing a Tall Tale

Use this form as you do the Writing Process lesson beginning on page 152. Put a check next to each item you can answer yes to.

Revising

☐ **Purpose:** Did I write a tall tale?

☐ **Audience:** Will my classmates understand my tall tale?

☐ **Focus:** Did I use humorous exaggerations in my tall tale?

☐ **Grammar Check:** Did I use vivid verbs to make my writing more lively?

☐ **Word Choice:** Have I used strong words?

☐ **Writing♦Similes and Metaphors:** Have I used similes and metaphors to make my writing vivid?

Proofreading

☐ Did I spell words correctly?

☐ Did I indent paragraphs?

☐ Did I use capital letters correctly?

☐ Did I use correct marks at the end of sentences?

☐ Did I use my best handwriting?

Publishing

☐ Have I shared my writing with readers or listeners?

☐ Has my audience shared reactions with me?

☐ Have I thought about what I especially liked in this piece of writing?

☐ Have I thought about what I would like to work on the next time?

Use the space on the other side to tell what you liked about your writing and to make notes of your plans for improvement.

Name

What I liked about my writing:

My plans for improvement:

Writing a Tall Tale

Use the questions below and on the other side of this page to help you review the writer's tall tale. Then give this form to the writer to read and save. Your comments can help the writer improve the tall tale.

A First Reaction

Here is what I thought in general about your tall tale:

_____

_____

_____

_____

_____

_____

A Second Reaction

Now I have looked at your tall tale more closely. I have more specific comments about it.

Here is something you have done well as a writer:

_____

_____

Here is an area that might be improved:

_____

_____

Here is an idea for improvement:

_____

_____

_____

Writing a Tall Tale

Check Yes or No for each item. If you check No, explain or give a suggestion for improvement.

Yes   No   *Revising*

☐   ☐   **Purpose:** Did the writer tell a tall tale?

_____

☐   ☐   **Audience:** Did I understand the tall tale?

_____

☐   ☐   **Focus:** Did the writer use humorous exaggerations?

_____

☐   ☐   **Grammar Check:** Did the writer use vivid verbs to make the writing lively?

_____

☐   ☐   **Word Choice:** Has the writer used strong words?

_____

☐   ☐   **Writing♦Similes and Metaphors:** Has the writer used similes and metaphors to make the writing vivid?

_____

Yes   No   *Proofreading*

☐   ☐   Are words spelled correctly?

_____

☐   ☐   Are paragraphs indented?

_____

☐   ☐   Are capital letters used correctly?

_____

☐   ☐   Are there correct marks at the end of sentences?

_____

☐   ☐   Is the handwriting neat and legible?

_____

Writing with Pronouns

A.

1-22. Nathan likes to write exaggerations in his notebook. When Nathan read his exaggerations, he noticed that he often repeated the same nouns. Help Nathan change some nouns to pronouns. Correct any other errors you find also. Use the revising and proofreading marks on this page.

Ours is one talented famaly. Anne is so tall

Anne can clean Anne's gutters without a

ladder. my brother Brett is so strong Brett

can lift a car with one hand In fact, Brett

can changing a tire on Brett's car without

using a jack. Our dog Fido is the most

Amazing family member. Fido becomes so

hungry that Fido eats a ten-pound turkey

in one gulp. if you hear Mom driving

home, it's because Mom uses Mom's horn

all the time The horn is so loud you can

hear the horn five Miles away. Altogether,

we smiths are so happy that the Smiths'

mouths hurt most of the time from laufing.

B. Try writing some exaggerations of your own. Use pronouns to avoid repeating the same nouns. Use revising and proofreading marks if you need to make changes.

23. _____

24. _____

25. _____

26. _____

C. Leon and Mike have an amazing toy. After reading about this toy you will be directed to do something. To find out what you will do, first write a pronoun to replace the underlined word or words in each sentence. Then use the first letter of each pronoun you wrote to fill in the blanks.

27. Anne said that <u>Anne</u> had never seen such an unusual bike. _____

28. Brett could not stop laughing when <u>Brett</u> saw it. _____

29. "That is <u>Leon and Mike's</u> bike," said Leon and Mike. _____

30. "<u>Leon and Mike</u> found it at the fair," said Leon and Mike. _____

31. Leon and Mike couldn't believe <u>Leon and Mike's</u> eyes when they first saw

it. _____

32. Leon said that <u>Leon</u> thought it was very colorful. _____

33. The bike had something strange at the top of <u>the bike</u>. _____

34. Anne thought that <u>Anne</u> saw the bike suddenly move. _____

35. Brett, Leon, and Mike laughed when <u>Brett, Leon, and Mike</u> saw Anne run away

from the bike. _____

36. "We must try to put the bike in <u>Leon and Mike's</u> shed," said Leon and

Mike. _____

37. "Good luck putting that thing into <u>Leon and Mike's</u> shed," said Brett to Leon and

Mike. _____

___ ___ ___ ___   ___ ___ ___ ___   ___ ___ ___

Name_____

Subject Pronouns

A. Natalie has written a book review for her school newspaper. The
editor noticed that Natalie should have used subject pronouns
1-23. instead of repeating some noun subjects. Help the editor replace
nouns in the subjects of sentences with pronouns. Correct any
errors you find also. Use the revising and proofreading marks on
this page.

<u>Dolphin Cove</u> is an exciting book. <u>Dolphin Cove</u>

has interesting charakters and a Great plot. One

character named joe becomes friends with the

dolphins. Joe swims with them in the water. Joe

tries to communicate with the dolphins. The

dolphins seem to enjoy swimming with Joe The

dolphins call out to Joe when they see him. Joe

likes the dolphins so much he wants to keep them

in the cove. Joe puts a larje holding net up to

Keep them in The net extends all the way across

the cove. Then Joe meets a girl named stacey.

Stacey wants Joe to take the net down. Stacey

and Joe argew about the dolphins a lot. Stacey

and Joe have trouble working things out. read

<u>Dolphin cove</u> to find out what happens Stacey

likes the dolphins, too.

Name_____

⭐ **B.** Write a short report telling about the characters, the setting, and the plot of a book you have read. Use some subject pronouns in your sentences. Use revising and proofreading marks if you need to make changes.

_____

_____

_____

_____

_____

_____

⭐ **C.** How do you think the book, <u>Dolphin Cove</u> ends? To find out, look at the underlined subject pronoun in each sentence. Fill in each numbered line below with the word or words the pronoun replaces. Then read the paragraph to discover the end of the story.

24. "<u>I</u> want to keep the dolphins," said Joe.

25. "Why?" asked Stacey. "<u>They</u> need to be free!"

26. "<u>You</u> just don't understand," exclaimed Joe.

27. "<u>We</u> like to swim and play together."

28. "<u>I</u> may never see the dolphins again if I let them go," he explained.

29. "This net is like a jail," cried Stacey. "<u>It</u> must be removed, Joe!"

30. <u>He</u> looked at Stacey and thought about what she had said.

31. <u>She</u> held Joe's hand and watched the dolphins at play.

_____ loved the _____ but he knew _____
      24   25   26

was right. _____ had been friends for a long time. As their friend,
        27

_____ decided to take _____ down. _____
    28   29   30

slowly removed the net as he and _____ watched the dolphins together.
                           31

The dolphins seemed to be smiling and waving as they swam out to sea.

Object Pronouns

A.

1-21. Miki has written an account of a soccer game, but she has forgotten that she can use the pronouns <u>me</u>, <u>you</u>, <u>him</u>, <u>her</u>, <u>it</u>, <u>us</u>, and <u>them</u> to stand for nouns used as direct objects. Help Miki revise what she wrote. Replace some direct objects that are nouns with object pronouns. Correct any other errors you find also. Use the revising and proofreading marks on this page.

Ms. Mackie is a good soccer coach. Everyone likes and respects Ms. Mackie. she has helped the Soccer team form a wining strategy. She gives the soccer team confidence. Ms. Mackie really guides the team and inspires all the players to do there best We are lucky Ms. Mackie is our coach.

The last home game was really exciting. Ms. Mackie cheered the team on as we made the Winning goal. Arthur caut the ball at the goal. He passed the ball to Jonathan. Two players on the Other team blocked Jonathan. We still had the ball. Brian took the ball down the feild. We made a goal! Everyone on the field was cheering except the other team We went over to the other team and shook their hands. We sure injoy winning a game. But good sportsmanship is the most important thing Ms. Mackie taught our team.

Name_____

B. Write a short account of a sports event that you have played in
or watched. Use object pronouns to avoid repeating nouns used
as direct objects. If you need to make changes, use revising and
proofreading marks.

_____

_____

_____

_____

_____

C. Your soccer team is playing against Ms. Mackie's team. To find out
who scores the winning goal, first read each sentence pair. Complete
the second sentence by filling in the correct object pronoun to
replace the underlined noun. Then underline the first letter of each
object pronoun. Draw a line from the soccer ball to the first letter.
Continue in this manner to trace the path of the ball.

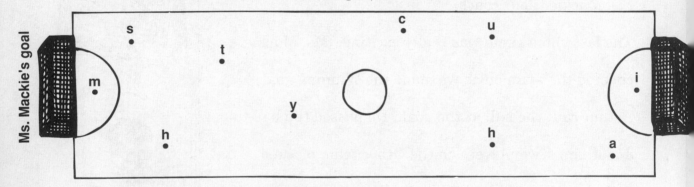

Ms. Mackie's goal

22. Marsha and I bought <u>tickets</u> for the game.

    We bought _____ at a bargain price.

23. Dad drove <u>Marsha and me</u> to the game.

    He showed _____ around the new soccer field.

24. Someone called <u>Marsha</u> from the top of the bleachers.

    They called _____ again, loudly.

25. Marsha saw <u>Jackie</u> up in the bleachers.

    She asked _____ to save seats.

26. Jackie tossed a <u>balloon</u> down to us.

    We carried _____ up to him.

Unit 4, Lesson 3 • Use after page 181.

96

Possessive Pronouns

Revising
Marks

cross _____
out

add   ∧

move   ⟳

A. Dana wrote a script for the upcoming fashion show. When she read

1-20. it, she realized she could have used possessive pronouns in place of
some possessive nouns. Help Dana make these changes. Correct any
other errors you find also. Use the revising and proofreading marks
on this page.

Proofreading
Marks

capital letter   ≡

small letter   /

indent paragraph ¶

check spelling   ⬭

Welcome to our School Fashion Show. My name is

○ dana, and today I will be showing you fashions for

preteens. Our First model is Marcy. Marcy's green

jumper with pink polka dots really makes a fashion

statement. On Marcy's head is a hat which reelly sets

off the outfit

Our next two models are Mark and Leroy. Mark's

and Leroy's jackets are made of real leather. Mark's and

○ Leroy's jackets match the glow-in-the-dark pants nicely.

Mark's striped shirt brings out the Color of Mark's orange

pants. Mark is carrying an unusual umbrella. The

umbrella's handle has several uses It contains a pencil

case on one side and a radio on the other. this is an item

that is sure to be popular with preteens. The umbrella

○ handle is Dana's own personal design. Leroy's checkered

sneakers pick up the check pattern in Leroy's shirt very

nicly. Leroy and Mark where Leroy's and Mark's outfits

very well. thank you Leroy and mark.

B. Write a short script for a fashion show. Try to use possessive pronouns to show ownership. Use the revising and proofreading marks if you need to make changes.

_____

_____

_____

_____

 C. A new fashion is coming out next season that all the kids will be wearing. To find out what the fashion is, first find the underlined possessive noun in each sentence. In the blank, write a possessive pronoun to replace the underlined noun or nouns. Then underline the first letter of each pronoun you write. Shade the spaces containing those letters to see the latest fashion.

21. Marcy, Leroy, and Mark took modeling lessons at

Marcy, Leroy, and Mark's school. _____

22. Marcy wishes the outfits she models could be

Marcy's. _____

23. "Marcy's clothes are not as stylish as the ones

I model," explains Marcy. _____

24. Mark loves Mark's job modeling clothes. _____

25. "My family comes to all my shows and many

friends of my family's come, too." _____

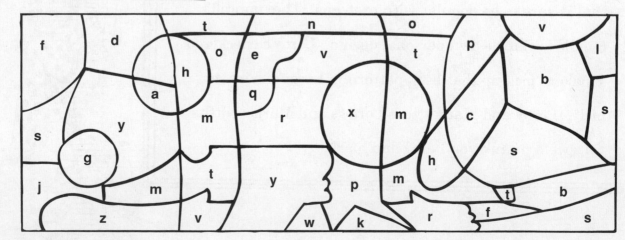

Using Pronouns

A. Calvin keeps notes at his weekly chess club meetings. As you will see, he made some mistakes using pronouns. Help Calvin by supplying the correct pronouns. Remember to use a subject pronoun as the subject of a sentence and an object pronoun after an action verb. Correct any other errors you find also. Use the revising and proofreading marks on this page.

1-19.

Revising Marks	
cross out	_____
add	∧
move	↺

Proofreading Marks	
capital letter	≡
small letter	/
indent paragraph	¶
check spelling	⬭

The chess club meeting came to order at 2:00 P.M., Thursday, January 15. Jane asked Susanna and I about the upcoming chess meet. Us and the other members will be facing tough competititon. susanna told I that a player on the opposing chess team had one a State competition Robert asked the team for ideas on how we can prepar for the upcoming meet. Him and Paul offered to hold special practice sessions in their home. the team and me agread that this was a good idea. Mark told we that his dad, Mr. Harmon, is a chess professional. His dad taught he and his family how to play chess. Benita had a good idea. Maria and her found Good chess tape at the library.

They will show it to we at the next meeting.

The meeting came to a close at 3:30 P.M

Name_____

 B. Imagine that you are the note taker of a nature club, model rocket club, or another club that interests you. Write minutes for an imaginary meeting. Be sure to use subject and object pronouns correctly. Use revising and proofreading marks to show any changes.

_____

_____

_____

_____

_____

_____

C. You can discover what the following mystery club is about by completing the sentences taken from the club meeting notes. Circle the correct subject or object pronoun to complete each sentence. Then write what you think the mystery club is for.

20. Valerie and (I, me) brought pictures to the club meeting.

21. (She, Her) and I had taken the pictures in the forest.

22. George showed the club and (me, I) some slides taken by his dad.

23. George's dad told George and (we, us) about each slide.

24. George and (me, I) made chirping sounds to go with the slides.

25. Valerie taped (him, he) and me as we made the sounds.

26. Cindy gave George and (I, me) some feathers that she found.

27. (Him, He) and I passed them around to all the club members.

28. Then, Kevin said that (him, he) and his mother were planning a trip to the zoo for all club members.

What could the mystery club be?
Did the clues above help you to see?
If your answer rhymes with words,   — — — — —
then you are right, the club is for the...

100

Contractions

A.

1-22. Tomás is spending his summer vacation with his grandparents on an island off the coast of Maine. He has written a letter to his friend Marnie. He has not used any contractions in his letter. Help Tomás capture the way people talk. Use contractions in place of pronouns and verbs. Correct any errors you find also. Use the revising and proofreading marks on this page.

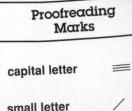

Revising Marks	
cross out	____
add	$\wedge$
move	

Proofreading Marks	
capital letter	$\equiv$
small letter	/
indent paragraph	
check spelling	

Dear Marnie,

I am so excited to be spending the summer with Grandma and Grandpa They have been so much Fun to be with. We have been to the movies and to a mini golf corse. Next week they are taking me to a county fair. I have never been to a fair, have you We will sea lots of prize-winning animals at the fair. Grandma says that i would be a sure winner in the Pie eating contest. I think i would like to Enter the watermelon eating contest instead. Well, I am going to see one next week

   I know you have wanted to visit. You are welcome to come next week. We will go to the fair and climb some rocks together. We are sure everyone will have a great time.

                        Your friend,

                        Tomás

B. Write a letter to a friend about a vacation or trip you have taken. Use contractions to capture the way you talk. Use revising and proofreading marks if you need to make changes.

_____

_____

_____

_____

_____

_____

_____

_____

_____

_____

C. Complete the sentences with contractions. Then use the numbered letters to complete the palindrome below. A palindrome is a word or phrase that is spelled the same way forward and backward.

23. If we don't hurry, __ __ ' __ __ be late.
                          1

24. Donna is sure __ __ __ ' __ forgotten something.
                        2

25. Tomás hopes __ __ ' __ __ be back soon.
                     3

26. Your parents said __ __ __ __ ' __ __ wait for you.
                            4

27. Margie said __ __ __ ' __ __ have too much homework.
                     5

28. Daryl thinks __ __ ' __ __ going to the race together.
                  6

29. The teachers think __ __ __ __ ' __ __ filled all their classes.
                        7

30. The coach told team members __ __ __ __ ' __ better come to
                                    8
practice on time.

__ __ ' __ __ __ __ __ __ a __ __ __ __ __ __ __ __
1 2   3 4   5 6 7 8   8   7 6 5 4   3 2 1

Name_____

A Thought Balloon

You can use these forms to make thought balloons for the
Creative Thinking lesson on pages 194–195.

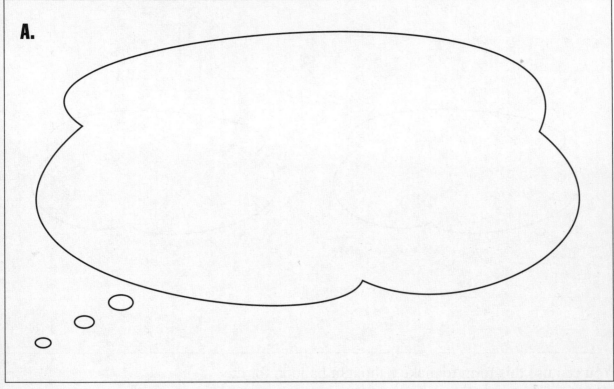

A.

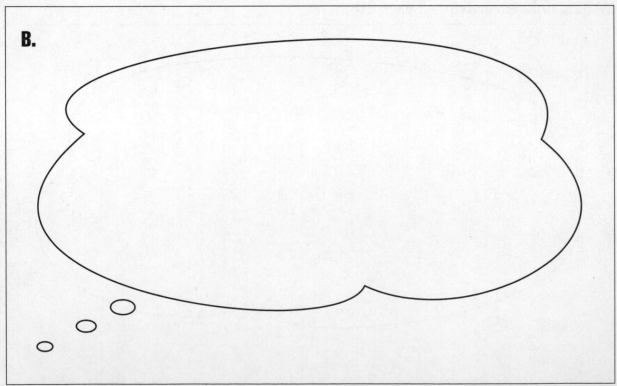

B.

Name_____

A Thought Balloon

You can use these forms to make thought balloons for the
Writing to Learn activity on page 199.

You can use this form to make a thought balloon for the
Writing to Learn activity on page 218.

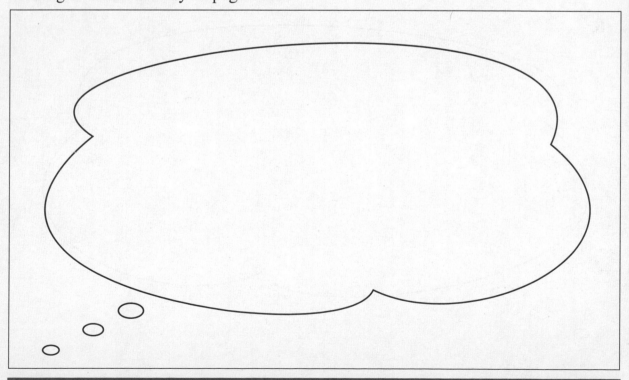

Story Starter

Persuading

You have read a selection from "The Littlest Sculptor" by Joan T. Zeier about a very persuasive young artist. Pretend that you are the artist pictured below. You decide to paint a portrait of a famous person, but first you must persuade the person to sit for you. Who will it be? The President? A rock star? An actor? An athlete? On the back of this page, write a paragraph that will convince the person to allow you to do the painting.

Writing Tips

◇ Use complete sentences to express your ideas. Use capital letters and punctuation carefully.

◇ Support your opinion with facts and reasons. List your reasons in order of importance.

◇ **Focus:** Remember to use the most persuasive words you can think of in your paragraph.

◇ You may wish to reread "The Littlest Sculptor" before you begin. Choose one thing that you like about the writer's way of writing, and try to use it in your own paragraph.

Name

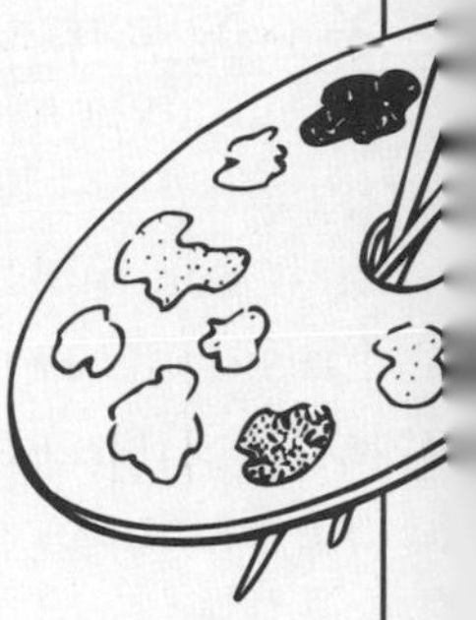

Name_____

Strategy: An Opinion Ladder

Use this page if you choose an opinion ladder as a
prewriting strategy for your persuasive letter.

Strategy: A Thought Balloon

Use this page if you choose a thought balloon as a prewriting strategy for your persuasive letter.

Name_____

cross ——— out	add ∧	move ⌒→

A Persuasive Letter

Practice your revising on the persuasive letter below. Use the revising
tips as a guide. Don't copy the letter. Use the revising marks to cross out,
add, or move words and sentences.

Revising Tips

Check to see that the writer has

◇ written a persuasive letter.
◇ given reasons that will persuade the reader.
◇ used persuasive words.
◇ used pronouns instead of nouns to make the writing less repetitive.
◇ given an opinion and listed reasons to support it.
◇ listed the supporting reasons in the order of their importance.

Dear Fellow Students,

    I think our school colors should be blue and yellow. Blue and yellow

would be a natural choice for our school. Blue and yellow can be found

both inside and outside our school. Blue morning glories and yellow

buttercups are growing all around the school grounds. Yellow shirts and

sweaters can be found in most stores. The floor in the hallway is light blue.

The walls in the main hallway are light yellow. It would be easy for

students to wear the school colors if the school colors were blue and

yellow. All students own a pair of blue jeans. All students could wear blue

jeans to school. We could even have some yellow T-shirts printed with

Kaley Elementary in blue.

    We will be voting next week. I hope that you will vote for the colors

blue and yellow.

                             Sincerely,

                             Nina Knowles

≡	/	⌐ℙ	⬭
capital letter	**small letter**	**indent paragraph**	**check spelling**

A Persuasive Letter

Practice your proofreading on the persuasive letter below. Use the proofreading tips as a guide. Don't copy the letter. Use the proofreading marks to make corrections.

Proofreading Tips

Check to see that the writer has
- ◇ spelled words correctly.
- ◇ indented paragraphs.
- ◇ used capital letters correctly.
- ◇ used correct marks at the end of sentences.

Dear Mayor Martin,

I think we need a playground in our neborhood. our neborhood has at least sixty children who would use the playground. Having a playground would help keep the children from playing in the street. A perfekt place for the playground would be the Empty lot on oak Stret. I heard on the news that the city received Approval for improvements. I think that a neighborhood playground would be an excellent improvement. It would add to the beauty of the neighborhood It would make both the children and their Parents very happy.

I hope that you will consider building a neighborhood playground for the children. we would all be very grateful to the sity.

Sincerely,

Tessie Carroll

Name _____

Writing a Persuasive Letter

Use this form as you do the Writing Process lesson beginning on page 210. Put a check next to each item you can answer yes to.

Revising

☐ **Purpose:** Did I write a persuasive letter?

☐ **Audience:** Will my reasons persuade the person I wrote to?

☐ **Focus:** Did I use persuasive words?

☐ **Grammar Check:** Have I replaced some nouns with pronouns to make my writing less repetitive?

☐ **Word Choice:** Have I used the best words?

☐ **Writing◆Business Letter:** Have I used all six parts of a proper business letter?

Proofreading

☐ Did I spell words correctly?

☐ Did I indent paragraphs?

☐ Did I use capital letters correctly?

☐ Did I use correct marks at the end of sentences?

☐ Did I use my best handwriting?

Publishing

☐ Have I shared my writing with readers or listeners?

☐ Has my audience shared reactions with me?

☐ Have I thought about what I especially liked in this piece of writing?

☐ Have I thought about what I would like to work on the next time?

Use the space on the other side to tell what you liked about your writing and to make notes of your plans for improvement.

Name _____

What I liked about my writing: _____

_____

_____

_____

_____

_____

_____

_____

_____

My plans for improvement: _____

_____

_____

_____

_____

_____

_____

_____

_____

_____

_____

_____

Reader's Name _____

Writer's Name _____

Writing a Persuasive Letter

Use the questions below and on the other side of this page to help you review the writer's persuasive letter. Then give this form to the writer to read and save. Your comments can help the writer improve the persuasive letter.

A First Reaction

Here is what I thought in general about your persuasive letter:

_____

_____

_____

_____

_____

_____

_____

A Second Reaction

Now I have looked at your persuasive letter more closely. I have more specific comments about it.

Here is something you have done well as a writer:

_____

_____

Here is an area that might be improved:

_____

_____

Here is an idea for improvement:

_____

_____

_____

Writing a Persuasive Letter

Check Yes or No for each item. If you check No, explain or give a suggestion for improvement.

Yes No   *Revising*

☐   ☐   **Purpose:** Is the letter persuasive?

_____

☐   ☐   **Audience:** Will the reasons in the letter persuade the person it is written to?

_____

☐   ☐   **Focus:** Did the writer use persuasive words?

_____

☐   ☐   **Grammar Check:** Has the writer replaced some nouns with pronouns to make the writing less repetitive?

_____

☐   ☐   **Word Choice:** Has the writer used the best words?

_____

☐   ☐   **Writing◆Business Letter:** Has the writer used all six parts of a proper business letter?

_____

Yes No   *Proofreading*

☐   ☐   Are words spelled correctly?

_____

☐   ☐   Are paragraphs indented?

_____

☐   ☐   Are capital letters used correctly?

_____

☐   ☐   Are there correct marks at the end of sentences?

_____

☐   ☐   Is the handwriting neat and legible?

_____

Writing with Adjectives

A. Elaine has decided to sell some things that she no longer needs.
She has written an ad which she will post at the local grocery store.
Elaine's ad does not have colorful and interesting details. Help
Elaine by adding some adjectives to her ad. Correct any errors you
find also. Use the revising and proofreading marks on this page.

1–24.

Revising Marks	
cross out	——
add	∧
move	↶

Proofreading Marks	
capital letter	≡
small letter	/
indent paragraph	¶
check spelling	⬭

For Sale

We're ready for new things We must make room, so we

have to sell meny items. All the items are in Good

condition. The items are gently used. They must be seen

Call elaine eny afternoon at 555-3190?

bike with training weels

jacket with decorations

"Solve the Mystery" bord game

<u>Ace Detective Marnie</u> books

doll and ferniture

book bag with pencil case

hat with eerflaps

girl's ice skates size 11

shirt, almost new

bear with overalls

B. Think of some things you might like to sell. Write an ad using adjectives to describe the things you are selling. Use revising and proofreading marks if you need to make changes.

25. _____

26. _____

27. _____

28. _____

29. _____

30. _____

C. Use adjectives to complete the crossword puzzle.

Across

1. Something that can be seen through is _____ .
2. A box with nothing in it is _____ .
4. A room with a lot of clutter is _____ .
6. wonderful; splendid
8. prepared; set
10. Something that tastes wonderful is _____ .
12. If the leg of a table is loose, the table will be _____ .

Down

1. not dirty
2. different or unusual; without exception
3. attractive; good-looking
5. My kitten has _____ fur.
6. full of mercy
7. large and impressive
9. Red paint and _____ paint make orange paint.
11. cross; hard to please

Name_____

Adjectives After Linking Verbs

A. The students in Mr. Perkins's class are writing travel brochures for their town. The brochures are supposed to attract visitors to the town. Roland did his best, but he was having trouble coming up with good descriptive words. Can you help him? Add details to his paragraph by putting in a predicate adjective after each linking verb. Correct any errors you find also. Use the revising and proofreading marks on this page.

1–28.

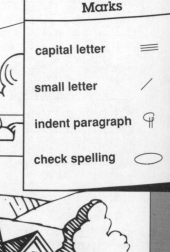

Visit thomasville where the people are

and . It is here. You will enjoy your stay

The old hotal is . All the rooms are . The

food in the hotel dining room tastes . The

food in the hotel snack bar is as well.

Spend afternoons wandering Through

our park. The trees look any tyme of

year The paths are . The playground is .

The small zoo is for children . wander

through our natural historie museum.

The rock collection is . In this part of the

country it is . Come and visit Thomasville.

The strets are . The air smells . You will

feel . you will be a welcome guest.

Name_____

B. How would you get people interested in visiting your town or area of the country? Write a paragraph for a travel brochure. Include some predicate adjectives. Use revising and proofreading marks if you need to make changes.

_____

_____

_____

_____

_____

_____

_____

_____

C. Complete the comic alphabet by supplying a predicate adjective that begins with the letter of the alphabet.

29. A is adorable.

30. B is _____ .

31. C is _____ .

32. D is drowsy.

33. E is exhausted.

34. F is _____ .

35. G is _____ .

36. H is helpful.

37. I is important.

38. J is _____ .

39. K is kind.

40. L is _____ .

41. M is messy.

42. N is _____ .

43. O is out-of-date.

44. P is _____ .

45. Q is quick .

46. R is _____ .

47. S is _____ .

48. T is _____ .

49. U is unclear.

50. V is vast.

51. W is _____ .

52. X is X-rayed.

53. Y is _____ .

54. Z is zany.

Adjectives That Compare

A. Tony wants to buy a radio he can wear while hiking in the woods.
To help him decide which radio to buy, he has written some notes
1–23. about three radios he has seen. Tony had difficulty with
comparative adjectives in his writing. Help him by writing the
correct form of each comparative adjective. Correct any other
errors you find also. Use the revising and proofreading marks on
this page.

Revising Marks	
cross out	_____
add	∧
move	↻

Proofreading Marks	
capital letter	≡
small letter	/
indent paragraph	¶
check spelling	⬭

Comparison of three radios:

the F–E is light than the R24.

The Xerophone radio is the light of all

The R24 haz a clear sounde.

the F–E and the Xerophone both have

clear sounds then the R24.

i think the Xerophone seems the clear of all?

it is also costly than the R24!

The R24 uses big batteries Than the F–E

The Xerophone uses the big Batteries

of all.

The Xerophone is fancy than the R24.

The F–E is the fancy of all three radeos.

Name_____

B. Write a comparison of three similar products, such as three bicycles or three kinds of jeans. Use the -er and -est forms of adjectives. Use revising and proofreading marks if you need to make changes.

_____

_____

_____

_____

_____

_____

C. Use the correct form of the adjective given to complete the puzzle.

Across

2. The one who got the most sun is the _____ . (tan)

3. The one who washed the most is the _____ . (clean)

6. The one who exercises the most is the _____ . (slim)

9. The least messy is the _____ . (neat)

10. The one who got more sun than the other is _____ . (tan)

Down

1. Jill got dunked more than Tom. She is _____ than he is. (wet)

4. The one who is more agreeable is _____ . (nice)

5. The road that is more level is _____ . (flat)

7. The nastiest one is the _____ . (mean)

8. The most level of all is the _____ .(flat)

120

Name_____

Using <u>more</u> and <u>most</u> with Adjectives

⚡**A.**
1–25. Tina wrote a movie review for her school newspaper. Tina had some trouble with comparative adjectives. Help her by supplying the correct form of the adjectives. Correct any other errors you find also. Use the revising and proofreading marks on this page.

Home Again is one of the powerful by Simon Taylor. The plot has the amazing twists and turns of any of his movies. The acshun in the second half is even exciting than in the first half The surprize ending is the suspensful of all the films out this year. I think the leading acktors give their good performances ever. John Jeremy was interesting than his brother Ben. he could make you lauff with just a look. The scenery was impressive in this movie than in Mr. Taylor's last movie. The action takes place in the beautiful town in all of Englend One of the fabulous castles is seen throughout the movie. the sunsets are probably the spectacular ever filmed.

All in all, you must see this picture It is the good of the year.

B. Write a review of a movie or television show that you particularly liked. Use a variety of adjectives, including several that need <u>more</u> or <u>most</u>, to make comparisons. Use revising and proofreading marks if you need to make changes.

_____

_____

_____

_____

_____

_____

_____

_____

_____

_____

C. Complete each of the following lines from different movie reviews. Remember to use the correct form of the adjective.

26. The best of the three movies was <u>The Shark</u> because it was

the _____ of all.

27. <u>The Long Journey</u> was _____ than the writer's first

movie, <u>Trails Westward</u>.

28. <u>The Fabulous Flight</u> was the _____ of all the science

fiction films.

29. <u>The Mystery at the Castle</u> was _____ than <u>The Case of

the Missing Letter</u>.

30. The special effects in <u>Planet Pranks</u> were _____ than

the ones in <u>Meteor Magic</u>.

31. The costumes in <u>Balloon Battles</u> were the _____ I have

seen in a long time.

Name_____

A Thought Balloon

You can use these forms to make thought balloons for the
Creative Thinking lesson on pages 248–249.

A.

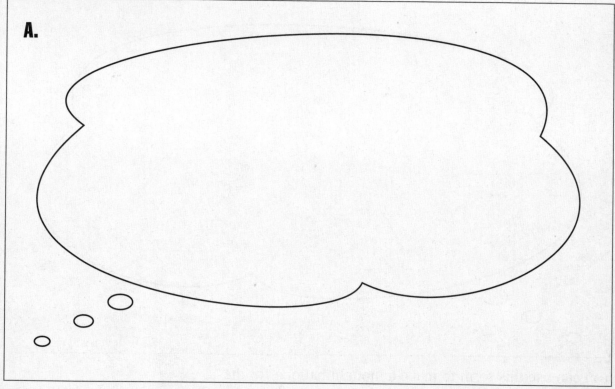

B.

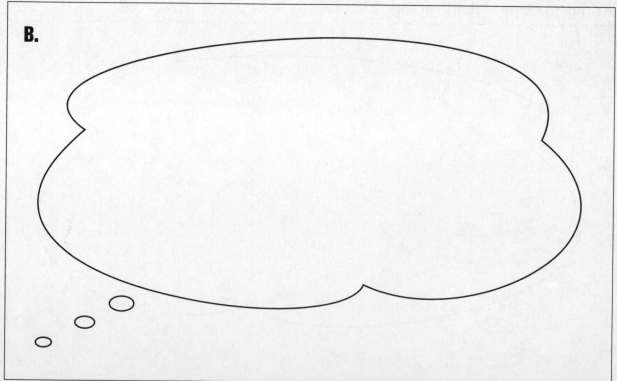

Name_____

A Thought Balloon

You can use this form to make a thought balloon for the
Writing to Learn activity on page 255.

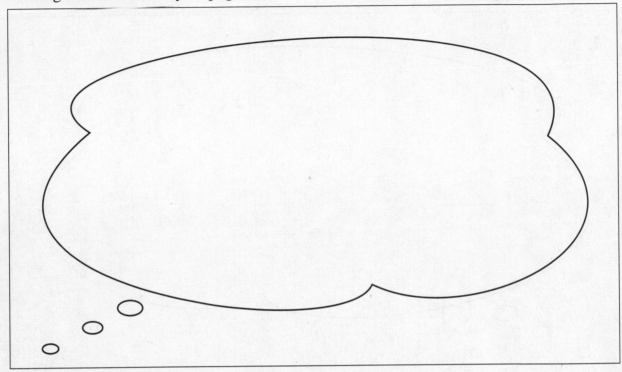

You can use this form to make a thought balloon for the
Writing to Learn activity on page 272.

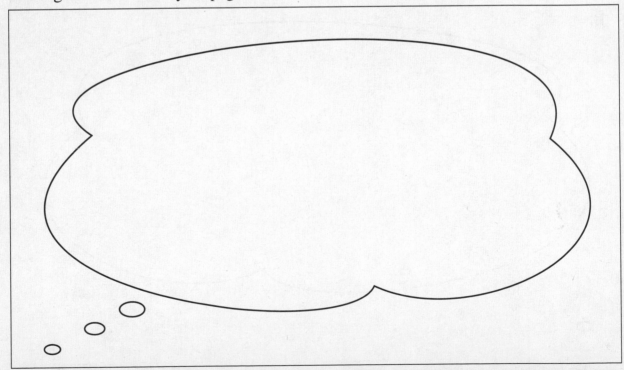

Name _____

Describing

You have read a selection from <u>Zeely</u> by Virginia Hamilton. Now imagine that you, Geeder, and Toeboy are in the picture below. You are hiking through the woods on the other side of Uncle Ross's farm. As you come to a clearing, you notice a shack. There are strange noises coming from inside. The door opens with a crash. On the back of this page, describe the character who walks out.

Writing Tips

◇ Use complete sentences to express your ideas. Use capital letters and punctuation carefully.

◇ Organize details by space order or order of importance to help the reader picture what you describe.

◇ **Focus:** Remember to use sensory words and other details to show what your character is like.

◇ You may wish to reread <u>Zeely</u> before you begin. Choose one thing that you like about the writer's way of writing, and try to use it in your description.

Unit 5 • LITERATURE • Use after the Reading-Writing Connection on pages 262–263.

125

Name

Strategy: A Character Map

Use this page to make a sketch if you choose a character map
as a prewriting strategy for your character sketch.

Strategy: A Thought Balloon

Use this page if you choose a thought balloon as a prewriting strategy for your character sketch.

Name _____

| cross out ——— | add ∧ | move ⟳ |

A Character Sketch

Practice your revising on the character sketch below. Use the revising tips as a guide. Don't copy the sketch. Use the revising marks to cross out, add, or move words and sentences.

Revising Tips

Check to see that the writer has

◇ given a vivid description of someone.

◇ made the character sketch enjoyable to read.

◇ included details and sensory words to help the reader get to know the character.

◇ used adjectives to add specific details to the writing.

◇ used precise words for words such as <u>good</u> and <u>cute</u>.

◇ organized descriptive details clearly, using space order or order of importance.

◆

Life is never dull when I'm with my sister Samantha. Sam is only five years old. She still has all of her baby teeth. She has long golden braids that go all the way down her back. Her eyes are dark. The freckles that dot her face are brown, too. Her good smile makes you want to smile right back.

Sam has energy. No one in the family can keep up with her. She works or plays busily from morning until night. Her voice chatters away all day. The cute things she says tickle everyone.

Sam makes me feel so special. She always asks me to braid her hair. I'm her favorite babysitter. Sam likes to wear my jeans and a T-shirt. She also likes to cuddle up with me while I read to her. Then she looks at a book while I do my homework. My sister Samantha is terrific.

≡	/	⊖	◯
capital letter	small letter	indent paragraph	check spelling

A Character Sketch

Practice your proofreading on the character sketch below. Use the proofreading tips as a guide. Don't copy the sketch. Use the proofreading marks to make corrections.

Proofreading Tips

Check to see that the writer has
- ◇ spelled words correctly.
- ◇ indented paragraphs.
- ◇ used capital letters correctly.
- ◇ used correct marks at the end of sentences.

If you walk through Baker Landing School and listen, you can hear the sweet voice of Ann Prentiss. ms. Prentiss is our music teacher. She has tauht here for fifteen years. Her cheery face lights up the halls. when she sings, everyone brightens up. She loves Music and children. That is why she chose to be a music teacher.

Ms. Prentiss's job is to intoduce music to all the students. She teaches kindergarten through eighth grade. she brings her sturdy old pitchpipe to each class. She begins each lessen with a song. Sleepy children's Ears perk up to listen. Her lively songs make everyone want to join in.

Ms. Prentiss beleives that every child should ixperience the joys of singing. She is particularly wonderful with students who are not naturally musical. I know because I am one After she sings with the students, Ms. Prentiss shares her knowledge with them. I'm so glad to know this caring teacher!

Writing a Character Sketch

Use this form as you do the Writing Process lesson beginning on page 264. Put a check next to each item you can answer yes to.

Revising

☐ **Purpose:** Did I write a vivid description of the person?

☐ **Audience:** Will my classmates enjoy my character sketch?

☐ **Focus:** Did I include details to show what this person is like?

☐ **Grammar Check:** Have I used adjectives to add specific details to my writing?

☐ **Word Choice:** Have I used precise words to make my meaning clear?

☐ **Writing◆Organizing Descriptive Details:** Have I used space order or order of importance to organize descriptive details in my character sketch?

Proofreading

☐ Did I spell words correctly?

☐ Did I indent paragraphs?

☐ Did I use capital letters correctly?

☐ Did I use correct marks at the end of sentences?

☐ Did I use my best handwriting?

Publishing

☐ Have I shared my writing with readers or listeners?

☐ Has my audience shared reactions with me?

☐ Have I thought about what I especially liked in this piece of writing?

☐ Have I thought about what I would like to work on the next time?

Use the space on the other side to tell what you liked about your writing and to make notes of your plans for improvement.

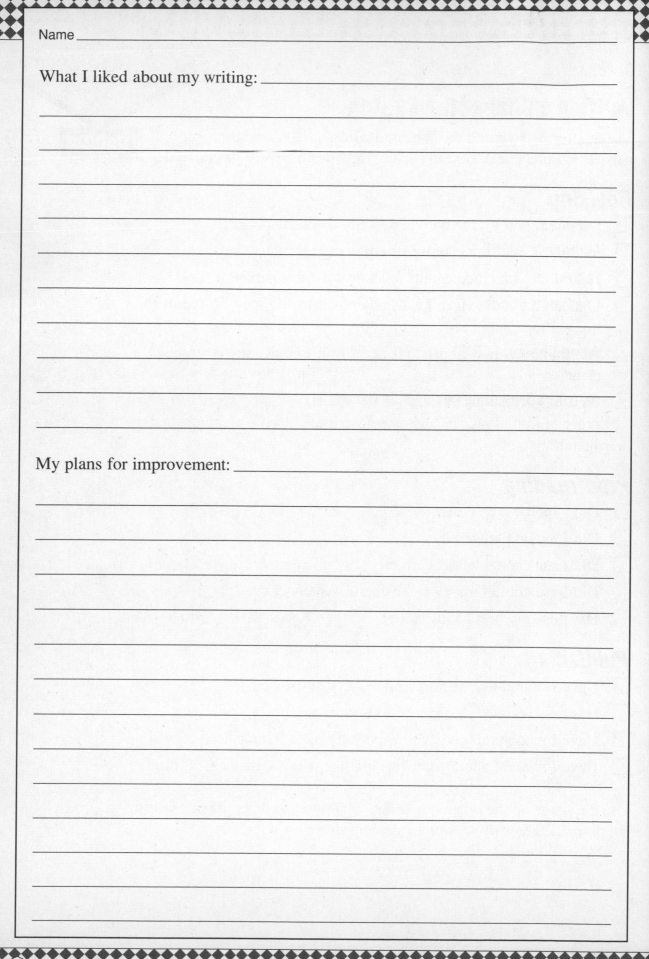

Name _____

What I liked about my writing: _____

_____

_____

_____

_____

_____

_____

_____

My plans for improvement: _____

_____

_____

_____

_____

_____

_____

_____

_____

_____

_____

Writing a Character Sketch

Use the questions below and on the other side of this page to help you review a classmate's character sketch. Then give this form to the writer to read and save. Your comments can help the classmate improve the character sketch.

A First Reaction

Here is what I thought in general about your character sketch:

_____

_____

_____

_____

_____

_____

A Second Reaction

Now I have looked at your character sketch more closely. I have more specific comments about it.

Here is something you have done well as a writer:

_____

_____

Here is an area that might be improved:

_____

_____

Here is an idea for improvement:

_____

_____

Writing a Character Sketch

Check Yes or No for each item. If you check No, explain or give a suggestion for improvement.

Revising

Yes No

☐ ☐ **Purpose:** Did the writer give a vivid description of a person?

_____

☐ ☐ **Audience:** Did I enjoy the character sketch?

_____

☐ ☐ **Focus:** Did the writer include details to show what the person is like?

_____

☐ ☐ **Grammar Check:** Has the writer included adjectives to add specific details to the writing?

_____

☐ ☐ **Word Choice:** Has the writer used precise words to make meanings clear?

_____

☐ ☐ **Writing◆Organizing Descriptive Details:** Does the writer use space order or order of importance to organize descriptive details?

_____

Proofreading

Yes No

Are words spelled correctly?
☐ ☐
_____

Are paragraphs indented?

☐ ☐
_____

Are capital letters used correctly?

☐ ☐
_____

Are there correct marks at the end of sentences?

☐ ☐
_____

Is the handwriting neat and legible?

☐ ☐
_____

Name _____

Writing with Adverbs

A.

1-27. Melissa started to write a bedtime story that she could tell her little sister. Read the story beginning and help Melissa add details to her writing. Add adverbs that describe _how_, _when_, or _where_ the action occurs. Correct any errors you find also. Use the revising and proofreading marks on this page.

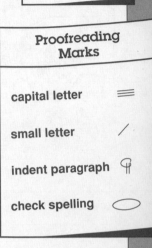

Revising Marks

cross out	____
add	∧
move	⟳

An old man and woman worked on their small farm. They led a very quiet life. they had visters. One morning a yung boy appeared. he had news from a nearby village He Spoke . The old man and woman listened. Then they questioned him. The boy said that a Huge frendly giant had wandered into his Village. Day after day, the giant explored the villagers waited. What would the giant do The giant announced that he would stay. the giant had wanted a new home What would the villagers do? Would they learn to live with the Huge friendly giant The old man and woman sat down. they thought about the situation. They thought about what they should say. They gave their advice.

Proofreading Marks

capital letter	≡
small letter	/
indent paragraph	¶
check spelling	⬭

Name _____

B. Now write your own story beginning to go with the picture. Use adverbs to add details to your writing. If you need to show changes, use revising and proofreading marks.

_____
_____
_____
_____
_____
_____
_____
_____
_____
_____

C. Read the story beginning below. Replace the adverb in each sentence with an adverb that has an opposite meaning. Reread the story beginning to a friend.

28-38.

Jenny rushed to the school gym. She was slightly out of breath. The tryouts for gymnastics were held today. Her friends waited patiently. The girls lined up outside. Jenny entered the gym slowly. She began her tumbles carefully. She tumbled forward. Then she spun slowly. She landed well. Jenny ended her tryouts happily. She calmly waited for the second round of tryouts.

136

Name_____

Adverbs That Compare

A. Lee's mother was interested in buying a copier for her office. When
1-27. Lee heard a commercial for copiers, he wrote down the information
for his mother. Lee had trouble writing adverbs that compare. Help
him correct the form of each adverb he wrote. You may need to
change the word or add <u>more</u> or <u>most</u>. Correct any other errors you
find also. Use the revising and proofreading marks on this page.

Now is the Perfect time to buy an office copier

The super x copies well of all machines

avallable today. It works the smoothly of all

three leading brans. it copys quietly than Artful

copier. it sorts carefully than Artful Copier? It

can be used easily than copier king It starts up

fast than than Copier King, too. you can

beleive us when we say, "The Super X Copier

copies clearly of all mashines." Buy one today

and work quickly than ever Shop at Mini Mall

Machines. The salespeople there will gladly

help you.

B. Pretend you are a writer of commercials. You have been asked to compare two bicycles. You want to show that Speed Racer is better than Dirt Zoomer. Write your commercial below. Use adverbs to compare how the bicycles go, stop, spin, brake, and last. If you need to show changes, use revising and proofreading marks.

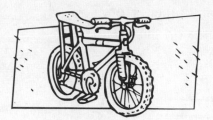 

_____

_____

_____

_____

_____

_____

 C. Read each question. Underline the adverb in parentheses ( ) that correctly completes each sentence. Then answer the question by circling the answer.

28. In stories, who acts (more cleverly, most cleverly)?   rabbit   ox   fox

29. Which month comes (earlier, earliest)?   June   August

30. Which breaks (more easily, most easily)?   eggshell   glass   gold ring

31. Which bends (more easily, most easily)?   rubber   steel

32. Which moves (more gracefully, most gracefully)?   penguin   swan

33. Which animal moves (more slowly, most slowly)?   snake   deer   snail

34. Which bird sings (more sweetly, most sweetly)?   crow   canary

35. Which animal acts (more playfully, most playfully)?   dolphin   zebra   shark

36. Which stands (taller, tallest)?   giraffe   elephant

37. Which winds move (more swiftly, most swiftly)?   hurricane   thunderstorm

Adverbs Before Adjectives and Other Adverbs

A. Rita received a mystery book as a gift from her Aunt Louisa. She
1-24. wrote the following thank-you note to her aunt. Help Rita improve
the thank-you note. Add adverbs to make adjectives and other
adverbs more exact. Correct any other errors you find also. Use
the revising and proofreading marks on this page.

Revising Marks	
cross out	_____
add	∧
move	↶

Proofreading Marks	
capital letter	≡
small letter	/
indent paragraph	¶
check spelling	⬭

14 Andrews drive

Portland, oregon 97208

June 20, 1992

Dear Aunt Louisa,

you are thoughtful. i was happy to recieve

the mystery book. It was beautifully wrapped?

It was a good present for me I always read

mystery storys. This was an exciting one. I

read it fast the ending toatally baffled me! The

author was clever. Thank you again for the

interesting book. It was kind of you to remember

my birthday with such a Wonderful gift

Love,

Rita

B. Pretend this gift box is for you. Decide from whom the gift is and what it might be. Then write a thank-you note. Use adverbs to make the adjectives and adverbs in your writing more exact. If you need to show changes, use revising and proofreading marks.

_____

_____

_____

_____

_____

_____

_____

_____

_____

_____

_____

_____

_____

_____

C. Think of some gift ideas of your own to complete each sentence below. Also add an adverb on the appropriate blank in the sentences.

25. The giant said, "Thank you for the _____ huge _____ ."

26. The tiger said, "Thank you for the _____ delicious _____ ."

27. The elephant said, "Thank you for the _____ enormous _____ ."

28. The ant said, "Thank you for the _____ tiny _____ ."

29. The princess said, "Thank you for the _____ delicate _____ ."

30. The dragon said, "Thank you for the _____ ferocious _____ ."

31. The frog said, "Thank you for the _____ cute _____ ."

32. The king said, "Thank you for the _____ serious _____ ."

Using Adverbs and Adjectives

A.
1-25. Mrs. Hart asked her students to help her develop a questionnaire. Each student wrote one question about schoolwork or homework. Read the questions. Correct errors in the use of adverbs and correct any other errors you find also. Use the revising and proofreading marks on this page.

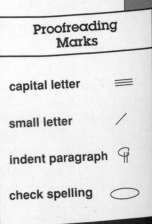

Revising Marks

cross out	_____
add	∧
move	↶

Proofreading Marks

capital letter	≡
small letter	/
indent paragraph	¶
check spelling	⬭

Questionnaire

Do you tire easy in school?   yes   no

is your handwriting neatly?   yes   no

Are you eagerly to do your homwork?   yes   no

Do you work careful   yes   no

do you usual study at Night   yes   no

Are You a well worker?   yes   no

Is your artwork wonderfully?   yes   no

do you read rapid   yes   no

Do you work slow   yes   no

Do you complet your work thorough?   yes   no

Do you do good in science!   yes   no

Are you a well math Student?   yes   no

B. Make up a questionnaire for your friends. Ask questions about sports or hobbies. The first one is started for you. Notice the answer choices are <u>sometimes</u> or <u>never</u>. Use adverbs and adjectives in your writing. If you nccd to make changes, use revising and proofreading marks.

26. Can you throw a baseball _____ sometimes never

27. _____ sometimes never

28. _____ sometimes never

29. _____ sometimes never

30. _____ sometimes never

31. _____ sometimes never

32. _____ sometimes never

33. _____ sometimes never

34. _____ sometimes never

35. _____ sometimes never

36. _____ sometimes never

C. Complete this questionnaire about animals. Use <u>good</u> or <u>well</u> to complete sentences 37–42. Use <u>bad</u> or <u>badly</u> to complete sentences 43–46. Then answer the questions.

37. Is an ostrich a _____ flier?   yes   no

38. Do leopards run _____ ?   yes   no

39. Have you ever heard a monkey speak _____ ?   yes   no

40. Is a mountain goat a _____ climber?   yes   no

41. Do seals fish _____ ?   yes   no

42. Are bears _____ swimmers?   yes   no

43. Do hawks have _____ eyesight?   yes   no

44. Do female lions treat their young _____ ?   yes   no

45. Do camels have _____ tempers?   yes   no

46. Does a donkey ever behave _____ ?   yes   no

Using Negative Words

A.
1-26.

Robert had the kind of day when everything seemed to go wrong. When he wrote about it in his diary, he used some double negatives. Help Robert revise the diary page so that each sentence has only one negative word. Correct any other errors you find in the diary entry. Use the revising and proofreading marks on this page.

Revising Marks	
cross out	_____
add	∧
move	↻

Proofreading Marks	
capital letter	☰
small letter	/
indent paragraph	¶
check spelling	⬭

Dear Diary,

You can't never imagine what hapened today? I have not never forgotten so many things in one Day. This was the day of Our class trip i didn't bring no lunch with me. none of my friends had no extra food. Luckily my teacher shared her lunch with me Also, You know that I never go nowhere without my mit. Well, today, of all days, I lefft it at home. I had to miss catching practize. Then, after School, I was lat for glee club because nobody never told me that it was three o'clock instead of four o'clock I hope tomorow is a better day! it couldn't be no worse!   Robert

B. Now write your own diary entry. You might want to tell about a day when you forgot something or missed going somewhere. If you need to make changes, use revising and proofreading marks.

_____

_____

_____

_____

_____

_____

_____

_____

C. Do a word search. Circle each negative word you find, except for the words <u>no</u> and <u>not</u>. You may look across or down. Then use each word to complete the following diary entry.

27–36.

U N N O B O D Y S A Q

N O T H I N G J F R D

X N R N O W H E R E O

N E J Z T H W X Z I W

A C O U L D N ' T Y U

Dear Diary,

     I _____ find my glasses. They were _____ to be found. _____ of my friends had found them. _____ remembered seeing them. There was _____ to do but read without them. Then I felt something strange. I reached up and found them right on my head!

Name_____

An Order Circle

You can use these forms to make order circles for the Critical
Thinking lesson on pages 300–301.

A.

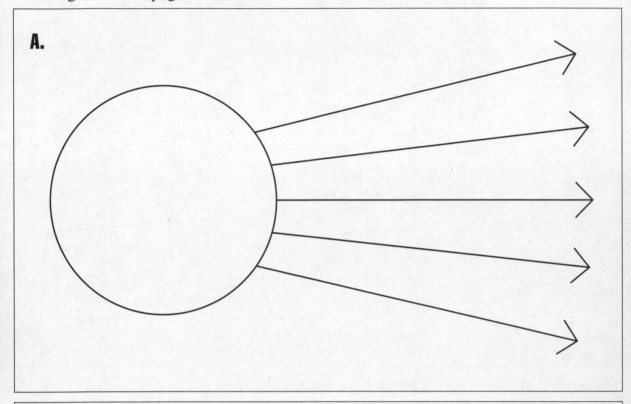

B.

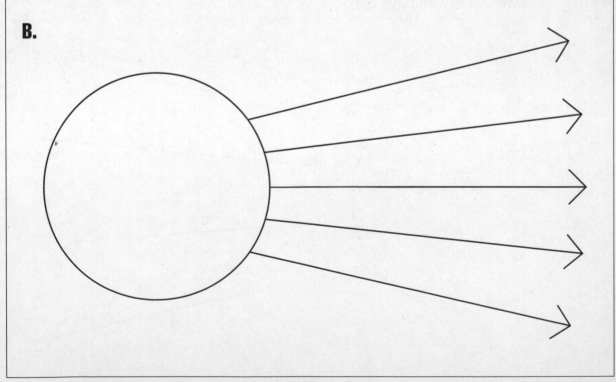

Name_____

An Order Circle

You can use this form to make an order circle for the
Writing to Learn activity on page 307.

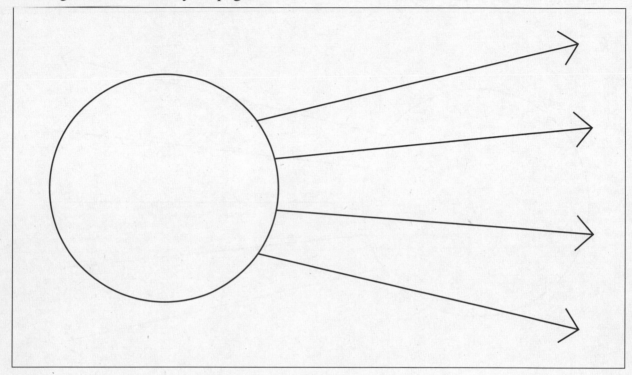

You can use this form to make an order circle for the
Writing to Learn activity on page 326.

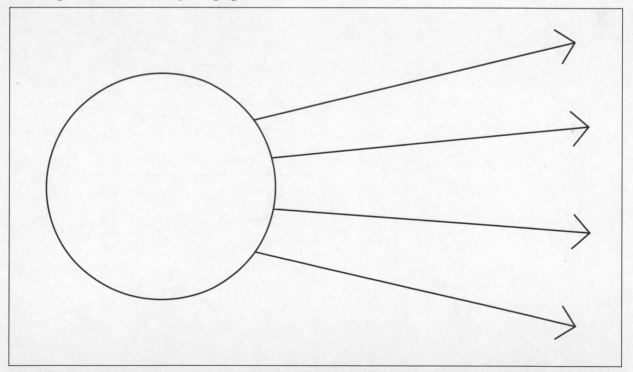

Name_____

Researching

You have read a selection from <u>Volcano</u> by Patricia Lauber. Now imagine you are preparing to give a short talk about these eruptions. You will use the diagram below to explain what causes a volcano to erupt. On the back of this page, write what you will say in your talk. You may also use information from <u>Volcano</u> that is written in your own words.

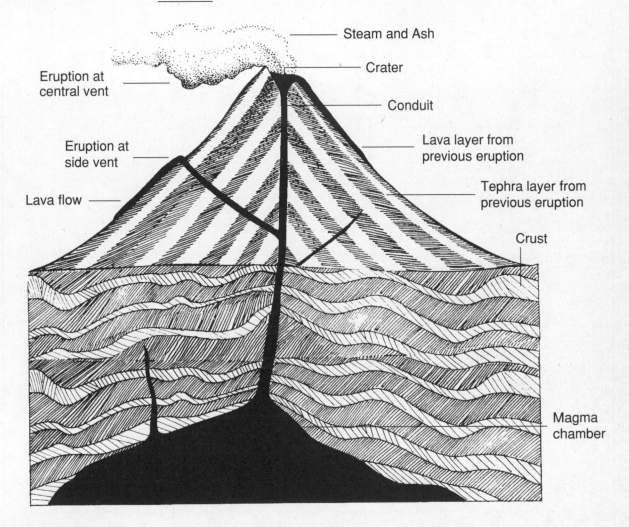

Steam and Ash

Crater

Eruption at central vent

Conduit

Eruption at side vent

Lava layer from previous eruption

Lava flow

Tephra layer from previous eruption

Crust

Magma chamber

Writing Tips

◇ Use complete sentences to express your ideas. Use capital letters and punctuation carefully.

◇ Organize your information into main ideas and supporting details.

◇ **Focus:** Choose a topic narrow enough for a short talk.

◇ When you reread <u>Volcano</u>, choose one thing that you like about the writer's way of writing, and try to use it in your report.

Name _____

Strategy: Taking Notes

Use this page if you choose taking notes as a prewriting strategy
for your research report. Use real note cards to take more notes.

Strategy: An Order Circle

Use this page if you choose an order circle as a prewriting
strategy for your research report.

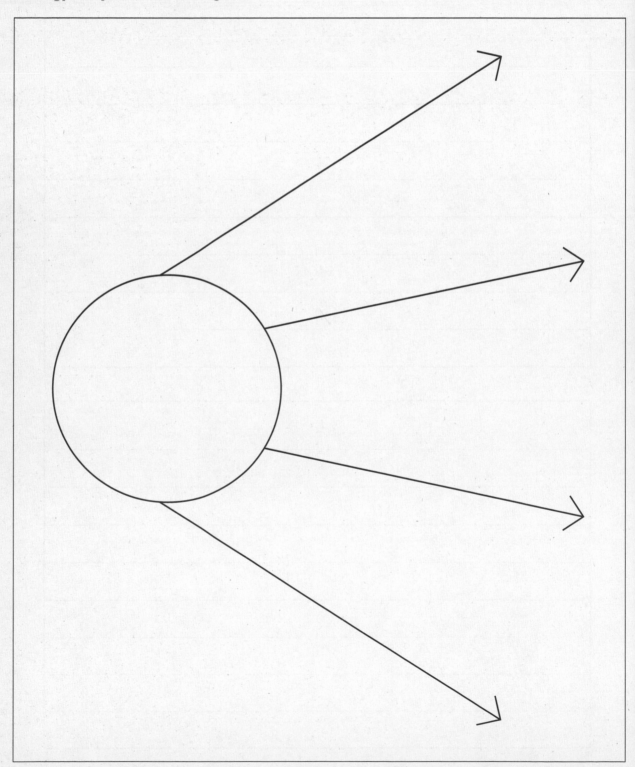

| cross out —— | add ∧ | move ⌒⟶ |

A Research Report

Practice revising on the research report below. Use the revising tips.
Don't copy the report. Use the revising marks to cross out, add, or move
words and sentences.

Revising Tips

Check to see that the writer has

◇   told about an unusual natural event.
◇   made sure the report is interesting and understandable.
◇   chosen a topic that was narrow enough for a short report.
◇   avoided using double negatives.
◇   avoided overused words such as <u>beautiful</u> and <u>said</u>.
◇   organized information into a main idea with supporting details.

◆

Do you think seventy-six years is a long time to wait for something?
No scientists do not think so. That is about how long they wait for Halley's
Comet to appear.

The majestic comet was first seen by Edmund Halley in 1682. The most
recent sighting was in 1986. He said that it would return in seventy-six
years. He was right.

A comet is a heavenly body. A star is also a heavenly body. A comet
travels in a path around the sun. When the comet is far from the sun, it
cannot never be seen. It follows an orbit, just as the Earth does. When a
comet gets nearer to the sun, it can be seen. A comet's ice and gases melt as
it nears the sun. That is the trail that can be seen in a nighttime sky. The
comet's tail is a beautiful sight. I hope I'll be able to see Halley's Comet
when it comes back!

≡	/	¶	◯
capital letter	small letter	indent paragraph	check spelling

A Research Report

Practice your proofreading on the research report below. Use the proofreading tips as a guide. Don't copy the report. Use the proofreading marks to make corrections.

Proofreading Tips

Check to see that the writer has

◇ spelled words correctly.

◇ indented paragraphs.

◇ used capital letters correctly.

◇ used correct marks at the end of sentences.

Can you imagine watching water shoot up from the earth? This is what happens every hour in Yellowstone national Park. People gather in a circle and wait for Old Faithful to spout its water and steam. Old Faithful ejects 5,000–7,000 gallons of hot water in one eruption. The tower of water shoots about as high as a 13-story building. Old Faithful is a geyser. A geyser is a spring that begins deep below the earth's surface. Water in the spring is heated by hot rocks deep in the erth. The water produces steam. The water and Steam then shoot up from the Geyser with great force

This great geyser got the name Old Faithful because it is so reliable. the eruptions occur 20–30 times per day, every day, year after year. The shortest interval between eruptions is 33 minutes, while the longest interval is 148 minutes. Other great geysers have been Inactive for months or even years. Old Faithful has never stopped.

people come from far and wide to see Old faithful. It is the most famis geyser in the word.

Writing a Research Report

Use this form as you do the Writing Process lesson beginning on page 318. Put a check next to each item you can answer yes to.

Revising

☐ **Purpose:** Did I write a research report about an unusual natural event?

☐ **Audience:** Will my classmates find my report understandable and interesting?

☐ **Focus:** Is my topic narrow enough to be covered well in a short report?

☐ **Grammar Check:** Have I avoided double negatives?

☐ **Word Choice:** Have I avoided overusing certain words?

☐ **Writing♦An Outline:** Did I organize my information into main ideas and supporting details?

Proofreading

☐ Did I spell words correctly?

☐ Did I indent paragraphs?

☐ Did I use capital letters correctly?

☐ Did I use correct marks at the end of sentences?

☐ Did I use my best handwriting?

Publishing

☐ Have I shared my writing with readers or listeners?

☐ Has my audience shared reactions with me?

☐ Have I thought about what I especially liked in this piece of writing?

☐ Have I thought about what I would like to work on the next time?

Use the space on the other side to tell what you liked about your writing and to make notes of your plans for improvement.

Name _____

What I liked about my writing: _____

_____

_____

_____

_____

_____

_____

_____

_____

My plans for improvement: _____

_____

_____

_____

_____

_____

_____

_____

_____

_____

_____

_____

Writing a Research Report

Use the questions below and on the other side of this page to help you review a classmate's research report. Then give this form to the writer to read and save. Your comments can help the classmate improve the research report.

A First Reaction

Here is what I thought in general about your research report:

_____

_____

_____

_____

_____

_____

A Second Reaction

Now I have looked at your research report more closely. I have more specific comments about it.

Here is something you have done well as a writer:

_____

_____

Here is an area that might be improved:

_____

_____

Here is an idea for improvement:

_____

_____

_____

Writing a Research Report

Check Yes or No for each item. If you check No, explain or give a suggestion for improvement.

| Yes | No | *Revising* |

☐ ☐ **Purpose:** Did the writer prepare a research report about an unusual natural event?

_____

☐ ☐ **Audience:** Did I find the report understandable and interesting?

_____

☐ ☐ **Focus:** Is the topic narrow enough to be covered well in a short report?

_____

☐ ☐ **Grammar Check:** Has the writer avoided double negatives?

_____

☐ ☐ **Word Choice:** Has the writer avoided overusing certain words?

_____

☐ ☐ **Writing◆An Outline:** Did the writer organize the information into main ideas and supporting details?

_____

Yes No ## *Proofreading*

☐ ☐ Are words spelled correctly?

_____

☐ ☐ Are paragraphs indented?

_____

☐ ☐ Are capital letters used correctly?

_____

☐ ☐ Are there correct marks at the end of sentences?

_____

☐ ☐ Is the handwriting neat and legible?

_____

Name_____

Writing with Prepositions

A.
1-26. Marta and her friends are putting on a backyard carnival. They are making posters to let people know about the event. Check the posters to see that prepositions have been used correctly. Correct any other errors you find also. Use the revising and proofreading marks on this page.

COME OF THE CARNIVAL!

See the funnyest clown of the World!

Enter the appel bobbing contest to your friends!

Watch Magic Marta pull a rabbit in a hat!

The fun does not stop

The carnival will be held of 32 Village street,

Saturday, May 10 on noon.

BRING ALL YOUR FRIENDS AND COME JOYN THE FUN!

We are having a carnival to everyone!

Enjoy a majic show a clown act, and a surprize Contest.

Have your face painted like a clown

Win a prize of the ring tos game.

Lots to refreshments Will be serve.

the fun begins at Saturday, May 10 at noon.

The carnival will be held at 32 village Street.

Name_____

B. Marta needs several different posters to display in the neighborhood. Help her advertise for the carnival by creating a poster. Be sure to use prepositions correctly. Use revising and proofreading marks if you need to make changes.

C. Discover the special event that will take place at the carnival. Read each sentence. If the letter <u>P</u> appears after a sentence, underline the preposition. If the letter <u>O</u> appears after a sentence, underline the object of the preposition. Write the first letter of each underlined word in the numbered spaces. The words that are formed name the special event.

27. Let's plan what we will have at the carnival. (P)

28. The clown is inside the tent. (P)

29. Should the magic show be in your room? (O)

30. No, it should be by the garage. (O)

31. I can climb up the ladder and hang this sign. (P)

32. The sign will look great in this tree. (P)

33. Place this game behind the tree. (O)

34. A better place might be somewhere around the garage. (P)

35. Don't put games near the road. (O)

36. At the carnival let's give prizes. (O)

37. The first person who walks over this line can get a prize. (P)

38. Let's have a refreshment stand near the picnic table. (P)

39. On the table we could have plates and napkins. (O)

40. Tickets should be sold at the entrance. (O)

41. Write the ticket prices on a sign. (O)

42. People will enjoy coming to our carnival! (P)

__ __ __ __ __ __ __ __ __ __ __ __ __ __ __ __

Prepositional Phrases

A. Danny and his father are writing a travel brochure for Quiet
Campgrounds. Danny's job is to write a section helping
1-21. visitors find their way around the park. Use the map to make sure
he has described the different locations correctly. Check his use of
prepositional phrases and add one if necessary to make the
meaning clear. Correct any other errors you find also. Use the
revising and proofreading marks on this page.

Revising Marks

cross out	_____
add	∧
move	↻

Proofreading Marks

capital letter	≡
small letter	/
indent paragraph	¶
check spelling	⬭

Quiet
Campgrounds

Finding Your Way Around Quiet Campgrounds

As you enter Quiet Campgrounds you will drive. A rushing river can be

seen. The river flows east over mirror Lake. Above the surface to the

lake are nachral springs. The campers' lodge is. You can learn aboat the

many campground activities for the lodge. Boats can be rented. Beside

the lodge you will find a large sun deck. The nature trails begin over

there. Campsites are located along the Old settlement Trail. Camping

supplies and Food can be found for Pioneer's Trading Post. Nightly

entertainment takes place on the deck. If you need help getting around

the park, Free maps can be found on the lodge. Hav an enjoyable stay at

quiet Campgrounds.

Name

B. Think of a place you have visited, such as a park or a playground. Write a description of how to get around this place. Be sure to include prepositional phrases. If you need to make changes, use revising and proofreading marks.

_____

_____

_____

_____

_____

_____

_____

_____

_____

_____

_____

_____

_____

C. Find your campsite at Quiet Campgrounds. Underline the prepositional phrase in each sentence. Then trace a path through the campground as directed by each sentence. Circle your campsite.

22. Begin at Settlement Trail.

23. Walk across the wooden bridge.

24. Follow the path by the lake.

25. Walk around the large stone.

26. Go to the tall lamppost.

27. Walk through the tall grass.

28. Climb up the stone steps.

29. Your campsite is by the wildflowers.

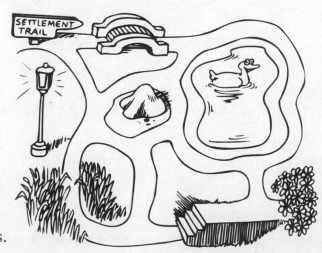

160

Prepositions and Adverbs

A. Chen has been working on an article for the newspaper about a monkey that has escaped from the zoo. But Chen's computer has a virus. It has printed many adverbs, but in each case a prepositional phrase would give more information. Help Chen revise the article. Change all the adverbs to prepositional phrases. Correct any other errors you find also. Use the revising and proofreading marks on this page.

1-25.

Merrille the Monkey Is on the Loose

Merrille the Monkey excaped from the city zoo

yesterday. The escape was Discovered this morning

for feeding time. "all the Monkeys were in the

monkey house except Merrille," exclaimed mr. allen,

the zoo keeper merrille was last seen inside.

Witnesses saw the monkey running around. "The

monkey climbed up," said one eyewitness. "When

I tryed to get him, he ran down. i chased him

around, but he ran faster than I could." The

monkey was seen running inside. Then he quickly

ran out. Another observer saw the monkey hiding

underneath. The monkey waved and jumped over.

Merrille was las seen racing along. If you have

any Information about merrille, please call the zoo

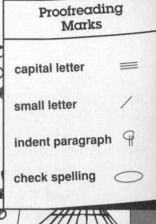

B. Write a newspaper article about another animal that escaped from a zoo. Use some of the following words in your article: along, around, below, down, in, inside, near, off, out, outside, under, up. Use these words as prepositions or as adverbs. If you need to show changes, use revising and proofreading marks.

_____

_____

_____

_____

_____

C. To learn where Merrille was hiding, follow these directions. Read each sentence. After each sentence write whether the underlined word is a preposition or an adverb. Circle the numbers of the sentences with adverbs. Shade the boxes having those numbers to find out where Merrille was found.

26. Merrille does not like to stay <u>inside</u>. _____

27. She will most likely be found <u>outside</u>. _____

28. A police officer saw a monkey hanging <u>in</u> a tree. _____

29. The tree was <u>near</u> the lake. _____

30. The monkey jumped <u>down</u> and ran. _____

31. Merrille hid <u>in</u> a hollow log. _____

32. The officer reached her hand <u>inside</u>. _____

33. The monkey quickly scrambled <u>out</u>. _____

34. The people standing <u>around</u> began laughing. _____

34	26	30	32	28	26	27	30	33	29	33	26	34	31	33	34	26
27	31	24	32	25	33	29	31	30	29	34	31	27	24	31	27	28
30	33	32	30	31	33	28	29	34	31	34	30	32	29	29	33	24
33	28	24	32	24	27	31	24	26	24	34	24	27	29	24	30	31
27	33	26	26	24	34	27	30	32	29	32	24	30	24	29	34	28

Using Prepositional Phrases

A. Virginia wrote a letter to her friend, Linda. She told Linda about her

1-24. trip to the circus. Help Virginia correct her letter. Check to see that she has used prepositional phrases correctly. Correct any other errors you find also. Show the changes that need to be made by using the revising and proofreading marks on this page.

Revising Marks	
cross out	_____
add	∧
move	↪

Proofreading Marks	
capital letter	≡
small letter	/
indent paragraph	¶
check spelling	⬭

Dear Linda

Mom and Dad took jill and I to the circus yesterday. To we the circus was very exiting We sat between all the peopel in the bleachers. Jill liked the clown-and-dog show the best. To she it was the funniest show of all. We saw two clowns with funy faces painted on they. The dogs pranced among two clowns. the one with the tall hat made the dogs jump with he. Then the clowns bilt a little dog house for they. The dogs ran inside the house and it Fell down. For dad and I this was the funnest part I hope we can go the Circus together some time soon. Seeing it together would be a lot of fun for you and I.

Your friend

Virginia

B. Write a letter to a friend. Tell about something exciting you have seen or experienced. Use some of the following object pronouns in your letter: me, you, him, her, it, us, them. Also use the prepositions between and among. If you need to show changes, use revising and proofreading marks.

_____

_____

_____

_____

_____

_____

_____

_____

_____

C. Circle the preposition or object pronoun that correctly completes the sentence. Complete the crossword puzzle by printing each word in the proper place on the puzzle.

Across

2. The lion tamer wore boots with stars all over (they, them).

4. We saw her standing (between, among) two lions.

6. The lion tamer told the lions to stand by (she, her).

Down

1. She stood (among, between) all the lions as they jumped through the ring.

3. This was the most exciting part to (I, me).

5. The lion tamer lit a ring of fire near the lions and hung it before (they, them).

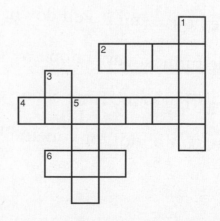

Name_____

Answering "What If?"

You can use these forms to make "what-if" charts for the
Creative Thinking lesson on pages 354–355.

A.

B.

Name_____

Answering "What If?"

You can use these forms to make "what-if" charts for the
Writing to Learn activity on page 359.

You can use this form to make a "what-if" chart for the
Writing to Learn activity on page 376.

Name_____

Creating

You have read poems by six different writers in which ordinary objects come to life and act like people. If you were an object, what would you be and what would you do? "Be" one of the objects below or think up one of your own. Then on the back of this page, write a poem to tell about yourself.

Writing Tips

◇ Use capital letters and punctuation carefully.

◇ Use repetition of words or phrases to bring sound to your poem.

◇ **Focus:** Remember to use personification to give life to the object you are writing about.

◇ You may wish to reread the poems before you begin. Which is your favorite? Choose one thing that you like about the poem, and try to use it in your poem.

Name_____

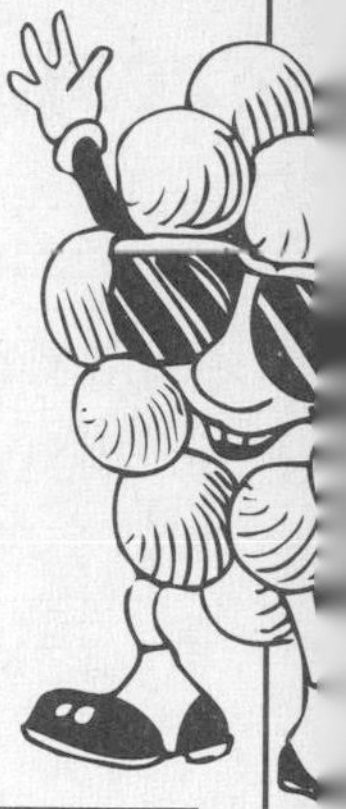

_____

_____

_____

_____

_____

_____

_____

_____

_____

_____

_____

_____

_____

_____

_____

_____

_____

_____

_____

_____

_____

_____

_____

_____

_____

Strategy: Playing a Role

Use this page to take notes if you choose playing a role as a prewriting strategy for your poem.

_____

_____

_____

_____

_____

_____

_____

_____

_____

_____

_____

_____

_____

_____

_____

_____

_____

_____

_____

_____

_____

_____

_____

_____

_____

_____

_____

Strategy: Answering "What If?"

Use this page if you choose a "what-if" chart as a prewriting strategy for your poem.

Name_____

| cross out —— | add ∧ | move ⤳ |

A Poem

Practice revising on the poem below. Use the revising tips. Don't copy the poem. Use the revising marks to cross out, add, or move words and sentences.

Revising Tips

Check to see that the writer has

◇ written a poem that expresses a fresh image or idea.
◇ made the poem enjoyable to the reader.
◇ used personification to help give life to the object.
◇ used prepositions or prepositional phrases to clarify the relationship between one thing and another.
◇ used poetic words.
◇ used some repetition of words or phrases to bring sound to the poetry.

◆

The Rainbow

The beautiful rainbow has

    across the blue-gray sky

    a coat of many colors.

Gently she lends her bright tones

    and soft pastels

    to the pale, white clouds.

She sings out a melody to hear.

    She moves

    bringing beauty for a moment,

    just a moment or two.

Then she says goodbye and

    slowly wanders away.

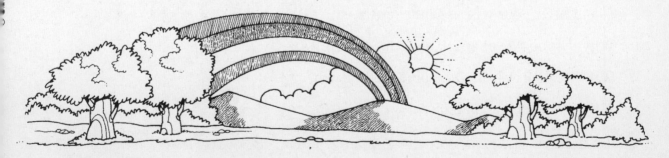

PROOFREADING PRACTICE

Name_____

A Poem

Practice your proofreading on the poem below. Use the proofreading tips as a guide. Don't copy the poem. Use the proofreading marks to make corrections.

Proofreading Tips

Check to see that the writer has

◇ spelled words correctly.

◇ used capital letters correctly.

◇ used correct marks at the end of sentences.

The Oak Tree

How wise you must be, you old oak tree,

but why do you never speak to me?

Your rich green leave shade me,

and your gentle Shade cools me.

How quitely you stand there.

You never say a word.

You always listen carfully

like a good old friend.

as I sit under your branches,

I think about Many things.

You seem to hear my thoughts

and offer your wise, silent counsel.

Why do you Never speak, oak tree?

Is it that your waiting for someone to listen,

A special friend and admirer?

i'm here!

Writing a Poem

Use this form as you do the Writing Process lesson beginning on page 368. Put a check next to each item you can answer yes to.

Revising

☐ **Purpose:** Did I write a poem that expresses a fresh image or idea?

☐ **Audience:** Will my friend enjoy the poem I wrote for him or her?

☐ **Focus:** Did I use personification? Did I show an object behaving like a person?

☐ **Grammar Check:** Have I used prepositions or prepositional phrases to clarify relationships?

☐ **Word Choice:** Have I used poetic words?

☐ **Writing◆Repetition in Poetry:** Have I used repetition to bring sound to my poem?

Proofreading

☐ Did I spell words correctly?

☐ Did I use capital letters correctly?

☐ Did I use correct marks at the end of sentences?

☐ Did I use my best handwriting?

Publishing

☐ Have I shared my writing with readers or listeners?

☐ Has my audience shared reactions with me?

☐ Have I thought about what I especially liked in this piece of writing?

☐ Have I thought about what I would like to work on the next time?

Use the space on the other side to tell what you liked about your writing and to make notes of your plans for improvement.

Name _____

What I liked about my writing: _____

_____

_____

_____

_____

_____

_____

_____

_____

My plans for improvement: _____

_____

_____

_____

_____

_____

_____

_____

_____

_____

_____

_____

_____

Writing a Poem

Use the questions below and on the other side of this page to help you review a classmate's poem. Then give this form to the writer to read and save. Your comments can help the classmate improve the poem.

A First Reaction

Here is what I thought in general about your poem:

_____

_____

_____

_____

_____

_____

A Second Reaction

Now I have looked at your poem more closely. I have more specific comments about it.

Here is something you have done well as a writer:

_____

_____

Here is an area that might be improved:

_____

_____

Here is an idea for improvement:

_____

_____

_____

Writing a Poem

Check Yes or No for each item. If you check No, explain or give a suggestion for improvement.

Yes	No	

Revising

☐ ☐ **Purpose:** Does the poem express a fresh image or idea?

_____

☐ ☐ **Audience:** Will the friend it is written for enjoy it?

_____

☐ ☐ **Focus:** Did the writer use personification? Did the writer show an object behaving like a person?

_____

☐ ☐ **Grammar Check:** Has the writer used prepositions or prepositional phrases to clarify relationships?

_____

☐ ☐ **Word Choice:** Has the writer used poetic words?

_____

☐ ☐ **Writing◆Repetition in Poetry:** Has the writer used repetition to bring sound to the poem?

_____

Proofreading

Yes No

☐ ☐ Are words spelled correctly?

_____

☐ ☐ Are capital letters used correctly?

_____

☐ ☐ Are there correct marks at the end of sentences?

_____

☐ ☐ Is the handwriting neat and legible?

_____

Reviewing the Parts of Speech

A. Six students wrote a story together. When the story was complete,
they looked it over and decided to make some changes. The story
1–25. needs more adjectives and adverbs to better describe things. Some
of the verbs need to be changed to add more action and excitement.
More pronouns are needed in place of nouns. Some prepositions are
missing or need to be replaced. Help the children improve their
story. Correct any other errors you find. Use the revising and
proofreading marks on this page.

Revising Marks	
cross out	_____
add	∧
move	↷

Proofreading Marks	
capital letter	≡
small letter	/
indent paragraph	¶
check spelling	⬭

It was a summer day . Some kids were looking for something to do.

○ The kids decided to set up a lemonade stand. with the money they

made, they hoped to make a clubhouse. The children had a lot of

customers that afternoon. They sold twelve pitchers. At the end

of the day they clozed the lemonade stand and counted the money.

They had earned $12.64! This Money could go towards bilding

○ their dream clubhouse!

The children started making a list of things they would need for

the clubhouse. then the children started listing the cost of

the materials. They knew they would need to sell more lemonade

to build the clubhouse. The $12.64 would get them started.

They desided that when the clubhouse were built, they would

name it the Lemonade Locker Room. They also decided to give out

○ free Lemonade every Saturday to thank their people for

the clubhouse

B. Write a story of your own. Choose one of the sentences below as a beginning, and work with a partner to complete the story. Remember to use a variety of parts of speech. If you need to make changes, use revising and proofreading marks.

It was a rainy, gloomy night.
The crowd could not wait for the game to begin.
The trip to the zoo was filled with surprises.

_____

_____

_____

_____

_____

_____

_____

C. Find the names of six parts of speech hidden in the puzzle. Then complete the sentences below the puzzle.

```
A A B N O U N Q V W E
A D J E C T I V E V L
D V A S D F G H R I K
P E O N Y U R T B X J
P R E P O S I T I O N
A B L P R O N O U N K
```

They are young skiers. Tony races down steep, snowy slopes. Cindy avoids them and skis carefully on smaller mountains.

26. The pronoun in the first sentence above is _____ .

27. The verbs in the sentences are _____ , _____ , _____ , and _____ .

28. The words <u>skiers</u>, <u>Tony</u>, <u>slopes</u>, <u>Cindy</u>, and <u>mountains</u>

are _____ , not verbs, in the sentences.

29. The adverb in the third sentence is _____ .

30. The adjectives in the sentences are _____ , _____ , _____ , and _____ .

Name_____

Compound Subjects

A. The Sloan family has decided to do some spring cleaning. They
have made a list of what needs to be done. At first they gave only
1–26. one person each chore. Then they decided that the work would go
faster if two or three people worked together. Help the Sloans
revise their list by using compound subjects. Correct any errors you
find also. Use the revising and proofreading marks on this page.

Workers: Mom, Dad, Mary, Jenny, Tad, Billy, and Mark

Mom will wash the windrows.

Dad will scour the oven

Billy will prepare Lunch.

Jenny will dust the furniture.

Mark will wax the floors.

Tad will polish the silverware?

Mary will prepare the grill for the cookout.

Tad will clean up from dinner.

Billy will scrub the sinks

Mary wiil empty the trash.

Dad will clean up from lunch.

Jenny will wash the curtains.

Dad will swepp the porch!

Mom will straighten the closets

Dad will grill the meat.

Mary will make the salad.

The whole family will go to the movey.

B. What things might you and the members of your family do to help around the house? Make a list of chores that you could do together. Use compound subjects to assign more than one person to each task. Use revising and proofreading marks if you need to make changes.

_____

_____

_____

_____

_____

_____

C. Read the following list. Find the sentences that have compound subjects. Circle the first letter in each of those sentences. Use these letters to discover a special message.

27. Lists and notes help you remember things.

28. Some people list activities for each day.

29. Anna and Luis use lists all the time.

30. People make lists for certain jobs.

31. Names and numbers can be listed in a special book.

32. Good friends and family members might be in the book.

33. I have a list of all my favorite authors.

34. Uncle Bill and Aunt Marie keep their address book up to date.

35. A friend or a relative will get a birthday card.

36. I have a list of all my favorite songs.

37. Gan and Chim make lists of their favorite games.

38. My friend makes lists of all his grades.

39. Even my little brother and sister like to make lists.

40. Important days and dates can be listed.

41. Dad never goes shopping without a list.

42. Susie, Taro, and Winona make lists of their favorite foods.

43. Food and drinks for a party should be written on a list.

44. I made a list of important phone numbers.

45. Uncle Pete and Aunt Jean make guest lists.

46. Names and numbers are not the only things you can put on lists.

___ ___ ___ ___ ___ ___   ___ ___   ___ ___ ___ !

Using Subjects and Verbs That Agree

A. The students in Mrs. Kramer's class gave a chili dinner for their
1–24. parents in the school cafeteria last week. Now they are making a
bulletin board display with pictures and captions. Help the class
check their captions to be sure the subjects and verbs agree. Correct
any other errors you find also. Use the revising and proofreading
marks on this page.

Revising Marks	
cross out	_____
add	∧
move	↻

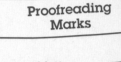

Proofreading Marks	
capital letter	≡
small letter	/
indent paragraph	¶
check spelling	⬭

Andrew and manuel

decorates the

Cafeteria.

Cindy and Her helper

places flowers on

each table

The kramers and

Tony tos salads?

Chili, salid, and bread

all tastes Great.

Kristy and mr. Hall

has fun Dancing.

Steve, patty, and Jose

plays Some musik.

the Parents and our

teacher is busy talking.

Tracy and Amy

clears the tables

Name_____

⭐ **B.** Think about a dinner your class might prepare for families and
friends. What kind of food would you like to serve? Who would
help, and what jobs would they have? Make up captions for pictures
of your class dinner. Make sure subjects and verbs agree. Use
revising and proofreading marks if you need to make changes.

_____

_____

_____

_____

_____

⭐ **C.** Some more bulletin board captions are written in the code shown
below. Decode and write the captions. Correct each caption so that
the subject and verb agree. Then tell what event the captions
describe. At the bottom, use the code to write your own caption. Be
sure that your subject and verb agree. Have a classmate decode your
caption.

| 1–A 2–B 3–C 4–D 5–E 6–F 7–G 8–H 9–I 10–J 11–K 12–L 13–M 14–N |
| 15–O 16–P 17–Q 18–R 19–S 20–T 21–U 22–V 23–W 24–X 25–Y 26–Z |

25. 2 9 12 12   19 13 9 20 8   1 14 4   16 1 20   19 12 15 1 14
13 1 11 5 19   2 1 19 11 5 20 19.

26. 20 8 5   3 8 5 5 18 12 5 1 4 5 18 19   1 14 4   20 8 5   2 1 14 4
5 14 20 5 18 20 1 9 14 19   20 8 5   3 18 15 23 4.

_____

27. 20 8 5   6 1 14 19   1 14 4   20 8 5   3 15 1 3 8   3 8 5 5 18 19
6 15 18   20 8 5   20 5 1 13.

_____

28. The captions describe a _____ .

29. _____

_____

Compound Predicates

A.

1–22. Ben's friend Cam just won the state championship for running the 100–yard dash. Ben wrote a note to Cam to congratulate her. Read Ben's note to see if any changes need to be made. Look for ways to avoid repeating the same subject by using compound predicates. Correct any errors you find also. Use the revising and proofreading marks on this page.

Revising Marks	
cross out	_____
add	∧
move	⤸

Proofreading Marks	
capital letter	≡
small letter	/
indent paragraph	¶
check spelling	⬭

dear Cam,

I think it is grate that you won the state championship

for the 100-yard dash You ran far every day. You

worked vary hard.

A good runner must concentrate. A good runner must

stay in good fisical shape. You have done your homework

well!

I am thinking about Joining the track team at school.

Being on the trak team would help me stay fit. Being on

the track team would let me meet friends. Maybe You

can give me some tips. Maybe you can tell me how to

prepare myself. I know i should run. I know I should

work out every day. What else do I need to do

I Congratulate you. I want to tell you how proud I am to

have you as a friend. Keep up the good work.

your Friend,

Ben

B. Ben has another friend, Marco, who has just won the school spelling bee. Help Ben write a note that congratulates Marco on his victory. Use some compound predicates in your sentences. Use revising and proofreading marks if you need to make changes.

_____

_____

_____

_____

_____

C. The pairs of verbs below are antonyms. Unscramble and write the verbs. Then use each pair to complete the sentences below with compound predicates. Select three antonym pairs to use as compound predicates in your own sentences.

ndfuo	stlo	_____
keat	vegi	_____
veeals	verrsia	_____
dselco	penode	_____
ardetst	dehiinfs	_____

23. I _____ my homework at three o'clock and

_____ at four o'clock.

24. Who _____ this window tightly and _____ that

door so wide?

25. Cindy _____ New York in the morning and

_____ in Texas in the afternoon.

26. I _____ my misplaced notebook and _____

my new pen.

27. I will _____ a pear and _____ it to a friend.

28. _____

29. _____

30. _____

Name_____

Compound Sentences

A.

1–31.

Kevin is entering a contest that he read about on the back of an
oatmeal box. He wrote a letter telling what he made from the
oatmeal box. The winner will be awarded an all-expenses-paid trip
to an amusement park. Kevin needs help revising his letter so it
reads more smoothly. Help Kevin combine simple sentences into
compound sentences. Place a comma before each conjunction you
use. Correct any errors you find also. Use the revising and
proofreading marks on this page.

Revising Marks	
cross out	_____
add	∧
move	⌒

Proofreading Marks	
capital letter	≡
small letter	/
indent paragraph	¶
check spelling	⬭

My brother and I eat Toasty Oats for brekfast every

morning. We like it better than any other cereal. Tim

likes his toasty oats with sugar. I like mine plain.

Yesterday we read about your oatmeal box contest. We

decided to enter. I wanted to make a toy from the epty

box. My brother wanted to make something else. He is

still deciding what to make.

The toy I made was a Rocket. First you cover the

outside of the box with tin foil Next you must make

a cone-shaped cover for the top of the box. Tag-board

is best for this. Construction paper will also work.

after you shape the cone, cut it to fit the top. You can

paste the cone on the top. You may prefer to tape it.

Decrate the box with an american flag and carefully

cut a door in the side.

When you play with the rocket, you can place

Action figures inside. An oatmeal box makes a

great rocket. Oatmeal makes a great brekfast.

Name _____

 B. Think of something you could make out of an oatmeal box or out of a cereal box. Write the directions on how to make the item. Use compound sentences to combine related ideas. If you need to make changes, use revising and proofreading marks.

_____

_____

_____

_____

_____

_____

_____

_____

C. Kevin won the oatmeal box contest! His family and friends are throwing a big party for him. Use a pencil to trace the path containing only compound sentences. Circle the place where the party is being held.

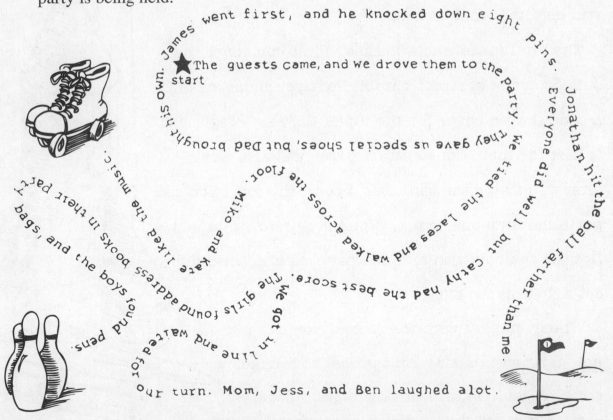

Name_____

Avoiding Run-on Sentences

A. Steve is a tour guide at an eighteenth-century village. He wrote a script to use for his tours. When he read it, he found some run-on sentences. Help Steve correct the run-on sentences in his script. Correct any other errors you find also. Use the revising and proofreading marks on this page.

1–26.

This tour will help you take a step back in Time. Your host today are dressed in tipical eighteenth-century clotheing. The men then wore trousers, shirts suspenders, and hats the women wore Long cotten dresses aprons, and bonnets. First we will visit the town inn we will see that the in was a hotel for travelers. it was also an important meeting plase for the townspeople. All town meetings were held in the inn people went for other purposes, too. Many wedings took place there. Quite often the inn was the only place in town for travelers to stay.

Now let us walk down this path to the Farmhouse. These people worked hard there were always plenty of chores to go around Women labored both inside and outside the farmhouse men tended the livestock and the feilds. children often helped by gathering berrys or feeding the chickens?

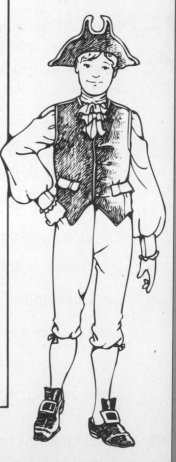

Name_____

★ **B.** Write the beginning of a tour guide's script for an interesting place
you have visited. Be sure to avoid run-on sentences. Use revising
and proofreading marks if you need to make changes.

_____
_____
_____
_____
_____
_____
_____
_____
_____

★ **C.** Read the following tour guide's script. Look for run-on sentences.
Use revising and proofreading marks to separate the run-on
sentences into simpler sentences. Then use the first letter of each
sentence to find the message below.

27–35.

     I will guide you on a walking tour of a park with marine
animals live dolphins and whales swim in water shows I see that the
seal and otter show is about to begin. Kids sometimes take part in
this show. Everyone will have a chance to feed the dolphins try to
walk faster so that we will be able to see the sharks on the left is a
special exhibit of beautiful seashells. Under the bridge you will see
a place to have lunch and rest rest for ten minutes, and then we will
begin the second half of the tour. Some people like the second half
of the tour better than the first half.

The special message is ___   ___ ___ ___ ___   ___ ___ ___ ___ ___ !

Name_____

An Observation Chart

You can use these forms to make observation charts for
the Critical Thinking lesson on pages 406–407.

A.

B.

Name_____

An Observation Chart

You can use this form to make an observation chart for the
Writing to Learn activity on page 411.

You can use these forms to make observation charts for the
Writing to Learn activity on page 428.

▅▅▅▅▅▅▅▅▅▅▅▅▅▅▅▅▅▅▅▅▅▅▅▅▅▅▅▅▅▅▅▅▅▅▅▅

Name_____

Classifying

You have read "Two of a Kind" by Ron Hirschi. Imagine that while on a camping trip last fall, you took lots of photographs of the different plants, trees, and animals that you saw. Two of your favorite photos are below. On the back of this page, write about how two things in the photos are alike.

Writing Tips

◇ Use complete sentences to express your ideas. Use capital letters and punctuation carefully.

◇ Show how things are alike in a paragraph of comparison.

◇ **Focus:** Remember to classify the information in your paragraph according to likenesses. You should leave out information about differences.

◇ You may wish to reread "Two of a Kind" before you begin. Choose one thing that you like about the writer's way of writing, and try to use it in your own writing.

Name

Name_____

Strategy: Sketch and Label

Use this page if you choose sketch and label as a prewriting strategy for your article that compares.

Strategy: An Observation Chart

Use this page if you choose an observation chart as a prewriting
strategy for your article that compares.

| cross ——— out | add ∧ | move ↻ |

An Article That Compares

Practice your revising on the article below. Use the revising tips. Don't copy the article. Use the revising marks to cross out, add, or move words and sentences.

Revising Tips

Check to see that the writer has

◇ written an article that compares two things.
◇ made sure the reader will be able to understand the article.
◇ clearly described the likenesses of two things.
◇ used subjects and verbs that agree.
◇ used precise words for words such as <u>give</u> and <u>good</u>.

◆

People don't think of soccer and basketball as being similar sports. However, these two sports are alike in ways.

Both soccer and basketball is played using a ball. The object of both games is to place a ball into a net. In basketball the net is under a hoop. In both sports players move the ball up and down a playing area. In soccer the net is the goal at the end of the field.

Some of the same terminology are used in the two sports. In basketball and soccer a player shoots for a goal. In both sports the ball is dribbled up and down the playing area. Basketball and soccer have players known as forwards and centers. Each sport has different uniforms, though.

Basketball and soccer have some of the same penalties as well. When one of the teams in basketball makes an error, the opposing team gets a free throw. In soccer the opposing team is given a free kick. Another similar penalty involves good handling of the ball. In basketball there is a penalty for moving the ball with the feet. There is a penalty for moving the ball with the hands.

≡	/	⊓	◯
capital letter	small letter	indent paragraph	check spelling

An Article That Compares

Practice your proofreading on the article below. Use the proofreading tips as a guide. Don't copy the article. Use the proofreading marks to make corrections.

Proofreading Tips

Check to see that the writer has

◇ spelled words correctly.

◇ indented paragraphs.

◇ used capital letters correctly.

◇ used correct marks at the end of sentences.

◆

Have you ever seen a moth or butterfly up close You may think they are very different, but they are very much alike.

First of all, butterflies and moths are both insects. Like all Insects they have three body parts. both butterflies and moths have two sets of wings that work as a single unit. They have larger front wings and smaller hind wings. The wings are covered with flat skales. it is these scales that give them their beautiful colors. Most adult moths and butterflies eat nectar, which they take from flowers. they may transfer pollen from one flour to another. Both butterflies and moths belong to a special groop of insects called Lepidoptera.

Butterflies and moths grow in much the same way. They both begin life as tiny eggs. The egs hatch into caterpillars. As caterpillars, they eat constantly and shed there skin. Then They enter a stage of change when they become adult butterflies and moths

Name _____

Writing an Article That Compares

Use this form as you do the Writing Process lesson beginning on page 420. Put a check next to each item you can answer yes to.

UNIT 8

Revising

☐ **Purpose:** Did I write an article that compares two things?

☐ **Audience:** Will my classmates understand my article?

☐ **Focus:** Did I clearly describe likenesses?

☐ **Grammar Check:** Did I use adjectives to add specific details to my writing?

☐ **Word Choice:** Have I used precise words?

☐ **Writing◆Comparison Paragraphs:** Did I begin paragraphs with a topic sentence?

Proofreading

☐ Did I spell words correctly?

☐ Did I indent paragraphs?

☐ Did I use capital letters correctly?

☐ Did I use correct marks at the end of sentences?

☐ Did I use my best handwriting?

Publishing

☐ Have I shared my writing with readers or listeners?

☐ Has my audience shared reactions with me?

☐ Have I thought about what I especially liked in this piece of writing?

☐ Have I thought about what I would like to work on the next time?

Use the space on the other side to tell what you liked about your writing and to make notes of your plans for improvement.

Name _____

What I liked about my writing: _____

_____

_____

_____

_____

_____

_____

_____

_____

My plans for improvement: _____

_____

_____

_____

_____

_____

_____

_____

_____

_____

_____

_____

_____

Writing an Article That Compares

Use the questions below and on the other side of this page to help you review a classmate's article that compares. Then give this form to the writer to read and save. Your comments can help the classmate improve the article that compares.

A First Reaction

Here is what I thought in general about your article that compares:

_____

_____

_____

_____

_____

_____

_____

A Second Reaction

Now I have looked at your article that compares more closely. I have more specific comments about it.

Here is something you have done well as a writer:

_____

_____

Here is an area that might be improved:

_____

_____

Here is an idea for improvement:

_____

_____

Writing an Article That Compares

Check Yes or No for each item. If you check No, explain or give a suggestion for improvement.

Yes   No   ## *Revising*

☐   ☐   **Purpose:** Does the article compare two things?

_____

☐   ☐   **Audience:** Did I understand the article?

_____

☐   ☐   **Focus:** Did the writer clearly describe likenesses?

_____

☐   ☐   **Grammar Check:** Has the writer included adjectives to add specific details to the writing?

_____

☐   ☐   **Word Choice:** Has the writer used precise words?

_____

☐   ☐   **Writing◆Comparison Paragraphs:** Did the writer begin paragraphs with a topic sentence?

_____

Yes   No   ## *Proofreading*

☐   ☐   Are words spelled correctly?

_____

☐   ☐   Are paragraphs indented?

_____

☐   ☐   Are capital letters used correctly?

_____

☐   ☐   Are there correct marks at the end of sentences?

_____

☐   ☐   Is the handwriting neat and legible?

_____

◆ A WRITER'S JOURNAL ◆

A writer's journal is a special place to do a special kind of writing. When you write just for yourself, that's journal writing.

What to Put in a Journal

You can use your journal as a place to

◇ express your thoughts and feelings.
◇ record experiences and events.
◇ save writing ideas that you can draw on later.
◇ practice and experiment with different kinds of writing, such as a story beginning or a conversation.
◇ write your opinions of a book or a movie.
◇ describe sensory observations.
◇ record new impressions of people or places.
◇ think through a difficult problem.
◇ write about something new you learned in math or science.

A Journal Is . . .

Here are some ways to think about what a journal is for:

A journal is an attic. In it you can store thoughts and observations you might use someday.

A journal is a rehearsal stage. It's a place to try out ideas you aren't ready to show an audience.

A journal is a costume. Try it on when you want to see what it feels like to be someone or something else.

A journal is a fountain. Dip into it when you need some refreshment for writing ideas.

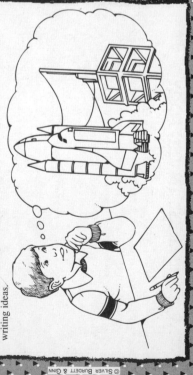

◆ A WRITER'S JOURNAL ◆

How to Make a Journal and a Writing Folder

Did you notice the heavier pages in the front and the back of this book? They are special materials for you. Use the set from the front to make a journal. Use the set from the back to make a writing folder for pages you want to keep from this book.

To make your journal, first remove the special pages at the front of the book. They are punched to hold three-hole looseleaf paper. Place some blank looseleaf paper between the journal covers. Line up the holes of the paper with the holes of the covers. Fasten the covers and inside pages together with ribbon, yarn, or brass fasteners. You can add pages as you need them.

You can make a writing folder the same way you made your journal. Use the two heavy pages at the back of this book for covers. For your writing folder, you will be inserting pages from this activity book.

When you see **SAVE** at the bottom of a page in this book, save that page in your writing folder.

Write your name on the covers of your journal and writing folder and decorate the covers. Have fun!

2

INTEREST INVENTORY

You may sometimes need help thinking up things to write about. This interest inventory can help you. It can help you discover things you are interested in or would like to know more about. Fill in the interest inventory. After you complete the interest inventory, remove it and place it in your writing folder. Look at it when you need writing ideas. You can redo the inventory as your interests change.

Name your favorite

game _____

school subject _____

sport to play _____

sport to watch _____

food _____

place to visit _____

thing to do _____

television show _____

animal _____

kind of book _____

hobby _____

singer _____

athlete _____

season _____

holiday _____

Circle everything you'd like to know more about.

puppets	monsters	dolphins
birds	the Solar System	clouds
plants	park rangers	hiking
insects	earthquakes	Eskimos
gymnastics	bats	pioneers
computers	the Olympics	airplanes

SAVE 3

INTEREST INVENTORY

Fill in the blanks with wishes.

I wish I could . . .

visit this place _____

play this intrument _____

play this sport _____

meet this person _____

build this thing _____

become an expert on this _____

have this animal for a pet _____

spend more time doing this _____

do this on a vacation _____

explore this place _____

have this job _____

For each subject, use a check (✔) to indicate your level of interest.

	No Interest	Some Interest	Much Interest
history	___	___	___
sports	___	___	___
nature	___	___	___
music	___	___	___
outer space	___	___	___
animals	___	___	___
underwater life	___	___	___
art	___	___	___
video games	___	___	___
inventions	___	___	___
science experiments	___	___	___
movies	___	___	___

4

T2

WRITING FORMS

Have you ever written an article about how to play your favorite game? Have you ever written a letter to a friend at camp? If so, you are a writer! Articles and friendly letters are two forms of writing.

Here are many more writing forms. Put a check next to the forms you have written and the ones you want to try.

Save this list in your writing folder. You can look at it when you need ideas for writing. Be sure to keep your "Have Written" list up to date.

	Have Written	Want to Try
adventure story		
advertisement		
book review		
bulletin		
business letter		
caption for a picture		
character sketch		
conversation		
description		
directions		
feature story		
folktale		
haiku		
how-to article		
interview		
journal entry		
legend		
limerick		
mystery story		
news release		
opinion poll		

SAVE 5

WRITING FORMS

	Have Written	Want to Try
personal narrative		
persuasive letter		
play		
poem		
record review		
research report		
short story		
speech		
sports column		
tall tale		
tongue twister		
want ad		
Add other forms you have written or would like to try.		
_____		

A writer who uses any of the forms in the list has at least one reason, and often more, for writing. Below are some reasons why writers write. For each reason, there is an example of a form that a writer might use.

Reason for Writing	Writing Form
Narrating	personal narrative
Informing	how-to article
Imagining	tall tale
Persuading	persuasive letter
Describing	character sketch
Researching	research report
Creating	poem
Classifying	article that compares

6

◆ BOOK LOG ◆

You can use the following pages to record information about each book you read. Keep the book log in your writing folder, and review it from time to time. Your teacher can give you additional pages if you need them. A book log can help you

◇ discover what kinds of books you enjoy.
◇ record information for friends who ask for book recommendations.
◇ learn about good writing from the books you read.

Title _____

Author _____

Kind of Book _____

Personal Rating (Circle 1 to 4 stars.) ★ ★★ ★★★ ★★★★

Reading as a Writer

Here's something the book made me think about: _____

I especially liked the way the author _____

Some words or phrases I liked in the book are: _____

The part on page _____ was interesting because _____

I'd like to tell _____ about this book.

He/She would like it because _____

You can duplicate copies of the book log pages as necessary for students to use throughout the year.

8

◆ BOOK LOG ◆

You can use the following pages to record information about each book you read. Keep the book log in your writing folder, and review it from time to time. Your teacher can give you additional pages if you need them. A book log can help you

◇ discover what kinds of books you enjoy.
◇ record information for friends who ask for book recommendations.
◇ learn about good writing from the books you read.

Title _____

Author _____

Kind of Book _____

Personal Rating (Circle 1 to 4 stars.) ★ ★★ ★★★ ★★★★

Reading as a Writer

Here's something the book made me think about: _____

I especially liked the way the author _____

Some words or phrases I liked in the book are: _____

The part on page _____ was interesting because _____

I'd like to tell _____ about this book.

He/She would like it because _____

You can duplicate copies of the book log pages as necessary for students to use throughout the year.

◇ BOOK LOG ◇

You can use the following pages to record information about each book you read. Keep the book log in your writing folder, and review it from time to time. Your teacher can give you additional pages if you need them. A book log can help you

◇ discover what kinds of books you enjoy.
◇ record information for friends who ask for book recommendations.
◇ learn about good writing from the books you read.

Title _____

Author _____

Kind of Book _____

Personal Rating (Circle 1 to 4 stars.) ★ ★★ ★★★ ★★★★

Reading as a Writer

Here's something the book made me think about: _____

I especially liked the way the author _____

Some words or phrases I liked in the book are: _____

The part on page ____ was interesting because _____

I'd like to tell _____ about this book.

He/She would like it because _____

You can duplicate copies of the book log pages as necessary for students to use throughout the year.

SAVE 9

◇ BOOK LOG ◇

You can use the following pages to record information about each book you read. Keep the book log in your writing folder, and review it from time to time. Your teacher can give you additional pages if you need them. A book log can help you

◇ discover what kinds of books you enjoy.
◇ record information for friends who ask for book recommendations.
◇ learn about good writing from the books you read.

Title _____

Author _____

Kind of Book _____

Personal Rating (Circle 1 to 4 stars.) ★ ★★ ★★★ ★★★★

Reading as a Writer

Here's something the book made me think about: _____

I especially liked the way the author _____

Some words or phrases I liked in the book are: _____

The part on page ____ was interesting because _____

I'd like to tell _____ about this book.

He/She would like it because _____

You can duplicate copies of the book log pages as necessary for students to use throughout the year.

10

◆ WRITER'S PROFILE ◆

On this sheet you will complete your writer's profile. The writer's profile will help you discover what kind of writer you are and what usually works best for you as a writer. Remember that everyone writes differently. Your writer's profile will probably be very different from classmates' profiles.

Put a check in the box that best describes you or your writing style. Then keep this sheet in your writing folder so you can refer to it from time to time before you begin writing.

	Sometimes	Always	Never
1. Before I write, I like to talk about my ideas with a friend.	☐	☐	☐
2. I like to list my ideas before I write my first draft.	☐	☐	☐
3. I like to know just what I'm going to say before I begin.	☐	☐	☐
4. I write out my piece quickly from start to finish. Then I make changes.	☐	☐	☐
5. My final version might be very different from my first version.	☐	☐	☐
6. It helps to have readers respond to my writing before I do the final version.	☐	☐	☐
7. I like to inform people through my writing.	☐	☐	☐
8. I enjoy expressing my thoughts and feelings in my writing.	☐	☐	☐
9. I like to entertain others through my writing.	☐	☐	☐
10. I like to know my readers' reactions.	☐	☐	☐

I like to write

___ quickly ___ slowly
___ with noise around ___ in a quiet place
___ anytime ___ at a particular time
___ anyplace ___ in a special place
___ with a pencil or a pen ___ on a word processor

SAVE 11

◆ WRITER'S PROFILE ◆

Sometimes you may hear or read language that really interests you. You can use this sheet to list the language you come across. You may want to use some of the language later in your own writing. Use extra pages as your collection grows.

Words and Phrases

_____

_____

_____

_____

_____

Sayings and Expressions

_____

_____

_____

_____

_____

12

T6

Name _____

B. Pretend you are Max's friend. You are on vacation with your family. Send a postcard to Max. Tell him where you are, what you are doing, and what exciting things you are seeing. You want to make sure Max can understand what you write. Are your sentences complete? Use revising and proofreading marks to show your changes. **Answers will vary.**

Max Anderson
14 Maple Lane
Greensburg, PA
      15601

C. Max sent a postcard to his teacher, but some of his sentences are incomplete. Add words to make complete sentences. The first letters of the complete sentences tell where Max was on his vacation. Write these letters on the lines below to find out the name of the place. **Answers will vary. Possible answers follow.**

I **Ʌ** Arrived last night. Friends from home have the next trailer. **Ʌ** Fished **We** together. Early in the morning the fish **Ʌ** bite well. Lois caught the biggest fish. **had a good time** Others got away. All the kids **Ʌ**. Row boats are for rent at the dock. **They are** I ordered my Ʌ Heavy and hard to row. It's best to take turns. **Ʌ** Favorite food from **We** the menu. Dinner at the pool is fun. The boats on the lake **Ʌ** **go fast** After Labor Day we go home.

F L O R I D A

14

Name _____

Writing Sentences

A. Max sent this postcard to Jamie while he was on vacation. Jamie was happy to get the postcard from his friend, but he could not **1-29.** understand it all. Max did not always use complete sentences. Add words to make complete sentences. Correct any other errors you find also so that Jamie can understand Max's postcard. Use the revising and proofreading marks on this page. Some corrections have been done for you. **Answers may vary. Possible answers follow.**

Revising Marks	
cross out	—
add	Ʌ
move	ꝺ

Proofreading Marks	
capital letter	≡
small letter	/
indent paragraph	¶
check spelling	◯

U.S. POSTAGE

Jamie Wilson

21 Sycamore Road

Greensburg, PA

       15601

Dear jamie,
                  We had
This is a ⟨grate⟩ vacation. Ʌ **Ʌ** An exciting day yesterday.
We were   **I saw**
Ʌ Out on a ship. Ʌ An enormous whale and
                              The whale was   **Dad**
her calf. Ʌ Leaped out of the water. Ʌ About
                                                   turn
fifty feet long. The captain Ʌ tern out so you can see
photos   **I enjoy**
photos ⟨fotos⟩. Ʌ Hope they Ʌ Riding the
We are   **beach**   today. **Wednesday**
the whales. Ʌ At the ⟨beech⟩ today. **We are coming**
was almost six feet high We are coming   **Wednesday**
waves. One wave, Ʌ Back home next ⟨Wenesday⟩.
I'll
Ʌ See you then.
                              friend
                    Your ⟨freind⟩
                         Max

13

T7

Name _____

Four Kinds of Sentences

A. Yoko and Mike are actors. They are trying to rehearse their parts for a camping scene. Unfortunately, they do not know where the sentences begin or end. Help Yoko and Mike by adding the capital letters and punctuation marks the script writer forgot. Correct any other errors you find also. Use the revising and proofreading marks on this page. **Answers will vary.**

1-36.

Revising Marks	
cross out	—
add	∧
move	○

Proofreading Marks	
capital letter	≡
small letter	/
indent paragraph	¶
check spelling	○

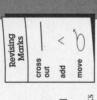

Yoko: did you hear that noise? it sounded lik[like] it
footsteps. [Yoko stiks[sticks] her head out of the sleeping bag.]

Mike: go back to sleep. it's just the wind here in the rockies.

Yoko: what if it's not the wind? what if it's a bare[bear] or a mountain lion?

it doesn't sound like the wind to me.

Mike: don't be scared. give me the flashlight; I'll investigate.

[Yoko hands Mike the flashlight. Mike goes outside the tent.]

Yoko: there's the noise again! it is coming from behind that rock;

Mike: hey, look at this! what a funny-looking cat it is!

Yoko: that's not a cat; that's a skunk! let's get out of here fast.

[Both Yoko and Mike run offstage.]

Name _____

B. Pretend you are a script writer. Here is the situation. The doorbell rings. Yoko and Mike go to the front door. At the door they find a gift-wrapped box about the size of a trunk. Write a script that tells what Yoko and Mike say as they stare at the box and then open it. Include the four kinds of sentences in your script. Use revising and proofreading marks to show any changes you make. **Answers will vary.**

Yoko: _____

Mike: _____

Yoko: _____

Mike: _____

Yoko: _____

Mike: _____

C. Here is the message that was attached to the box. Can you figure it out? Write the message above the clues. Insert the correct punctuation and capital letters.

Dear Mike and Yoko,

Happy Birthday to you. Can you guess what is in the box?

Open it carefully. I hope you like it.

Aunt Ellen

D + — t + o   M + — b   and — b   + o,

— d + th + — M + d 2 U

U   guest − t + s w +   hiss − h − s   N   the

− f + b   O +   K +   +

h +   − r U   l + − b it   LN

T8

Complete Subjects and Predicates

A. Kids' Korner store is having a back-to-school sale. Alicia wrote
a sale notice for the newspaper. She was in such a hurry that she
1-22. left out some important information. Help Alicia. Add subjects or
predicates to make complete sentences. Correct any other errors you
find also. Use the revising and proofreading marks on this page.
Answers will vary. Possible answers follow.

Revising Marks	
cross out	—
add	∧
move	○

Proofreading Marks	
capital letter	≡
small letter	/
indent paragraph	¶
check spelling	○

Save   Save   Save!

Kid's Korner

starts today
The annual back-to-School sale.

What bargains. Our everyday low prices.
are even lower

Hundreds of items.
are on sale
are on all floors

Our sale continue through
Will continu threw september. All
are 50% off
warm fall clothes.

cost   The first fifty shoppers
Shoes 25% less. Will bee a winner?
you be
Will receive a gift.

are
Our prices are low. Our styles the latest.

We are
to
Open from 9:00 A.M. too 9:00 P.M.
to
Monday two Friday.
we are open
On Saturdays until 5:30 P.M.

B. Pretend you are having a garage sale. Write a sale notice about the
things you will sell. Each sentence must have a subject and a
predicate. Check to see that your sentences are complete. Use
revising and proofreading marks to show any changes you make.
Answers will vary.

Garage Sale Today!

C. In five minutes write as many sentences as possible using the
subject and predicate parts listed below. All the sentence parts in
23-32. Column A are subjects but not all of the sentence parts in Column B
are predicates. Compare your answers with a friend. How many
different sentences did you make?

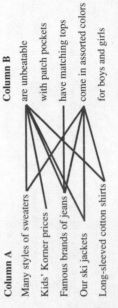

Column A	Column B
Many styles of sweaters	are unbeatable
Kids' Korner prices	with patch pockets
Famous brands of jeans	have matching tops
Our ski jackets	come in assorted colors
Long-sleeved cotton shirts	for boys and girls

Left page (19)

Name _____

Simple Subjects

A. Wendy is a reporter. She covered a story about Frank and John Shore. The two brothers spotted and reported a fire in an apartment
1-22. house. Tomorrow the boys are being honored at City Hall. As Wendy reread her article about the incident, she noticed she had left out some simple subjects. Help Wendy make changes and correct any errors in the article, using the revising and proofreading marks on this page. **Answers will vary. Possible answers follow.**

Revising Marks	
cross out	—
add	∧
move	↶

Proofreading Marks	
capital letter	≡
small letter	/
indent paragraph	¶
check spelling	○

The Gazette

boys
Two young smelled smoke on their way to school last week.

Frank
frank and John Shore noticed flames coming from a building

on Maple Street. Immediately alerted the fire department.

brothers   knock
Then the ran back to ring the doorbells and nock on the

Firefighters   minutes
windows and doors. Responded within minits and put out

person
the fire. Not one was hurt because of the brothers' quick

actions
acshuns
city   honor
Tomorrow the will honer the brothers for their good deed.

ceremony
The will receive a special award from the mayor. The will

It
be held in the auditorium at City Hall. Begins at noon.

boys
The will meet with the

public   class
The is invited to attend. Afterward will meet with the

then their whole from Hilltop
residents of the building.

School will tour the fire station with them.

Right page (20)

Name _____

B. Pretend you are a reporter. Write your own news story about an event that has taken place in your family, neighborhood, or school. Think about these questions as you write your article:
Who? What? Where? When? Why? How?
Remember to include a simple subject in each of your sentences.
Use revising and proofreading marks to show any changes. **Answers will vary.**

_____

_____

_____

_____

_____

_____

_____

C. Unscramble these sentences to learn what the work of the firefighter is. Underline the simple subject for each. Be sure to use capital letters and end the sentence with the correct punctuation mark.

23. the department of the community members whole the serve fire
The members of the fire department serve the whole community.

24. very is important it
It is very important.

25. firefighter has a job the dangerous
The firefighter has a dangerous job.

26. these risk brave people their lives
These brave people risk their lives.

27. help they accident and victims too disaster firefighters training
They help accident and disaster victims too.

28. special in receive aid first firefighters training
Firefighters receive special training in first aid.

29. fire talk they prevention children to about school
They talk to school children about fire prevention.

30. hard engines their good of take workers these care
These hard workers take good care of their engines.

Simple Predicates

A. Sergio writes ads for new food products. He wrote this ad for
1-21. Crunchy Oats, the newest cereal on the market. Sergio was
interrupted before he could finish checking over his ad. Some
simple predicates are missing. Show the changes you would make
to improve the ad. Correct any other errors you find also. Use the
revising and proofreading marks on this page. **Answers may vary.**
Possible answers follow.

Kids of all ages/Crunchy Oats in the morning.
(choose) (like)

Americans/Crunchy Oats first. One taste/your
(wakes) (gives)

sleepy taste buds. One portion/you all the
(have)

important vitamins and minerals.

I/more good news/The top of your Crunchy
(is) (too) (New/Knew)

Oats box/very valuable/customers/a gift.
(can receive)

Each box top/you/baseball cards. just make/your
(will bring) (four/for) (mail)

tops to Crunchy Oats, Box 32, Akron, Ohio 07538.
(comes)

The best news/last. The makers of this great cereal/
(put)

a surprise right in the box. Can you guess the
(will help) (need)

surprise? Maybe this hint/you. You/a pencil to
(need)

use the surprise.

Revising Marks

cross out	—
add	∧
move	◯

Proofreading Marks

capital letter	≡
small letter	/
indent paragraph	¶
check spelling	◯

21

B. Now you can create your own ad. Think about your favorite cereal
or breakfast food. What would you say to persuade someone to try
it for the first time? Explain how it tastes and why it is good for you.
Remember to include precise action words as simple predicates in
your sentences. Use the revising and proofreading marks to show
any changes you want to make. **Answers will vary.**

_____

_____

_____

_____

_____

C. Read the sentences about cereal. How quickly can you find the
correct simple predicate hidden in each sentence? Underline the
word with the hidden predicate. Write the hidden predicate above.
Time yourself. Then compare your answers with those of a
classmate.

22. Americans breathe over twenty billion bowls of cereal a year. *(eat)*
23. Most ready-to-eat cereals consistent of wheat and oats. *(consist)*
24. People usually deserved cereal with milk or cream. *(serve)*
25. Companies refuse several different ways to make cereal. *(use)*
26. They grinder and troll the grains into flakes. *(grind / roll)*
27. Sometimes they sadden sugar. *(add)*
28. Hot cereals welcome in three forms: regular, quick cooking, and instant. *(come)*
29. Regular hot cereal mistakes about fifteen minutes to cook. *(takes)*
30. Most cereals shaved vitamins and minerals. *(have)*

22

T11

Name _____

Subjects in Imperative Sentences

A. Lani moved to a town thirty miles away. Her friend Heather is coming to visit next weekend. Lani sent Heather directions and a map to show the way to her new house. Lani did not need to use the subject *you* in each imperative sentence. Help her improve the directions by taking out *you* in the imperative sentences and correcting any other errors you find. Use the revising and proofreading marks on this page.

1-24.

~~You~~ take Route 20 west for twenty-five ⟨miles⟩ ~~mils~~ ~~You~~
turn left at Mountain Avenue. ~~You~~ continue to the end
of the ⟨road⟩ ~~rode~~ where you have to turn either left or right.∧
~~You~~ go right. That's Route 120. ~~You~~ follow the road
until you get to the top of the hill. Then ~~you~~ make a
⟨station⟩
left turn at the gas ~~stashun~~ onto West Point Drive. At
⟨turn⟩
the next corner ~~You~~ make a right ~~tern~~ onto Newport
⟨eight⟩
Road. ~~You~~ keep going about ~~ate~~ hundred feet. Our
⟨fourth⟩
house is the ~~forth~~ on the left. There is a long driveway.
⟨way⟩
~~You~~ drive all the ~~weigh~~ back to the barn. You will
probably find me there with the new kittens.

Revising Marks	
cross out	—
add	∧
move	◯

Proofreading Marks	
capital letter	≡
small letter	/
indent paragraph	¶
check spelling	◯

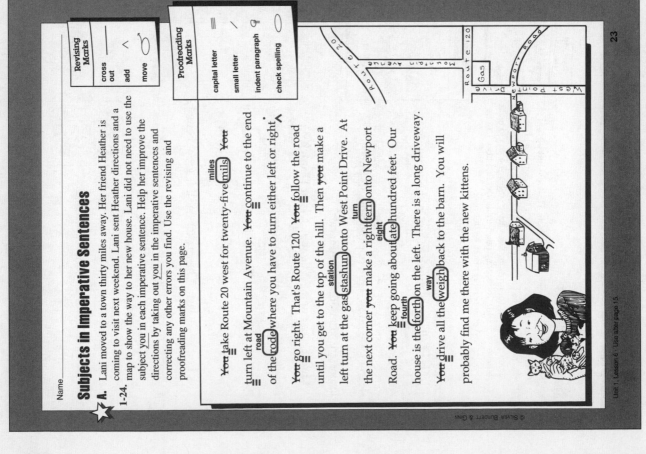

23

Name _____

B. How do you tie your shoelaces? How do you make an airplane? How do you make a sandwich? Write a set of directions to tell how to do something. After you finish writing, check to make sure the directions are clear. Are the imperative sentences written correctly? Use revising and proofreading marks to show any changes. **Answers will vary.**

C. Ann has directions to the post office, but some of the important words are missing. Use the map to help you write sentences that tell Ann how to get to the post office. Use imperative sentences.
Answers will vary. Possible answers follow.

25. Go east on Park Street.
26. Turn left at Poplar Place⊙
27. Turn right on to Linden Road⊙
28. Turn left on to Locust Street⊙
29. Go left at Woodland Road⊙
30. Make a right turn on Elm Street⊙
31. Cross Maple Way⊙
32. Go to the building in the middle of the block.

24

Name

An Observation Chart

You can use this form to make an observation chart for the Writing to Learn activity on page 29.

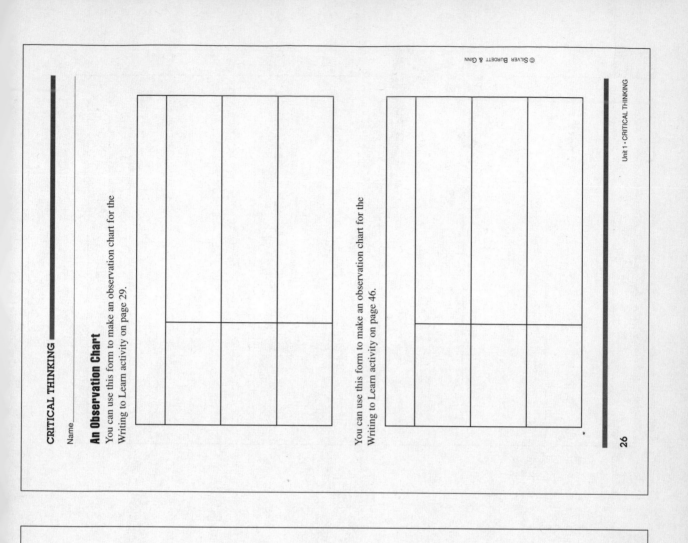

You can use this form to make an observation chart for the Writing to Learn activity on page 46.

Name

An Observation Chart

You can use these forms to make observation charts for the Critical Thinking lesson on pages 22–23.

A.

B.

T14

Name

Narrating

You have read a selection from The Midnight Fox by Betsy Byars. Now imagine that you are visiting Aunt Millie's farm. You are sitting on the rock next to the stream pictured below. When you look up, you see something on the other side of the stream that startles you. On the back of this page, tell what you see and what happens.

Writing Tips

◇ Use complete sentences to express your ideas. Use capital letters and punctuation carefully.

◇ Make character, setting, and plot work together in your story.

◇ **Focus:** Remember to use the words <u>I</u> and <u>me</u> to tell your story.

◇ You may wish to reread The Midnight Fox before you begin. Choose one thing that you like about the writer's way of writing, and try to use it in your own narrative.

Unit 1 · LITERATURE · Use after the Reading-Writing Connection on pages 36–37.

27

Name

Name _____

Strategy: A Conversation

Use this page to take notes if you choose a conversation as a prewriting strategy for your personal narrative.

PREWRITING

Name _____

Strategy: An Observation Chart

Use this page if you choose an observation chart as a prewriting strategy for your personal narrative.

T15

PROOFREADING PRACTICE

Name _____

≡	/	¶	◯
capital letter	small letter	indent paragraph	check spelling

A Personal Narrative

Practice your proofreading on the personal narrative below. Use the proofreading tips as a guide. Don't copy the story. Use the proofreading marks to make corrections.

Proofreading Tips

Check to see that the writer has
◇ spelled words correctly.
◇ indented paragraphs.
◇ used capital letters correctly.
◇ used correct marks at the end of sentences.

♦

Yesterday was field day at school. The whole school spent the day outdoors. We even ate lunch outside on picnic tables. It really was a lot of fun. My favorite activities were relay racing, climbing the rope, and jumping on the trampoline. Have you ever jumped on a trampoline? A funny thing happened to me yesterday when I jumped on the trampoline during field day. Our teacher told us to jump very high and then drop to our knees. I started jumping until I was very high in the air. I was jumping so high that my stomach felt funny on the way down. At last I was ready to drop to my knees. When I dropped to my knees, I held my nose. Everyone laughed loudly.

"why did you hold your nose?" my friend Julie asked.

"The reason I held my nose is because when I jump into a pool, I always hold my nose."

This just made them laugh harder. now I have a new nickname.

Everyone calls me "the swimmer."

32

REVISING PRACTICE

Name _____

cross out ———	add ∧	move ◯

A Personal Narrative

Practice your revising on the personal narrative below. Use the revising tips as a guide. Don't copy the story. Use the revising marks to cross out, add, or move words and sentences.

Revising Tips

Check to see that the writer has
◇ told about a personal experience.
◇ made the reader understand what has happened and how the writer feels.
◇ used the first person point of view.
◇ used interrogative, imperative, and exclamatory sentences for variety.
◇ used precise words for words such as play and happened.
◇ used quotations to show the exact words of a speaker.

Answers will vary.
Possible answers follow.

♦

I have been playing the drums since the third grade. I never thought that I would play in front of a big group of people though. (perform) Would you believe? I played in front of my whole school. (performed)

It all started when three friends wanted me to enter a talent show with them. Each of us plays a different instrument. We practiced together for weeks. We were beginning to sound pretty good. Jerry plays the guitar, Luis plays the bass, and Jolan sings.

The day of the talent show finally arrived. Jolan was very nervous. I felt so scared my knees were shaking! Then a strange thing happened. occurred We started playing the first song, and Jolan did not sing. He just stood there with his mouth open. A microphone was next to my drums, so I started singing. I sang the whole song while playing the drums. I forgot about being scared. Afterwards I asked Jolan what happened. He said he couldn't remember the words to the song and thanked me for taking over.

"I just froze!" said Jolan. "I couldn't remember the words. Thanks for taking over!"

Now Jolan wants to play drums. He wants me to be the singer. I will have to think about this!

31

Name _____

SELF-EVALUATION

UNIT 1

Writing a Personal Narrative

Use this form as you do the Writing Process lesson beginning on page 38. Put a check next to each item you can answer yes to.

Revising

- [ ] **Purpose:** Did I write about a personal experience I had with an animal?
- [ ] **Audience:** Will my classmates understand what happened and how I felt?
- [ ] **Focus:** Did I use first-person point of view?
- [ ] **Grammar Check:** Have I used some interrogative, imperative, or exclamatory sentences to make my story more interesting?
- [ ] **Word Choice:** Have I used precise words?
- [ ] **Writing◆Quotations:** Have I used quotation marks to show the exact words of a speaker?

Proofreading

- [ ] Did I spell words correctly?
- [ ] Did I indent paragraphs?
- [ ] Did I use capital letters correctly?
- [ ] Did I use correct marks at the end of sentences?
- [ ] Did I use my best handwriting?

Publishing

- [ ] Have I shared my writing with readers or listeners?
- [ ] Has my audience shared reactions with me?
- [ ] Have I thought about what I especially liked in this piece of writing?
- [ ] Have I thought about what I would like to work on the next time?

Use the space on the other side to tell what you liked about your writing and to make notes of your plans for improvement.

SAVE 33

Name _____

What I liked about my writing: _____

_____

_____

_____

_____

_____

_____

My plans for improvement: _____

_____

_____

_____

_____

34

Reader's Name _____

Writer's Name _____

Writing a Personal Narrative

Check Yes or No for each item. If you check No, explain or give a suggestion for improvement.

Revising

Yes   No

☐   ☐   **Purpose:** Did the writer tell about a personal experience with an animal?

☐   ☐   **Audience:** Did I understand what happened and how the writer felt?

☐   ☐   **Focus:** Did the writer use first-person point of view?

☐   ☐   **Grammar Check:** Are there some interrogative, imperative, or exclamatory sentences to make the story more interesting?

☐   ☐   **Word Choice:** Has the writer used precise words?

☐   ☐   **Writing♦Quotations:** Has the writer used quotation marks to show the exact words of a speaker?

Proofreading

Yes   No

☐   ☐   Are words spelled correctly?

☐   ☐   Are paragraphs indented?

☐   ☐   Are capital letters used correctly?

☐   ☐   Are there correct marks at the end of sentences?

☐   ☐   Is the handwriting neat and legible?

36

PEER EVALUATION

UNIT 1

Reader's Name _____

Writer's Name _____

Writing a Personal Narrative

Use the questions below and on the other side of this page to help you review a classmate's personal narrative. Then give this form to the writer to read and save. Your comments can help the classmate improve the personal narrative.

A First Reaction

Here is what I thought in general about your personal narrative:

_____

_____

_____

_____

A Second Reaction

Now I have looked at your personal narrative more closely. I have more specific comments about it.

Here is something you have done well as a writer:

_____

Here is an area that might be improved:

_____

Here is an idea for improvement:

_____

SAVE 35

T18

Name _____

B. Imagine that you work for a store. You have been asked to write an ad that will appear in the Yellow Pages. Choose one of the stores below, or make up one of your own.

BART'S BIKES   PETE'S PET PALACE   COMPUTER COTTAGE

Use specific nouns to include as much information as possible in your ad. If you need to make changes, use revising and proofreading marks.   **Answers will vary.**

C. Read the following lines from several Yellow Pages ads. Many words have been scrambled. Unscramble them to complete the line from each ad. Then circle the unscrambled words that are nouns.

16. Visit our decorating *center* for all your *paint* and wallpaper.
17. We are the equipment *experts* you can trust.
18. Our *excellent* service is the secret of our *success*.
19. Come to our warehouse for the *biggest* *bargain* in *towns*.
20. Our *company* has served the tri-state area for thirty *years*.
21. Beauty is our *business*.
22. We serve good *food* at reasonable *prices*.
23. You'll find special *jewelry* at special savings.

Name _____

Writing with Nouns

A. Gayle is preparing some ads for the Yellow Pages of the telephone directory. She does not think they give enough information. Help

1-15. Gayle change the nouns so that the ads are more specific. Correct any errors you find also. Use the revising and proofreading marks on this page.   **Answers will vary. Possible answers follow.**

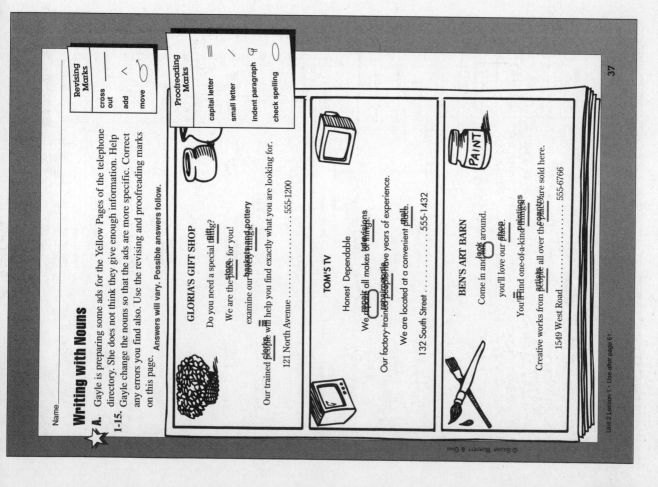

Revising Marks

cross out	—
add	∧
move	

Proofreading Marks

capital letter	≡
small letter	/
indent paragraph	¶
check spelling	

GLORIA'S GIFT SHOP
Do you need a special thing?
We are the place for you!
examine our pottery
Our trained people will help you find exactly what you are looking for.
121 North Avenue 555-1200

TOM'S TV
Honest Dependable
We repair all makes of things
Our factory-trained people ... years of experience.
We are located at a convenient place.
132 South Street 555-1432

BEN'S ART BARN
Come in and look around.
you'll love our place.
You'll find one-of-a-kind paintings
Creative works from people all over the place are sold here.
1549 West Road 555-6766

T19

Name _____

Singular and Plural Nouns

A. Ms. Bennett asked Mark to make a list of all the art supplies in the classroom closet. She needs to see what supplies must be reordered. Help Mark by

1-21. Mark wants to make sure his list is free of errors. Correct any other errors you find also. Use the revising and proofreading marks on this page.

Revising Marks	
cross out	—
add	<
move	◯

Proofreading Marks	
capital letter	≡
small letter	/
indent paragraph	¶
check spelling	◯

Art Supplies

12 gum erasers

2 dozen ~~brush~~ brushes

boxes
8 ~~box~~ of crayons

markers
15 ~~marker~~

knives
4 paint ~~knife~~

2 easels

frames
8 8 × 10 ~~frame~~

tubes
24 ~~toobs~~ of oil paint

dozen
1 ~~duzzen~~ rulers

canvases
16 stretched ~~canvass~~

pads
8 sketch ~~pad~~

1 pack of drawing paper

compasses
4 ~~compass~~

jars
9 ~~jar~~ of paste

pounds
20 ~~pound~~ of clay

sets
4 water color ~~set~~

keys
3 ~~key~~ to supply closet

4 pairs of scissors

bunches
5 ~~bunch~~ of artificial ~~cherry~~ cherries

1 can of paint thinner

bottles
2 ~~bottle~~ of blue ink

feet
100 ~~feet~~ of silver foil paper

batteries
1 pack of ~~battery~~

packages
3 ~~package~~ of colored pencils

Unit 2, Lesson 2 · Use after page 63.

© Silver Burdett & Ginn

39

Name _____

B. In the space below, make a list of all the items you can find in one of the following places: school desk, a closet at home, or the classroom. Then check your list to make sure you have spelled the plural nouns correctly. Use revising and proofreading marks if you need to make changes. **Answers will vary.**

_____

C. Think of a related item that you can add to each of the following lists. Be sure to use the plural forms of nouns correctly. **Some answers will vary. Possible answers follow.**

22. forks
spoons
knives

23. brownies
fairies
elves

24. taxis
subways
buses

25. legs
ankles
feet

26. tales
jokes
riddles

27. trees
branches
leaves

28. infants
newborns
babies

29. articles
features
stories

30. fourths
thirds
halves

31. shoes
sneakers
boots

32. elk
deer
moose

33. apples
oranges
peaches

40

Unit 2, Lesson 2 · Use after page 63.

© Silver Burdett & Ginn

T20

Right page (42)

Name _____

B. Interview one of your classmates, a teacher, or a new student in your school. Then write an article to tell some interesting facts about the person. Use proper nouns to make your article more specific. Use the revising and proofreading marks to improve your work. **Answers will vary.**

_____

_____

_____

_____

_____

_____

_____

C. How are you at breaking codes? Read the clues below and guess the famous person, place, and thing. Then use the alphabet code to check your answers. For the code, write the letters from A to Z. Then number each letter from 1–26, beginning with the letter A.

26. This gift from France greets those entering New York's harbor.

S	t	a	t	u	e		o	f		L	i	b	e	r	t	y
19	20	1	20	21	5		15	6		12	9	2	5	18	20	25

27. John Adams was the first to live here. Everyone who followed John Adams has lived here, too.

T	h	e		W	h	i	t	e		H	o	u	s	e
20	8	5		23	8	9	20	5		8	15	21	19	5

28. A child's letter suggested he would look better with a beard. He became the first president to wear one.

A	b	r	a	h	a	m		L	i	n	c	o	l	n
1	2	18	1	8	1	13		12	9	14	3	15	12	14

42

Left page (41)

Name _____

Common and Proper Nouns

A. Jessica interviewed a new girl in her class for the school newspaper and wrote an article about her. Read Jessica's first draft below. Notice that she did not give enough specific information in her article. Help Jessica get her article ready for the newspaper deadline. Replace some of the common nouns with proper nouns. Correct any other errors you find also. Use the revising and proofreading marks on this page. **Answers will vary. Possible answers follow.**

1–25.

Revising Marks	
cross out	—
add	∧
move	◡

Proofreading Marks	
capital letter	≡
small letter	/
indent paragraph	¶
check spelling	○

The Gazette

Pine Ridge Elementary School
Samantha Lewis is a new student at school. Samantha
fifth   family   there
is in the fifth grade. She and her family recently moved to
Pine Ridge   their   two
town from a foreign country. She lived there for too years.
Citizens Bank
Her father works for the bank. Her mother teaches
Eastern Junior High
English at the junior high. Samantha
language   interesting
She is teaching. but she is glad to be
living in europe was intresting. Her new home is on the main
the United States   Center Street
back home in this country.
Lake Adams   has
road near the lake.
hear
Samantha naz lots of hobbies and plans to join the club.
Drama Club
Hill Tigers
She also enjoys sports and will try out for the team this
Sweet Sounds
November   here
month. You can also here her singing with the school
Chorus group.
Good luck, Samantha. we are glad you are here.

41

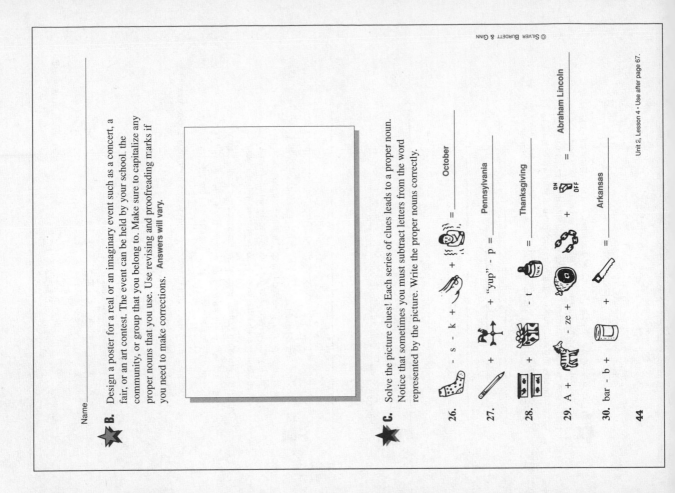

Name _____

Capitalizing Proper Nouns

A. Willow Valley is having a poster contest for its summer festival.

1-25. The winning poster will be printed and used throughout the valley to advertise the event. Jessie made a poster, but she forgot to capitalize some of the proper nouns. Help Jessie fix the poster. Capitalize all the proper nouns and correct any other errors you find also. Use the revising and proofreading marks on this page.

Revising Marks	
cross out	—
add	∧
move	◯

Proofreading Marks	
capital letter	≡
small letter	/
indent paragraph	¶
check spelling	◯

20th Annual willow valley festival at

entertainment   food   games and rides

Come join in fun!

friday, july 28th through saturday, august 4th

mount pleasant fair grounds

route 136 and Scottdale road

adults $2.50   children $1.50   senior citizens $1.00

Profits will be donated to

willow valley children's library.

For additional informashun call:

mary ann zimmer......555-1900

or peter rivera......555-9765

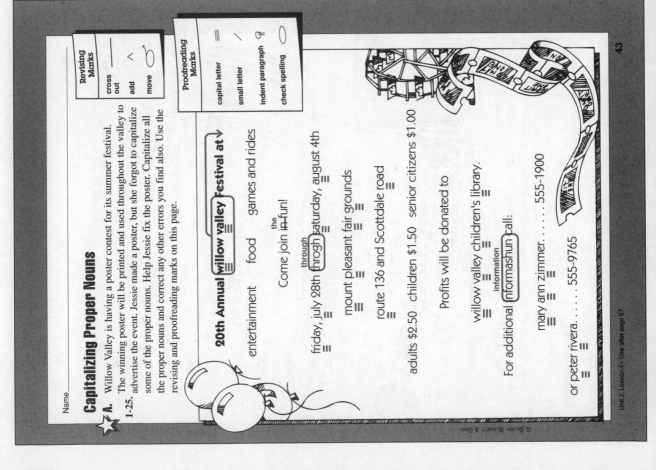

43

Name _____

B. Design a poster for a real or an imaginary event such as a concert, a fair, or an art contest. The event can be held by your school, the community, or group that you belong to. Make sure to capitalize any proper nouns that you use. Use revising and proofreading marks if you need to make corrections.   Answers will vary.

C. Solve the picture clues! Each series of clues leads to a proper noun. Notice that sometimes you must subtract letters from the word represented by the picture. Write the proper nouns correctly.

26. [picture] - s - k + [picture] = _____ October

27. [picture] + "yup" - p = _____ Pennsylvania

28. [picture] + [picture] - t = _____ Thanksgiving

29. A + [picture] - ze + [picture] = _____ Abraham Lincoln

30. bar - b + [picture] = _____ Arkansas

44

T22

Abbreviations

A. Harry took these telephone messages for his family. He made
1-27. several mistakes writing the initials and abbreviations. Help Harry
write them correctly. Correct any other errors you find also. Use
the revising and proofreading marks on this page.

Revising Marks	
cross out	———
add	∧
move	↶

Proofreading Marks	
capital letter	≡
small letter	/
indent paragraph	¶
check spelling	○

Time: 9:00 ~~A.M.~~ A.M.
Date: Tues. Jan. ~~tu, jan~~ 31
To: Dad
From: ~~mr~~ Mr. Alexander
Message: ~~you~~ you can pick up
the part for the car at the
shop on 6th ~~av~~ Ave.
Message taken by: Harry

Time: 6:30 p.m.
Date: Feb 1
To: Beth
From: ~~mrs~~ Ms. Warren at ~~libary~~ library
Message: The book you
reserved is in. Pick it up by
8:00 ~~pm~~ P.M. ~~ff~~ Fri. night.
Message taken by: Harry

Time: 12:15 P.M.
Date: Wed. ~~wed~~
To: Mom
From: Dr. Carlson
Message: Appointment
has been changed from
Thurs. Mar. ~~thu, mar~~ 29, to mon., ~~apr~~ Apr. 4.
Message taken by: Harry

Time: 11:30 ~~am~~ A.M.
Date: Apr. ~~Ap~~ 2
To: Mom
From: Dad
Message: Pick Dad up
between 5:45 ~~pm~~ P.M. and 6:00
~~pm~~ P.M. at the bus stop on ~~rt~~ Rte. 136.
Message taken by: Harry

© SILVER BURDETT & GINN

B. Make up a name and title for yourself. Pretend to be that person as
you make a telephone call to a partner. Take turns giving and taking
messages. Include in the message the time, place, and location of a
birthday party you are giving for a friend. Use abbreviations in your
message. Use revising and proofreading marks if you need to make
changes. **Answers will vary.**

Time: _____	**Date:** _____

To: _____

From: _____

Message: _____

_____

Message taken by: _____

C. Some words in the following sentences can be abbreviated. Write the
abbreviations and the initials that can be used in sentences above the
words. Then use the first letter of each abbreviation and each initial to
find a hidden message.

28. ~~Mister Oliver~~ Small, ~~Mister Marcus~~ Brown, and my cousin, Michael, met
    Mr. O.   Mr. M.
    unexpectedly last week.

29. It was at 10:00 ~~in the morning~~.
    A.M.

30. They were all in ~~Doctor~~ Chu's sports medicine office on Pine Street.
    Dr.

31. There were some magazines from last January and some newer ones too.

32. ~~Edward~~ Fernandez, ~~Junior~~, the doctor's assistant, greeted us.
    E.   Jr.

33. He told us the doctor was delayed but would see us all by 11:30 ~~in the morning~~.
    A.M.

34. ~~Mister~~ Small said he would have to come back another time.
    Mr.

35. The nurse gave him an appointment for next Tuesday.

Message: M O M   M A D E   J A M

© SILVER BURDETT & GINN

Name _____

Possessive Nouns

A. The Lucky Label Company makes labels for anything. Their artist has just designed some new labels, but he has made mistakes in possessive nouns. Help the artist fix the labels. Correct each possessive noun. Correct any other errors you find also. Use the revising and proofreading marks on this page.

1-15.

Revising Marks
cross out —
add ∧
move ○

Proofreading Marks
capital letter ≡
small letter /
indent paragraph ¶
check spelling ○

Uncle ~~Billys~~ Billy's Barbecue Sauce

~~Tessies~~ Tessie's Tasty Taters

The ~~Joneses~~ Joneses' Jams & Jellies

~~Mcintoshs~~ McIntosh's Marvelous Corn Muffins

Seven ~~Sisters~~ Sisters' Spaghetti ~~Sause~~ Sauce

The ~~Rosses~~ Rosses' Raisins

~~Silass~~ Silas's Spicy Salami

My ~~Dogs~~ Dog's Dinner

~~Krauss~~ Krauss's Crispy Corn

~~Too~~ Two ~~Brothers~~ Brothers' Burgers

Working ~~Womens~~ Women's Waffles

~~Dukes~~ Duke's ~~dr.~~ Cough Syrup

Name _____

B. The Lucky Label Company needs labels for some new products. Think of a clever name for each item below. Exercise A will give you some ideas. Use a possessive noun in each label. Use revising and proofreading marks if you need to make changes. **Answers will vary.**

16. popcorn _____

17. cereal _____

18. rice _____

19. yogurt _____

20. pet food _____

21. spaghetti sauce _____

22. applesauce _____

23. orange juice _____

C. Look at the picture of the Fun-For-You Pet Shop. Find one or more things belonging to each pet or person on the list. Write what is owned next to the owner. Be sure to form possessive nouns to show ownership. **Answers will vary. Possible answers follow.**

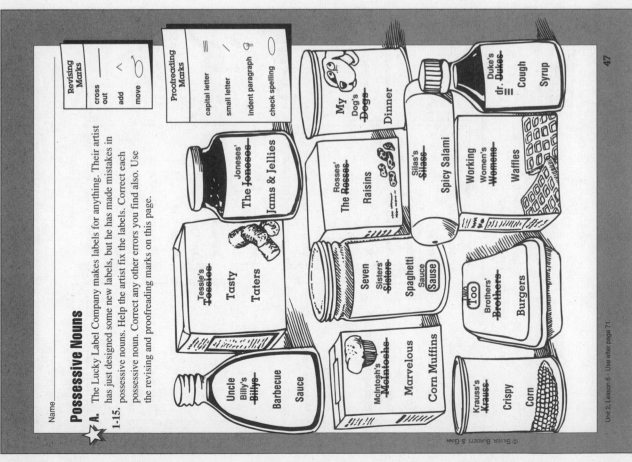

24. the hamsters ___'s cage___

25. Polly ___'s toy___

26. the puppy ___'s bones___

27. Mr. James ___'s store___

28. the mouse ___'s food___

29. The rabbit ___'s owner___

30. the fishes ___' bowl___

31. Ms. Adams ___'s pets___

32. The rabbit ___'s carrot___

33. The dog ___'s collar___

Name

An Order Circle

You can use this form to make an order circle for the Writing to Learn activity on page 83.

You can use this form to make an order circle for the Writing to Learn activity on page 102.

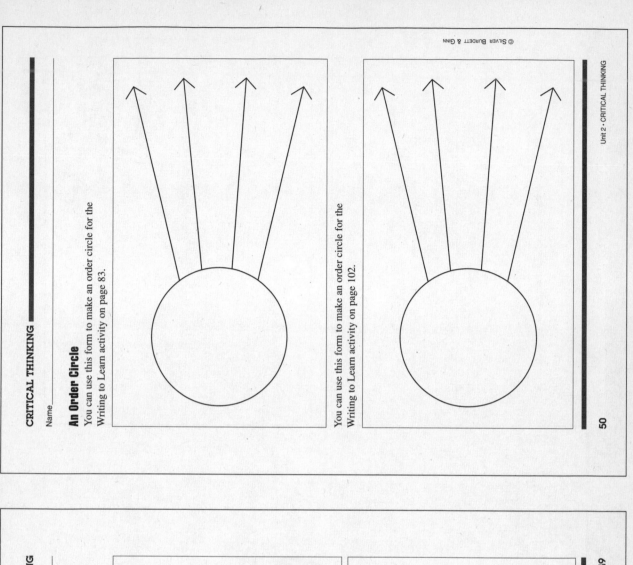

Name

An Order Circle

You can use these forms to make order circles for the Critical Thinking lesson on pages 78–79.

A.

B.

T25

T26

Story Starter

Name _____

Informing

You have read "Handicrafts" by Patricia Fent Ross. Now imagine that you and your classmates are having an international festival with foods from different countries. Think about what dish you would bring. On the back of this page, explain how to prepare the dish.

TACOS PIZZA GREEK SALAD SUKIYAKI

Writing Tips

◇ Use complete sentences to express your ideas. Use capital letters and punctuation carefully.

◇ State the main idea of your paragraph in a topic sentence. Develop the main idea in your supporting sentences.

◇ **Focus:** Remember to use words like <u>first</u>, <u>next</u>, <u>then</u>, and <u>last</u> to show the order of the steps.

◇ You may wish to reread "Handicrafts" before you begin. Choose one thing that you like about the writer's way of writing, and try to use it in your own writing.

Unit 2 · LITERATURE · Use after the Reading-Writing Connection on pages 92–93.

51

Name _____

Name _____

Strategy: An Order Circle

Use this page if you choose an order circle as a prewriting strategy for your how-to article.

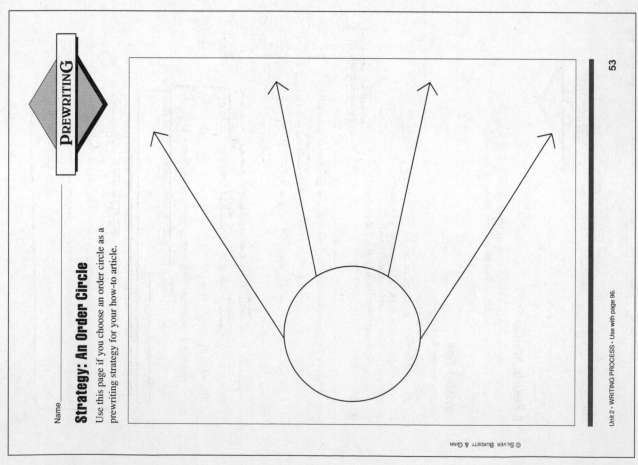

53

Name _____

Strategy: A Clock Graph

Use this page if you choose a clock graph as a prewriting strategy for your how-to article.

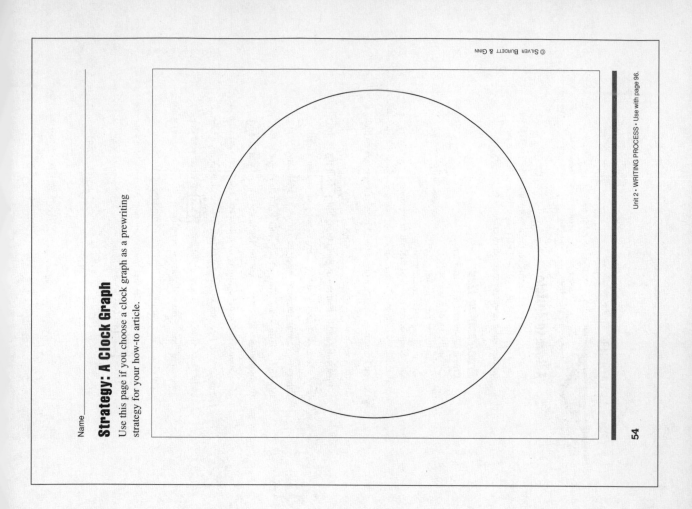

54

T27

PROOFREADING PRACTICE

Name _____

| ≡ capital letter | / small letter | ¶ indent paragraph | ◯ check spelling |

A How-to Article

Practice your proofreading on the how-to article below. Use the proofreading tips as a guide. Don't copy the article. Use the proofreading marks to make corrections.

Proofreading Tips

Check to see that the writer has
◇ spelled words correctly.
◇ indented paragraphs.
◇ used capital letters correctly.
◇ used correct marks at the end of sentences.

Do you know how to give a dog a bath? i will tell you how to bathe a dog the easy way.

First you need to find the dog and bring him outside. If you don't have a fenced-in yard, you may need to put your dog on a leash. Otherwise he may run run away when he knows it's Bath time. Next get a large tub, a hose, some soap, a brush, and some flea powder. Begin by filling the tub with water. Place the dog in the tub and wet his fer [fur]. Then Soap him down, beginning with the ears. You must start with the ears because fleas sometimes try to hide in them. Lather his whole body. Next rinse your dog with the hose. Wach [Watch] out when your dog gets out of the tub. He will shake water all over. dry your dog off with a towel. If it is a warm day, allow him to run around the yard to dry. Finally apply flea powder and brush your dog. After his bath your dog will look beter [better] and feel great.

REVISING PRACTICE

Name _____

| cross out —— | add ∧ | move ↶ |

A How-to Article

Practice your revising on the how-to article below. Use the revising tips as a guide. Don't copy the article. Use the revising marks to cross out, add, or move words and sentences.

Revising Tips

Check to see that the writer has
◇ explained how to do something.
◇ described the steps so that classmates can follow them.
◇ used words like first, next, and last to make the order clear.
◇ used exact nouns to make meaning clearer.
◇ used precise words for words such as get, things, and good.
◇ given complete directions and explained the steps in order.

Answers will vary.
Possible answers follow.

Granola is my favorite snack. We always used to get [buy] granola at the store. The kind at the store is good, but homemade granola is really good [delicious]. Now I know how to make homemade granola. You can do it, too. It is very easy to make.

First you need to buy the things [ingredients] you want to put in your granola. You may be creative with the things [ingredients]. I change my recipe a little [slightly] every time I make it. You put all the ingredients in a bowl and add 1/4 cup of honey. Then stir the mixture well. Now your homemade granola is done. Store it in an air-tight container to keep it good [fresh]. I like to use peanuts, raisins, banana chips, cashews, and dried dates.

Maybe you can try to make your own granola sometime. Next you may want to package the granola so that you can take it to school. Place some granola on a piece of plastic wrap. Put the four corners of the plastic wrap together and twist them around. Then use a [tie it with a] piece of ribbon. I usually make about five packages at a time. Sometimes I like to give my granola snacks to friends. They always ask for my [for the] recipe.

Name _____

What I liked about my writing: _____

My plans for improvement: _____

58

Name _____

SELF-EVALUATION

UNIT 2

Writing a How-to Article

Use this form as you do the Writing Process lesson beginning on page 94. Put a check next to each item you can answer yes to.

Revising

☐ **Purpose:** Did my article explain how to do something?

☐ **Audience:** Will my classmates be able to follow the steps?

☐ **Focus:** Have I used words like first, next, and last to make the order clear?

☐ **Grammar Check:** Have I used exact nouns?

☐ **Word Choice:** Have I used precise words?

☐ **Writing◆Topic Sentence and Supporting Sentences:** Have I used topic sentences and supporting sentences to make my writing clear?

Proofreading

☐ Did I spell words correctly?

☐ Did I indent paragraphs?

☐ Did I use capital letters correctly?

☐ Did I use correct marks at the end of sentences?

☐ Did I use my best handwriting?

Publishing

☐ Have I shared my writing with readers or listeners?

☐ Has my audience shared reactions with me?

☐ Have I thought about what I especially liked in this piece of writing?

☐ Have I thought about what I would like to work on the next time?

Use the space on the other side to tell what you liked about your writing and to make notes of your plans for improvement.

SAVE 57

T29

Reader's Name _____

Writer's Name _____

Writing a How-to Article

Check Yes or No for each item. If you check No, explain or give a suggestion for improvement.

Revising

Yes No

☐ ☐ **Purpose:** Did the article explain how to do something?

☐ ☐ **Audience:** Was I able to follow the steps?

☐ ☐ **Focus:** Were words like first, next, and last used to make the order clear?

☐ ☐ **Grammar Check:** Did the writer use exact nouns?

☐ ☐ **Word Choice:** Did the writer use precise words?

☐ ☐ **Writing◆Topic Sentence and Supporting Sentences:** Has the writer used topic sentences and supporting sentences to make the writing clear?

Proofreading

Yes No

☐ ☐ Are words spelled correctly?

☐ ☐ Are paragraphs indented?

☐ ☐ Are capital letters used correctly?

☐ ☐ Are there correct marks at the end of sentences?

☐ ☐ Is the handwriting neat and legible?

◆ 60

Reader's Name _____

Writer's Name _____

Writing a How-to Article

Use the questions below and on the other side of this page to help you review the writer's how-to article. Then give this form to the writer to read and save. Your comments can help the writer improve the how-to article.

A First Reaction

Here is what I thought in general about your how-to article:

_____
_____
_____
_____

A Second Reaction

Now I have looked at your how-to article more closely. I have more specific comments about it.

Here is something you have done well as a writer:

_____
_____

Here is an area that might be improved:

_____
_____

Here is an idea for improvement:

_____
_____

SAVE 59 ◆

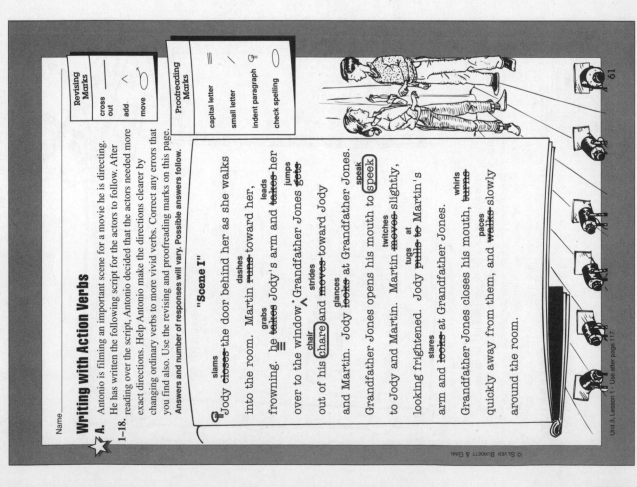

Writing with Action Verbs

A. Antonio is filming an important scene for a movie he is directing. He has written the following script for the actors to follow. After reading over the script, Antonio decided that the actors needed more exact directions. Help Antonio make the directions clearer by changing ordinary verbs to more vivid verbs. Correct any errors that you find also. Use the revising and proofreading marks on this page. **Answers and number of responses will vary. Possible answers follow.**

1–18.

Revising Marks	
cross out	—
add	∧
move	⟲

Proofreading Marks	
capital letter	≡
small letter	/
indent paragraph	¶
check spelling	○

"Scene I"

Jody ~~closes~~ [slams] the door behind her as she walks into the room. Martin ~~runs~~ [dashes] toward her, frowning. he ~~takes~~ [grabs] Jody's arm and ~~takes~~ [leads] her over to the window. Grandfather Jones ~~gets~~ [strides] [jumps] out of his ~~chair~~ and ~~moves~~ [glances] toward Jody and Martin. Jody ~~looks~~ [glances] at Grandfather Jones. Grandfather Jones opens his mouth to ~~speek~~ [speak] to Jody and Martin. Martin ~~moves~~ [twitches] slightly, looking frightened. Jody ~~pulls to~~ [tugs at] Martin's arm and ~~looks~~ [stares] at Grandfather Jones. Grandfather Jones closes his mouth, ~~turns~~ [whirls], paces quickly away from them, and ~~walks~~ slowly around the room.

61

B. Now you try writing some script directions. Read the following description. Then write what you think each actor or actress will be doing for the next few moments of the scene. Be sure to use vivid verbs to make your directions clear. If you need to show changes, use revising and proofreading marks. **Answers will vary.**

The scene takes place at a horse corral. "Tex" is sitting on the coral fence holding a lasso. Betty is wearing jeans, cowboy boots, a plaid shirt, and a hat. She is sitting on a horse. Betty's mother, Mrs. Lane, stands inside the corral. She is watching Betty with a worried look on her face.

C. Help one of Antonio's actors find his way to the treasure. Beside each diamond write a vivid verb that tells what he must do to pass each obstacle.
Answers will vary. Possible answers follow.
19–25.

climb   swim   leap   descend   dodge   scale   avoid

62

T31

B.

Imagine that you are a casting director interviewing student actors and actresses for parts in a film. Write notes about them. Use linking verbs to connect the subject with a word or words in the predicate. If you need to indicate changes, use revising and proofreading marks. **Answers will vary.**

_____

_____

_____

C.

Use a linking verb from the box to complete each sentence. Some verbs are used more than once. Then use the numbered letters to spell out a message that tells something about you.

am	is	are	was	were	seem
taste	tastes	feel	feels	felt	seems

25. Tammy **i** s a good dancer. (1)
26. Some actors **a r e** superstitious. (2)
27. They **s e e m** nervous sometimes. (3)
28. Fresh corn **t a s t e s** delicious. (4)
29. Those fabrics **f e e l** soft. (5)
30. The actors **a r e** ready for a picnic. (6)
31. The tables **a r e** filled with food. (7)
32. Cal **i s** the cook. (8)
33. The sun **f e l t** warm. (9)
34. Pat **i s** smart. (10)

I	a m	t e r r i f i c!
1	2 3	4 5 6 7 8 9 10

Linking Verbs

A.

Carla is Antonio's casting director. She interviews actors and actresses for parts in his films. Below are some notes Carla made 1–24. about the people who tried out for the various parts. In her notes, Carla left out some linking verbs. Help Carla add linking verbs that connect the subject with a word or words in the predicate. Correct any other errors that you find also. Use the revising and proofreading marks on this page.

Answers will vary. Possible answers follow.

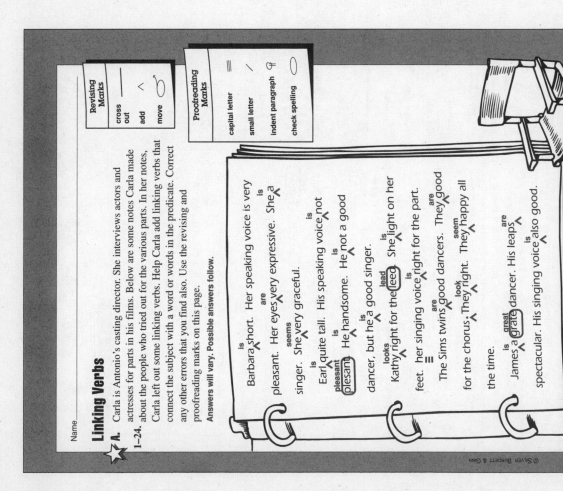

Revising Marks	
cross out	—
add	∧
move	⟳

Proofreading Marks	
capital letter	≡
small letter	/
indent paragraph	¶
check spelling	○

Barbara **is** short. Her speaking voice is very pleasant. Her eyes **are** very expressive. She **is** a singer. She **seems** very graceful.

Earl **is** quite tall. His speaking voice **is** not pleasant. He **is** handsome. He **is** not a good dancer, but he **is** a good singer.

Kathy **looks** right for the **lead**. She **is** light on her feet. her singing voice **is** right for the part.

The Sims twins **are** good dancers. They **look** good for the chorus. They **seem** right. They **are** happy all the time.

James **is** a **great** dancer. His leaps **are** spectacular. His singing voice **is** also good.

T32

Main Verbs and Helping Verbs

A. Kelly has written a campaign speech to convince her classmates she would make a good class president. As you can see, she has made some mistakes with helping verbs and main verbs. Help Kelly make the helping verbs work with the main verbs. Correct any other errors that you find also. Use the revising and proofreading marks on this page.

1–16.

Revising Marks	
cross out	—
add	^
move	○

Proofreading Marks	
capital letter	≡
small letter	/
indent paragraph	¶
check spelling	○

First I ~~have~~ (will) tell you about my experience. As class secretary I have written the (meating→meeting) notes. I ~~was~~ (have) presented them to the class. as ≡ class vice-president, I ~~were~~ (have) presided over many class meetings. I ~~was~~ (have) worked on many class projects.

I ~~am~~ (will) work hard to make our school better. I ~~have~~ (will) set aside time each week when all of you can speak to me privately. ^ You may (can) ~~want~~s to suggest activities that we ~~have~~ (can) do as a class. I will ~~listens~~ (listen) to each suggestion you make. I ~~had~~ (will) make a (fare→fair) and honest class president. I ~~have~~ (am) (hopping→hoping) you will vote for me.

B. Write a campaign speech for yourself. Be sure to use main verbs and helping verbs correctly. If you need to indicate changes, use revising and proofreading marks. **Answers will vary.**

_____

_____

_____

_____

C. Complete each sentence with the correct helping verb or main verb from the box. You may use a verb more than once. To answer the riddle at the end, write the numbered words and letters on the line provided.

are	need	will	am	tried
serve	bat	were	had	tasted

17. Sean _____will_____ read a mystery story to us.

18. He will _____need_____ to find his glasses.

19. Will Carla b a t the ball?

20. Mr. Joseph's students a r e planning to win the game.

21. The batter on second has t r i e d to steal third.

22. Have you t a s t e d maple syrup?

23. The players a r e practicing this afternoon.

24. The chefs will s e r v e a breakfast favorite.

25. What do baseball players and pancakes have in common?

For both you will need b a t t e r s
             1 2 3 4 5 6 7 8 9

T33

Name _____

Verbs with Direct Objects

A. Amy has written captions for pictures of last week's baseball game. Help
1–19. Amy add the direct objects. Use the revising and proofreading
marks on this page. Correct any other errors you find also.
Answers and number of responses may vary. Possible answers follow.

Revising Marks	
cross out	——
add	∧
move	◌

Proofreading Marks	
capital letter	≡
small letter	/
indent paragraph	¶
check spelling	◯

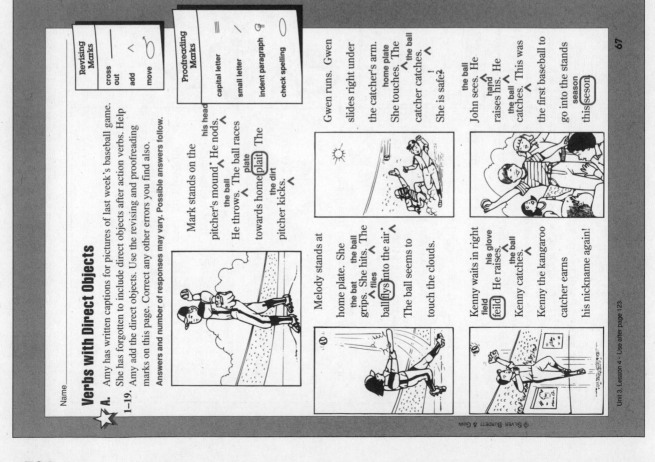

Mark stands on the
pitcher's mound. He nods. his head ∧
He throws. The ball races ∧ the ball
towards home plait(plate). The
pitcher kicks. ∧ the dirt

Melody stands at
home plate. She the bat ∧ the ball
grips. She hits. The
ball flys into the air. ∧
The ball seems to
touch the clouds.

Gwen runs. Gwen
slides right under
the catcher's arm.
She touches. The home plate ∧ the ball
catcher catches. ∧
She is safe!

Kenny waits in right
field(field). He raises. his glove ∧
Kenny catches. ∧ the ball
Kenny the kangaroo
catcher earns
his nickname again!

the ball ∧
John sees. He
raises his. He hand ∧
catches. This was ∧ the ball
the first baseball to
go into the stands
this season(season)

Unit 3, Lesson 4 · Use after page 123.

© SILVER BURDETT & GINN

Name _____

B. Now write your own captions for the following pictures. Try to
make your captions brief and exact. If you need to indicate changes,
use revising and proofreading marks. **Answers will vary.**

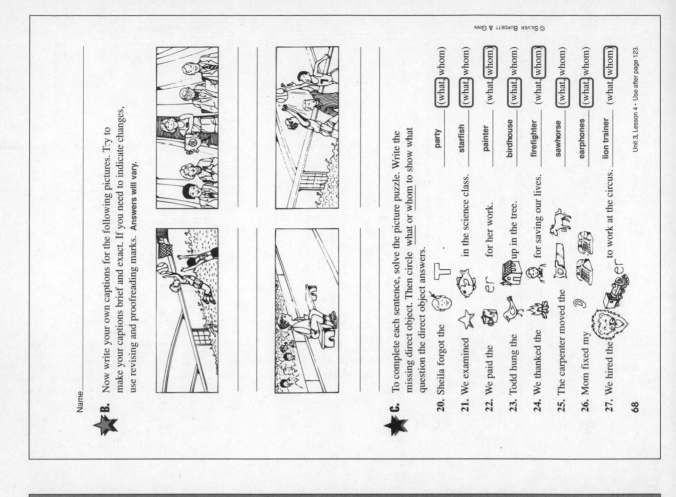

C. To complete each sentence, solve the picture puzzle. Write the
missing direct object. Then circle what or whom to show what
question the direct object answers.

20. Sheila forgot the _____ party (what, whom)

21. We examined _____ in the science class. starfish (what, whom)

22. We paid the _____ for her work. painter (what, whom)

23. Todd hung the _____ up in the tree. birdhouse (what, whom)

24. We thanked the _____ for saving our lives. firefighter (what, whom)

25. The carpenter moved the _____ sawhorse (what, whom)

26. Mom fixed my _____ earphones (what, whom)

27. We hired the _____ to work at the circus. lion trainer (what, whom)

Unit 3, Lesson 4 · Use after page 123.

© SILVER BURDETT & GINN

Name _____

Tenses of Verbs

A. Don has written the beginning of a research report on the
Abominable Snowman. As you can see, he has made some mistakes
1–24. with verb tenses. Help Don correct the verbs. Correct any other
errors you find also. Use the revising and proofreading marks on
this page. Answers will vary. Possible answers follow.

Revising Marks
cross out —
add ∧
move ○

Proofreading Marks
capital letter ≡
small letter /
indent paragraph ¶
check spelling ○

            legend
     According to le̶j̶e̶n̶d̶ the Abominable Snowman
      lived
w̶i̶l̶l̶ ̶l̶i̶v̶e̶ in the h̲imalayan Mountains. It stand
                        stood
                   resembled
over seven feet tall. its face resem̶b̶l̶e̶ a human
being's face. The snowman's arms r̶e̶a̶c̶h̶ its
         reached
knees. The Abominable Snowman is also called
             means
Yeti. This word m̶e̶a̶n̶i̶n̶g̶ evil-smelling man of
                looked
the snows. The monster is said to have a very
                   explored
strong odor. In 1960 scientists w̶i̶l̶l̶ ̶l̶o̶o̶k̶ for the
 creature
creature. They explore in the mountains
                studied
for many cold months. They study large
            decided
footprints in the snow. scientists d̶e̶c̶i̶d̶e̶ that
                  melted
other animals made the tracks and the sun
       larger
made the tracks l̶a̶r̶g̶e̶r̶ as they w̶i̶l̶l̶ ̶m̶e̶l̶t̶. Today
                      seen
some people still believe that the Abominable
                    seen
Snowman exists. have you ever s̶e̶a̶n̶ the
Abominable Snowman? Do you believe it exists?

© Silver Burdett & Ginn

Name _____

B. Write a paragraph for a report about one of the topics below or one
you choose. Tell what you know about the topic. Be sure to use
present, past, and future tenses of verbs correctly. If you need to
show changes, use revising and proofreading marks.

     robots   space travel   computers   video games

Answers will vary.

_____
_____
_____
_____

C. Complete each sentence using the correct tense of the verb in
parentheses. Then write that verb in the crossword puzzle.

Across

1. We ___wanted___ to go to the fair
yesterday. (want)
5. She ___labeled___ the box two days ago. (label)
8. I ___wish___ I could go to the movies
today. (wish)
9. He will soon ___disappear___ into the
large crowd. (disappear)
12. Susan ___belted___ the skirt
around her waist. (belt)
13. I will ___trace___ the picture
on my paper. (trace)

Down

2. Last night the fireworks ___exploded___
above the castle. (explode)
3. Sherry and I will ___fill___ the glasses
to the top. (fill)
4. They ___fish___ every day. (fish)
6. Today we will ___dream___ about the
future. (dream)
7. He ___piled___ the books in a
corner. (pile)
10. She ___paints___ very quickly. (paint)
11. It ___rained___ all day long
yesterday. (rain)

Crossword puzzle answers:
- F I L L
- W A N T E D
- E X P
- L A B E L E D
- D I S A P P E A R
- R A I N E D
- B E L T E D
- T R A C E S
- W I S H
- P A I N T S
- D R E A M

© Silver Burdett & Ginn

B. Be a headline writer. Write four headlines about school events or other real or imaginary events. Use the present tense. If you need to indicate changes, use revising and proofreading marks.

Answers will vary.

_____

_____

_____

_____

C. Complete each sentence by choosing the correct form of the verb in parentheses. Write the verb on the line and circle the letters as indicated. Then write the letters on the lines below to find Mary's prediction.

24. Mary **thinks** that something exciting will happen tomorrow. (think, thinks) Circle last letter.

25. Exciting things **happen** every day. (happen, happens) Circle third letter.

26. Yes, but Mary **says** that this will be really exciting. (say, says) Circle second letter.

27. They **race** to Mary's house. (race, races) Circle last two letters.

28. I **wish** I knew how Mary can predict the future. (wish, wishes) Circle last two letters.

29. Two people **trip** on the sidewalk. (trip, trips) Circle last two letters.

30. Some children **play** baseball near Mary's house. (plays, play) Circle second letter.

31. You **ask** Mary what the newspaper headlines will be tomorrow. (ask, asks) Circle first letter.

32. Mary **senses** that we don't believe in her ability to predict the future. (sense, senses) Circle third letter.

33. He **reads** stories about people who can predict the future. (reads, read) Circle the last two letters.

s p a c e   S h i p   L a n d s

Using the Present Tense

A. Lee has written headlines for some stories for the school newspaper. The editor of the newspaper has found some mistakes in subject and verb agreement. Help the editor by changing the present-tense verbs so that they agree with their subjects. Correct any other errors you find also. Use the revising and proofreading marks on this page. Remember that each important word in a headline begins with a capital letter.

1–23.

Revising Marks	
cross out	—
add	∧
move	◯

Proofreading Marks	
capital letter	≡
small letter	/
indent paragraph	¶
check spelling	◯

Urges
Teacher ~~Urge~~ Good (Studey) Habits
Study

Declares
Principal ~~Declare~~ Holaday ↔ Holiday

Compete
Runners ~~Competes~~ in State meet

Join
Students ~~Joins~~ Debating team

Hear
Sixth Graders ~~Hears~~ Speech

Agree
Council Members ~~Agrees~~ on Rules

Begins
Spring Show ~~Begin~~ Thursday

Wins
Softball Team ~~Win~~ Championship

Begin
Football Tryouts ~~Begins~~ Next week

Attracts
Field Day ~~Attract~~ Many Students

Students Are Reading More Than Ever
Success
Field Trip to the Zoo Was a Wild (Suces)

Brings
Bake Sale business ~~Bring~~ Big Profits

Make
New Bike Racks ~~Makes~~ Parking Easier

Visits
Mayor ~~Visit~~ School in May

Write
Fifth Graders ~~Writes~~ to Pen Pals in russia

T36

Name _____

Using Irregular Verbs

A. Tony has written a letter to his friend Jack describing a trip he has taken. When he read the letter, Tony noticed that he had made some

1–23. mistakes with the tenses of irregular verbs. Help him correct the verbs in the letter. Correct any other errors you find also. Use the revising and proofreading marks on this page.

Revising Marks	
cross out	—
add	∧
move	⟳

Proofreading Marks	
capital letter	≡
small letter	/
indent paragraph	¶
check spelling	○

Dear Jack,

    went   **beach**

I ~~go~~ to the (beech) last week with my folks. It ~~taked~~ **took**

  came

us almost an ~~A~~our to pack the car. My grandparents

        rode

also ~~come~~ with us. to get to the beach, we ~~rided~~

    saw

in the car for three hours. We ~~seen~~ a flock of canvas-

    flown

back ducks near the beach. They had ~~flew~~ down

from ~~a~~laska.

    When we got to the beach, the first thing ~~i~~ did

    given   **lessons**

was swim. My dad had ~~gave~~ me (lesons) last year.

        rode

it was so much fun. The waves were so high that I

  fallen   **twenty**

must have ~~fell~~ about (tweny) times. I actually ~~ridden~~

one wave right back onto the beach! after that

ran

fierce wave, I ~~run~~ back to my family's beach blanket.∧

    written

Sorry I haven't ~~wrote~~ sooner. I've been so busy!

        See you soon,

           Tony

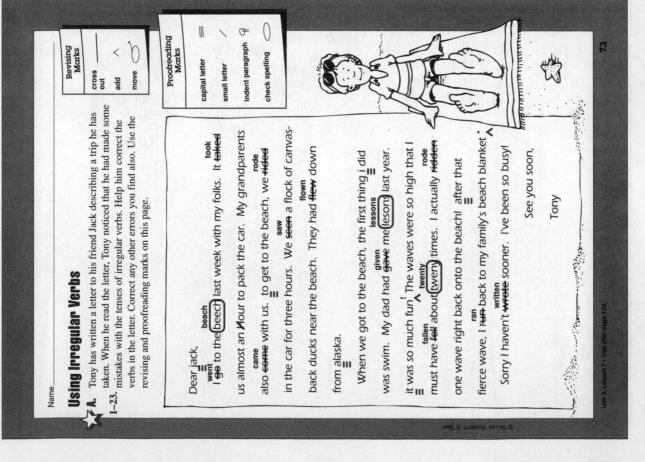

Name _____

B. Write a description of a trip you have taken. It could be a trip to the local park or mall. Use irregular verbs such as <u>see</u>, <u>eat</u>, <u>grow</u>, <u>run</u>, <u>wear</u>, or <u>write</u> in your description. If you need to indicate changes, use revising and proofreading marks. **Answers will vary.**

_____

_____

_____

_____

_____

C. Use the past and past participles of the verbs given to complete each puzzle.

24. FALL / FELL

25. FLY / FLOWN

26. EAT / EATEN

27. WRITE / WROTE

28. RIDE / RIDDEN

29. TAKE / TAKEN

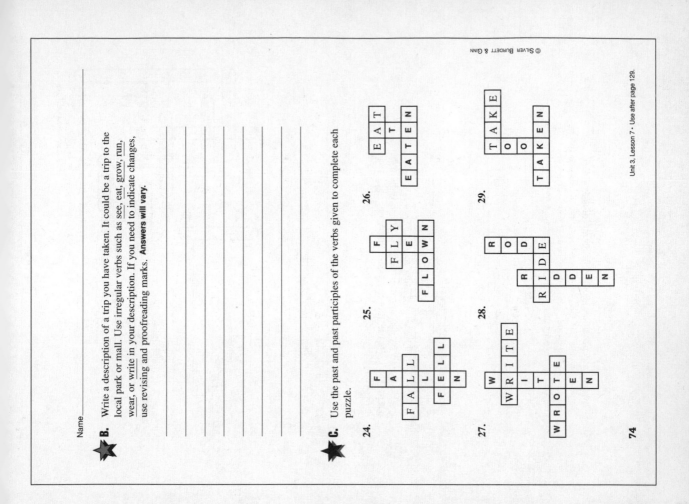

T37

Name _____

Using Irregular Verbs

A. Jill has written a newspaper article. Her editor noticed that she used irregular verbs incorrectly. Help the editor correct the irregular verbs in Jill's article. Correct any other errors you find also. Use the revising and proofreading marks on this page.

1–25.

Revising Marks	
cross out	—
add	∧
move	↶

Proofreading Marks	
capital letter	≡
small letter	/
indent paragraph	¶
check spelling	○

In an interview earlier today, ace detective Rita
~~said~~ "Farmer Jones can relax. I have ~~find~~ the
found
thief. Chicken egg thief." Rita had been trying to catch
the egg thief for months. She had almost ~~thinked~~
thought
that the case could not be solved. "At first I ~~think~~
thought
it was a dog," explained Rita. "Then yesterday I
~~choosed~~ to watch the hen house. I ~~bringed~~ a thermos
chose **brought**
of juice and a ~~sandwhich~~. I ~~drinked~~ the juice and
sandwich **drank**
waited. I ~~catched~~ the fox in the Act. He had ~~broke~~
caught **broken**
many eggs." When Farmer Jones was interviewed,
he ~~sung~~ Rita's praises. He spoke of her patience
sang
and cleverness. "Rita ~~breaked~~ this case!" exclaimed
broke
Farmer Jones. "She ~~catched~~ that chicken egg thief in
caught
a jiffy. I had ~~think~~ that Rita was a very ~~pashent~~
thought **patient**
and clever detective. I am glad I ~~goed~~ to her
went
with my problem."

Once again Rita has baffled the experts with
her detective work.

75

Name _____

B. Write a newspaper article about school events or other real or imaginary events. Use the past and past participle of irregular verbs such as say, think, find, speak, and choose. If you need to show changes, use revising and proofreading marks.   **Answers will vary.**

_____

_____

_____

_____

_____

C. Find and circle the past or past participles of these verbs in the puzzle: break, choose, find, say, freeze, speak, ring, sing, swim, think. Write a sentence for each one.

26. _____

27. _____

28. _____

29. _____

30. _____

31. _____

32. _____

33. _____

34. _____

35. _____

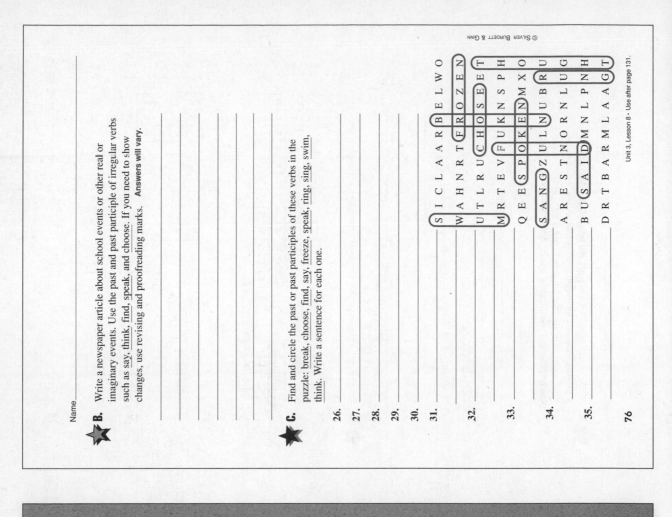

```
S I C L A A R B E L W O
W A H N R T F R O Z E N
U T L R U C H O S E T
M R T E V F U K N S P H
Q E E S P O K E N M X O
S A N G Z U L N U B R U
A R E S T N O R N L U G
B U S A I D M N L P N H
D R T B A R M L A A G T
```

76

T38

Using Troublesome Verb Pairs

A. Melissa would like to be a greeting card writer. She is practicing writing some verse for cards. After reading her verses Melissa
1–23. realized that she had used the verb pairs can, may and sit, set incorrectly. Help Melissa correct the verbs. Correct any other errors you find also. Use the revising and proofreading marks on this page.

Revising Marks	
cross out	—
add	<
move	(symbol)

Proofreading Marks	
capital letter	≡
small letter	/
indent paragraph	
check spelling	◯

can
I ~~may~~ imagine your excitement (exsitement)
     sit
As you ~~set~~ and wait
For the wonderful celebration
That's coming your way today.
there will be candles glowing
and friends who come to play.
     may
Do as you ~~can~~ wish,
It's your tenth birthday!

                              yourself
Though you are not (you're self)
And feel a little down,
                           sit
You'll soon be up and around.
i know you wont ~~set~~ for long.
                      friend
But if you need a (freind)
     sit
I'll ~~set~~ aside some time
           cheer
And try to (chear) you up at once,
             can
A Project I ~~may~~ not mind!

May
~~Can~~ I tell you I like you?
May   friend
~~Can~~ I tell you you're my (frend)?
       sit
Will you ~~set~~ beside me,
So this happy time won't end?

although we may be sisters,
    ≡
You are my best friend too
May   chance
~~Can~~ I take this (chanse)
to tell you?
I will always love You!

B. Write your own greeting card verses. Use the verbs can, may, sit, and set. If you need to show changes, use revising and proofreading marks. **Answers will vary.**

_____

_____

_____

_____

_____

C. Complete each sentence with can, may, sit or set. Then use the numbered letters to answer the riddle at the bottom.

24. M a y I speak to Maria?
    —
    1

25. We will s i t at the table to eat.
              —
              2

26. S e t the tapes on the shelf.

27. We c a n tell that it will rain.
        —
        3

28. If we all s i t down, we will be able to see.
                —
                4

29. You m a y watch TV after dinner.
          —
          5

30. Carol c a n play the clarinet well.

31. Don s e t that book on the table.
          —
          6

32. Would you s e t the package down?
                —
                7

33. Let's s i t near the front of the theater.
          —
          8

34. What is a good name for Tom Thumb's teeny-tiny, sloppy bedroom?

m i n i   m e s s
— — — —   — — — —
1 2 3 4   5 6 7 8

78

T39

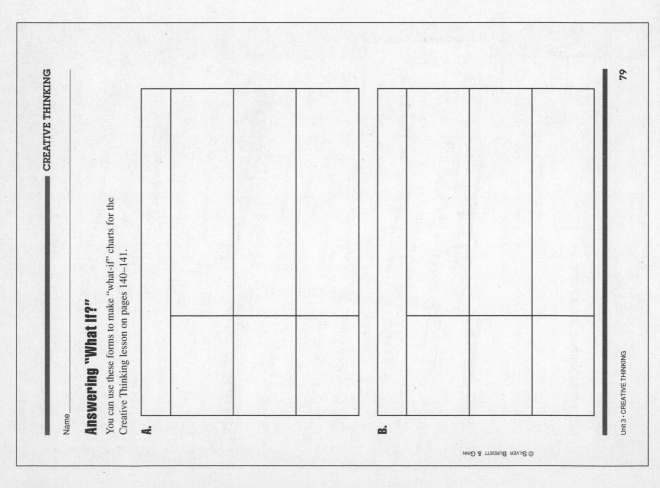

CREATIVE THINKING

Name _____

Answering "What If?"

You can use these forms to make "what-if" charts for the Writing to Learn activity on page 145.

You can use this form to make a "what-if" chart for the Writing to Learn activity on page 160.

CREATIVE THINKING

Name _____

Answering "What If?"

You can use these forms to make "what-if" charts for the Creative Thinking lesson on pages 140–141.

A.

B.

Story Starter

Imagining

You have read a selection from "Sky-Bright Axe" by Adrien Stoutenberg. Now imagine that you and your friends are visiting the great northern timber country where Paul Bunyan and Babe the Blue Ox once logged. You never really believed in these legendary characters, but something amazing happens to change your mind. On the back of this page, write a short tale about Paul and Babe. Tell what they do.

Writing Tips

◇ Use complete sentences to express your ideas. Use capital letters and punctuation carefully.

◇ Use similes and metaphors to make creative comparisons.

◇ **Focus:** Use humorous exaggeration in your tall tale.

◇ You may wish to reread "Sky-Bright Axe" before you begin. Choose one thing that you like about the writer's way of writing, and try to use it in your own tall tale.

Unit 3 · LITERATURE · Use after the Reading-Writing Connection on pages 150–151.

81

T41

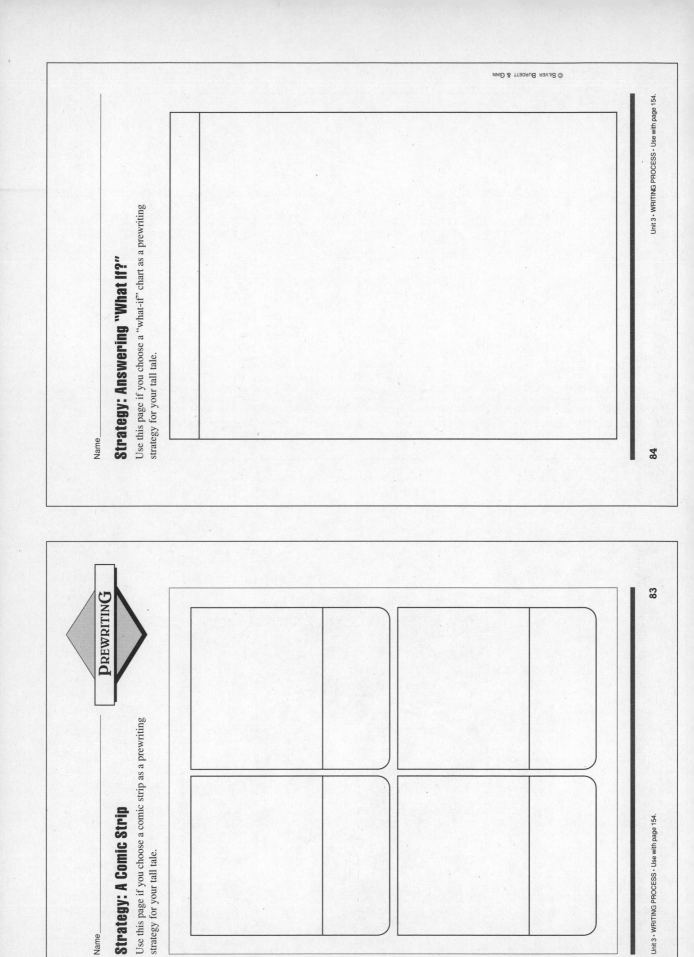

Name _____

Strategy: A Comic Strip

Use this page if you choose a comic strip as a prewriting strategy for your tall tale.

PREWRITING

83

Name _____

Strategy: Answering "What If?"

Use this page if you choose a "what-if" chart as a prewriting strategy for your tall tale.

84

T42

REVISING PRACTICE

| cross out | add ∧ | move ↶ |

A Tall Tale

Practice your revising on the tall tale below. Use the revising tips as a guide. Don't copy the tall tale. Use the revising marks to cross out, add, or move words and sentences.

Revising Tips

Check to see that the writer has
◇ told a tall tale.
◇ narrated the tall tale so that classmates will understand it.
◇ used humorous exaggerations in the tall tale.
◇ used vivid verbs to make the writing more lively and interesting to read.
◇ used similes and metaphors to make the writing vivid. **Answers will vary. Possible answers follow.**

My brother, David, is very strong for a baby. The doctor said that he is the strongest baby he's ever seen. David's muscles are big. His legs are hard. "He's a little powerhouse!" said the doctor.
as as iron   as wagon wheels

The first day David was home from the hospital, he lifted his baby crib over his head and moved it by the window. We were all surprised. I guess David wanted to look outside.
shocked   just

One day Dad, David, and I were on our way to the store. We saw a man with his foot under a big rock. We stopped to see if we could help. David lifted the rock up off the man's foot. His arm looked like a crane as he held the rock up high. "Thank you!" said the man.
gigantic   lifted moved   exclaimed

My friends and I were playing baseball yesterday. David wanted to play. He took a tree out of the ground and used it as a bat. He hit the ball so hard it landed far away. We had to take a trip on an airplane to get the ball back.
yanked   slammed   in China

I just don't know what we will do if David gets much stronger!

85

PROOFREADING PRACTICE

| capital letter ≡ | small letter / | indent paragraph | check spelling |

A Tall Tale

Practice your proofreading on the tall tale below. Use the proofreading tips as a guide. Don't copy the tall tale. Use the proofreading marks to make corrections.

Proofreading Tips

Check to see that the writer has
◇ spelled words correctly.
◇ indented paragraphs.
◇ used capital letters correctly.
◇ used correct marks at the end of sentences.

Jeff had wanted a puppy for a long time. At last his mother got him one from the pet store. Mr. Sneed, the pet shop owner, seemed glad to sell the puppy. "This is a cute puppy," said the pet shop owner. "I must warn you though. He has a big appetite."
puppy   appetite

Mr. sneed was not joking. Jeff's new puppy was always hungry. He was a walking garbage disposal. For breakfast he usually ate three huge bags of dog food. For lunch he ate 75 peanut-butter-and-jelly sandwiches and 4 gallons of milk. For dinner he normally ate a dozen steaks, 3 pounds of Potatoes and 10 cans of green beans.
breakfast   green

Jeff named the puppy Chubby. Chubby was eating Jeff's family out of house and home. in fact, one day while Chubby was waiting for his dinner, he took a bite of the house. He liked the flavor so much that he ate the whole thing. after that, Jeff's family had to live in a tent. Chubby didn't like the flavor of the tent, so he started eating trees. Finally the family got Chubby a job clearing land. The money from this job gave the family Enough money to buy another house.
dinner   flavor   started

86

T43

Name _____

What I liked about my writing: _____

_____

_____

_____

_____

_____

_____

My plans for improvement: _____

_____

_____

_____

_____

_____

Name _____

Self-Evaluation — UNIT 3

Writing a Tall Tale

Use this form as you do the Writing Process lesson beginning on page 152. Put a check next to each item you can answer yes to.

Revising

- [ ] **Purpose:** Did I write a tall tale?
- [ ] **Audience:** Will my classmates understand my tall tale?
- [ ] **Focus:** Did I use humorous exaggerations in my tall tale?
- [ ] **Grammar Check:** Did I use vivid verbs to make my writing more lively?
- [ ] **Word Choice:** Have I used strong words?
- [ ] **Writing◆Similes and Metaphors:** Have I used similes and metaphors to make my writing vivid?

Proofreading

- [ ] Did I spell words correctly?
- [ ] Did I indent paragraphs?
- [ ] Did I use capital letters correctly?
- [ ] Did I use correct marks at the end of sentences?
- [ ] Did I use my best handwriting?

Publishing

- [ ] Have I shared my writing with readers or listeners?
- [ ] Has my audience shared reactions with me?
- [ ] Have I thought about what I especially liked in this piece of writing?
- [ ] Have I thought about what I would like to work on the next time?

Use the space on the other side to tell what you liked about your writing and to make notes of your plans for improvement.

Reader's Name

Writer's Name

Writing a Tall Tale

Check Yes or No for each item. If you check No, explain or give a suggestion for improvement.

Revising

Yes   No

☐   ☐   **Purpose:** Did the writer tell a tall tale?

☐   ☐   **Audience:** Did I understand the tall tale?

☐   ☐   **Focus:** Did the writer use humorous exaggerations?

☐   ☐   **Grammar Check:** Did the writer use vivid verbs to make the writing lively?

☐   ☐   **Word Choice:** Has the writer used strong words?

☐   ☐   **Writing◆Similes and Metaphors:** Has the writer used similes and metaphors to make the writing vivid?

Proofreading

Yes   No

☐   ☐   Are words spelled correctly?

☐   ☐   Are paragraphs indented?

☐   ☐   Are capital letters used correctly?

☐   ☐   Are there correct marks at the end of sentences?

☐   ☐   Is the handwriting neat and legible?

◆ 90

PEER EVALUATION

UNIT 3

Reader's Name

Writer's Name

Writing a Tall Tale

Use the questions below and on the other side of this page to help you review the writer's tall tale. Then give this form to the writer to read and save. Your comments can help the writer improve the tall tale.

A First Reaction

Here is what I thought in general about your tall tale:

A Second Reaction

Now I have looked at your tall tale more closely. I have more specific comments about it.

Here is something you have done well as a writer:

Here is an area that might be improved:

Here is an idea for improvement:

SAVE ◆ 89

Name _____

Writing with Pronouns

A. Nathan likes to write exaggerations in his notebook. When Nathan read his exaggerations, he noticed that he often repeated the same nouns. Help Nathan change some nouns to pronouns. Correct any other errors you find also. Use the revising and proofreading marks on this page. **Number of responses may vary.**

1–22.

Revising Marks	
cross out	—
add	∧
move	↶

Proofreading Marks	
capital letter	≡
small letter	/
indent paragraph	¶
check spelling	○

                                                        family
¶ Tours is one talented (family) Anne is so tall
   she
Anne can clean Anne's gutters without a
                         he
ladder. my brother Brett is so strong Brett
                            he
can lift a car with one hand. In fact, Brett
   his   change
can changing a tire on Brett's car without
using a jack. Our dog Fido is the most
                        He
Amazing family member. Fido becomes so
            he
hungry that Fido eats a ten-pound turkey
               she
in one gulp. if you hear Mom driving
          her
home, it's because Mom uses Mom's horn
                  it
all the time. The horn is so loud you can
     she
hear the horn five Miles away. Altogether,
        our   laughing
we smiths are so happy that the Smiths
mouths hurt most of the time from (aufing)

91

Name _____

B. Try writing some exaggerations of your own. Use pronouns to avoid repeating the same nouns. Use revising and proofreading marks if you need to make changes. **Answers will vary.**

23. _____

24. _____

25. _____

26. _____

C. Leon and Mike have an amazing toy. After reading about this toy you will be directed to do something. To find out what you will do, first write a pronoun to replace the underlined word or words in each sentence. Then use the first letter of each pronoun you wrote to fill in the blanks.

27. Anne said that Anne had never seen such an unusual bike. _____ **she**

28. Brett could not stop laughing when Brett saw it. _____ **he**

29. "That is Leon and Mike's bike," said Leon and Mike. _____ **our**

30. "Leon and Mike found it at the fair," said Leon and Mike. _____ **we**

31. Leon and Mike couldn't believe Leon and Mike's eyes when they first saw it. _____ **their**

32. Leon said that Leon thought it was very colorful. _____ **he**

33. The bike had something strange at the top of the bike. _____ **it**

34. Anne thought that Anne saw the bike suddenly move. _____ **she**

35. Brett, Leon, and Mike laughed when Brett, Leon, and Mike saw Anne run away from the bike. _____ **they**

36. "We must try to put the bike in Leon and Mike's shed," said Leon and Mike. _____ **our**

37. "Good luck putting that thing into Leon and Mike's shed," said Brett to Leon and Mike. _____ **your**

s h o w   t h i s   t o y

T46

Subject Pronouns

A. Natalie has written a book review for her school newspaper. The editor noticed that Natalie should have used subject pronouns
1–23. instead of repeating some noun subjects. Help the editor replace nouns in the subjects of sentences with pronouns. Correct any errors you find also. Use the revising and proofreading marks on this page.

Revising Marks	
cross out	—
add	∧
move	⟳

Proofreading Marks	
capital letter	≡
small letter	/
indent paragraph	¶
check spelling	○

Dolphin Cove is an exciting book. ~~Dolphin Cove~~ **It**
                                            characters
has interesting ⟨Charakters⟩ and a ⱡreat plot. One
                         He
character named Joe becomes friends with the
                  He
dolphins. ~~Joe~~ swims with them in the water. ~~Joe~~
                                         They
tries to communicate with the dolphins. ~~The~~
                                     They
dolphins seem to enjoy swimming with Joe. ~~the~~
        He
dolphins call out to Joe when they see him. Joe
                  large
likes the dolphins so much he wants to keep them
                     It
in the cove. ~~Joe~~ puts a ⟨large⟩ holding net up to
              He
keep them in. ~~The net~~ extends all the way across
         She
the cove. Then Joe meets a girl named stacey.
~~Stacey~~ wants Joe to take the net down. Stacey
        argue   **They**
and Joe ~~argew~~ about the dolphins a lot. ~~Stacey~~
                                        Stacey
and Joe have trouble working things out. read
        D
Dolphin cove to find out what happens. ~~Stacey~~
likes the dolphins, too.

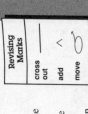

B. Write a short report telling about the characters, the setting, and the plot of a book you have read. Use some subject pronouns in your sentences. Use revising and proofreading marks if you need to make changes. **Answers will vary.**

_____

_____

_____

_____

_____

_____

C. How do you think the book, Dolphin Cove ends? To find out, look at the underlined subject pronoun in each sentence. Fill in each numbered line below with the word or words the pronoun replaces. Then read the paragraph to discover the end of the story.

24. "I want to keep the dolphins," said Joe.
    _____Joe_____
          24

25. "Why?" asked Stacey. "They need to be free!"
                          _____Joe and the dolphins_____
                                      25

26. "You just don't understand," exclaimed Joe.
    _____Stacey_____
          27

27. "We like to swim and play together."
    _____Joe and the dolphins_____
                    27

28. "I may never see the dolphins again if I let them go," he explained.
    _____Joe_____   _____the dolphins_____
          28   29

29. "This net is like a jail," cried Stacey. "It must be removed, Joe!"
                                              _____the net_____
                                                    29

30. He looked at Stacey and thought about what she had said.
    _____Joe_____   _____Stacey_____
          30   31

31. She held Joe's hand and watched the dolphins at play.
    _____Stacey_____
          31

_____Joe_____ loved the _____dolphins_____ but he knew _____Stacey_____
     24   25   26
was right. _____Joe and the dolphins_____ decided to take _____the net_____
                      27   29
down. _____Joe_____ and _____Stacey_____ watched the dolphins together.
            30   31
The dolphins seemed to be smiling and waving as they swam out to sea.

T47

Name _____

Object Pronouns

A. Miki has written an account of a soccer game, but she has forgotten that she can use the pronouns me, you, him, her, it, us, and them to stand for nouns used as direct objects. Help Miki revise what she wrote. Replace some direct objects that are nouns with object pronouns. Correct any other errors you find also. Use the revising and proofreading marks on this page. **Number of responses may vary.**

1–21.

Revising Marks	
cross out	—
add	∧
move	↻

Proofreading Marks	
capital letter	≡
small letter	/
indent paragraph	¶
check spelling	○

¶ Ms. Mackie is a good soccer coach. Everyone likes and respects ~~Ms. Mackie~~ **her**. ~~she~~ **S**he has helped the soccer team form a wining (winning) strategy. She gives ~~the soccer team~~ **us** confidence. Ms. Mackie really guides ~~the team~~ **us** and inspires all the players to do there (their) best. ∧We are lucky. Ms. Mackie is our coach.

¶ The last home game was really exciting. Ms. Mackie cheered the team on as we made the winning goal. **it** Arthur caut (caught) the ball at the goal. He passed ~~the ball~~ **it** to Jonathan. Two players on the other team blocked ~~the ball~~ **it** ~~Jonathan~~ **him**. We still had the ball. Brian took ~~the ball~~ **it** down the feild (field). We made a goal! Everyone on the ∧field was cheering except ~~the other team~~ **them**. We went over to ~~the other team~~ **them** and shook their hands. We sure injoy (enjoy) winning a game. But good sportsmanship is the most important thing Ms. Mackie taught ~~our team~~ **us**.

95

Name _____

B. Write a short account of a sports event that you have played in or watched. Use object pronouns to avoid repeating nouns used as direct objects. If you need to make changes, use revising and proofreading marks. **Answers will vary.**

_____

_____

_____

_____

C. Your soccer team is playing against Ms. Mackie's team. To find out who scores the winning goal, first read each sentence pair. Complete the second sentence by filling in the correct object pronoun to replace the underlined noun. Then underline the first letter of each object pronoun. Draw a line from the soccer ball to the first letter. Continue in this manner to trace the path of the ball.

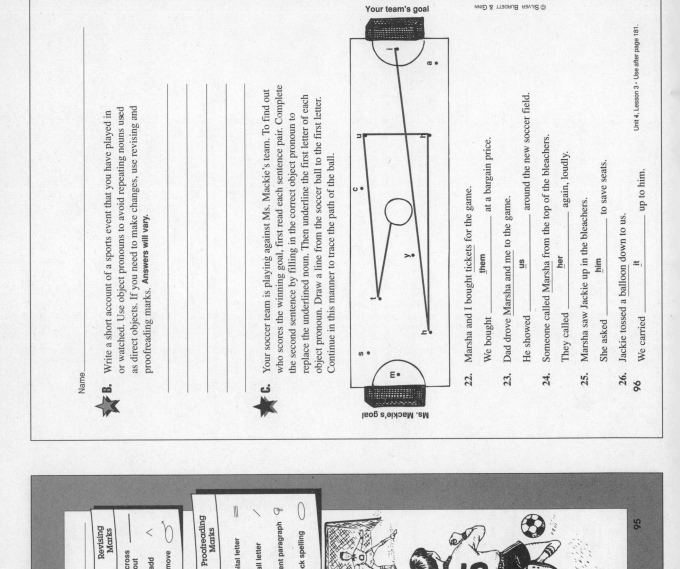

Your team's goal

Ms. Mackie's goal

22. Marsha and I bought tickets for the game.
We bought __them__ at a bargain price.

23. Dad drove Marsha and me to the game.
He showed __us__ around the new soccer field.

24. Someone called Marsha from the top of the bleachers.
They called __her__ again, loudly.

25. Marsha saw Jackie up in the bleachers.
She asked __him__ to save seats.

26. Jackie tossed a balloon down to us.
We carried __it__ up to him.

96

Possessive Pronouns

A. Dana wrote a script for the upcoming fashion show. When she read it, she realized she could have used possessive pronouns in place of some possessive nouns. Help Dana make these changes. Correct any other errors you find also. Use the revising and proofreading marks on this page.

1–20.

Revising Marks	
cross out	—
add	∧
move	⟲

Proofreading Marks	
capital letter	≡
small letter	/
indent paragraph	¶
check spelling	⬭

Welcome to our School Fashion Show. My name is
dana, and today I will be showing you fashions for
preteens. Our first model is Marcy. *Her* ~~Marcy's~~ green
jumper with pink polka dots really makes a fashion
statement. On *her* ~~Marcy's~~ head is a hat which *really* ⟲ sets
off the outfit.
Our next two models are Mark and Leroy. *Their* ~~Mark's and Leroy's~~ jackets are made of real leather.
~~Leroy's~~ jackets match the glow-in-the-dark pants nicely.
Mark's striped shirt brings out the color of *his* ~~Mark's~~ orange pants. Mark is carrying an unusual umbrella. *Its* ~~The umbrella's~~ handle has several uses. It contains a pencil case on one side and a radio on the other. this is an item that is sure to be popular with preteens. The umbrella handle is *my* ~~Dana's~~ own personal design. Leroy's checkered sneakers pick up the check pattern in *his* ~~Leroy's~~ shirt very *nicely* ⬭. Leroy and Mark *wear* ~~where Leroy's and Mark's~~ *their* outfits very well. thank you Leroy and mark.

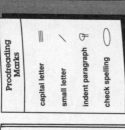

B. Write a short script for a fashion show. Try to use possessive pronouns to show ownership. Use the revising and proofreading marks if you need to make changes. **Answers will vary.**

C. A new fashion is coming out next season that all the kids will be wearing. To find out what the fashion is, first find the underlined possessive noun in each sentence. In the blank, write a possessive pronoun to replace the underlined noun or nouns. Then underline the first letter of each pronoun you write. Shade the spaces containing those letters to see the latest fashion.

21. Marcy, Leroy, and Mark took modeling lessons at Marcy, Leroy, and Mark's school. ___their___

22. Marcy wishes the outfits she models could be Marcy's. ___hers___

23. "Marcy's clothes are not as stylish as the ones I model," explains Marcy. ___my___

24. Mark loves Mark's job modeling clothes. ___his___

25. "My family comes to all my shows and many friends of my family's come, too." ___ours___

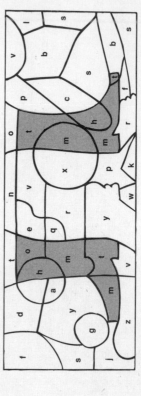

T49

T50

Name _____

Using Pronouns

A. Calvin keeps notes at his weekly chess club meetings. As you will see, he made some mistakes using pronouns. Help Calvin by supplying the correct pronouns. Remember to use a subject pronoun as the subject of a sentence and an object pronoun after an action verb. Correct any other errors you find also. Use the revising and proofreading marks on this page.

1-19.

Revising Marks	
cross out	—
add	∧
move	◠

Proofreading Marks	
capital letter	≡
small letter	/
indent paragraph	¶
check spelling	○

The chess club meeting came to order at 2:00 P.M..

Thursday, January 15. Jane asked Susanna and
We
~~me~~ about the upcoming chess meet. ~~Us~~ and the other

members will be facing tough competititon.
me
susanna told ~~I~~ that a player on the opposing chess
won
team had ~~one~~ a state competition. ∧ Robert asked
prepare
the team for ideas on how we can ~~prepair~~ for the
He
upcoming meet. ~~Him~~ and Paul offered to hold
him
special practice sessions in their home. the team
I **agreed**
and ~~me~~ ~~agreed~~ that this was a good idea. Mark
us
told ~~we~~ that his dad, Mr. Harmon, is a chess

professional. His dad taught ~~he~~ and his family how

to play chess. Benita had a good idea. Maria and
she **a**
~~her~~ found ~~good~~ chess tape at the library.
us
They will show it to ~~we~~ ∧ at the next meeting.

The meeting came to a close at 3:30 P.M. ∧

Unit 4, Lesson 5 • Use after page 185.

99

Name _____

B. Imagine that you are the note taker of a nature club, model rocket club, or another club that interests you. Write minutes for an imaginary meeting. Be sure to use subject and object pronouns correctly. Use revising and proofreading marks to show any changes. **Answers will vary.**

_____

_____

_____

_____

C. You can discover what the following mystery club is about by completing the sentences taken from the club meeting notes. Circle the correct subject or object pronoun to complete each sentence. Then write what you think the mystery club is for.

20. Valerie and (**I**, me) brought pictures to the club meeting.
21. (**She**, Her) and I had taken the pictures in the forest.
22. George showed the club and (**me**, I) some slides taken by his dad.
23. George's dad told George and (we, **us**) about each slide.
24. George and (me, **I**) made chirping sounds to go with the slides.
25. Valerie taped (him, **he**) and me as we made the sounds.
26. Cindy gave George and (I, **me**) some feathers that she found.
27. (Him, **He**) and I passed them around to all the club members.
28. Then, Kevin said that (him, **he**) and his mother were planning a trip to the zoo for all club members.

What could the mystery club be?
Did the clues above help you to see?
If your answer rhymes with words,
then you are right, the club is for the...

b i r d s

100

Unit 4, Lesson 5 • Use after page 185.

Name _____

Contractions

☆ **A.** Tomás is spending his summer vacation with his grandparents on an island off the coast of Maine. He has written a letter to his friend Marnie. He has not used any contractions in his letter. Help Tomás

1-22. capture the way people talk. Use contractions in place of pronouns and verbs. Correct any errors you find also. Use the revising and proofreading marks on this page.

Revising Marks	
cross out	—
add	∧
move	⟋◯

Proofreading Marks	
capital letter	≡
small letter	╲
indent paragraph	¶
check spelling	◯

Dear Marnie,

    I'm
I am so excited to be spending the summer with

                They've
Grandma and Grandpa. They have been so much Fun

       We've
to be with. We have been to the movies and to a

       course   they're
mini golf corse. Next week they are taking me to a

          I've
county fair. I have never been to a fair, have you?

  We'll   see
We will sea lots of prize-winning animals at the fair.

                     I'd
Grandma says that I would be a sure winner in the

                           I'd
Pie eating contest. I think i would like to Enter the

                                 I'm
watermelon eating contest instead. Well, I am going

to see one next week.

            you've   You're
    I know you have wanted to visit. You are welcome

               We'll
to come next week. We will go to the fair and climb

               We're
some rocks together. We are sure everyone will

have a great time.

                  Your friend,

                  Tomás

© SILVER BURDETT & GINN

Name _____

© SILVER BURDETT & GINN

☆ **B.** Write a letter to a friend about a vacation or trip you have taken. Use contractions to capture the way you talk. Use revising and proofreading marks if you need to make changes. **Answers will vary.**

_____

_____

_____

_____

_____

_____

☆ **C.** Complete the sentences with contractions. Then use the numbered letters to complete the palindrome below. A palindrome is a word or phrase that is spelled the same way forward and backward.

23. If we don't hurry, __w__ __e__ ' __l__ __l__ be late.
                      1

24. Donna is sure __s__ __h__ __e__ ' __s__ forgotten something.
                    2

25. Tomás hopes __h__ __e__ ' __l__ __l__ be back soon.
              3

26. Your parents said __t__ __h__ __e__ __y__ ' __l__ __l__ wait for you.
                        4

27. Margie said __s__ __h__ __e__ ' __l__ __l__ have too much homework.
                  5

28. Daryl thinks __w__ __e__ ' __r__ __e__ going to the race together.
                  6

29. The teachers think __t__ __h__ __e__ __y__ ' __v__ __e__ filled all their classes.
                          7

30. The coach told team members __t__ __h__ __e__ __y__ ' __d__ better come to practice on time.
                                   8

__W__ __e__ ' __l__ __l__ __l__ __e__ __t__ __D__ __a__ __d__ __t__ __e__ __l__ __l__ __L__ __e__ __w__
 1   2   3   4   5   6   7   8   8   7   6   5   4   3   2   1

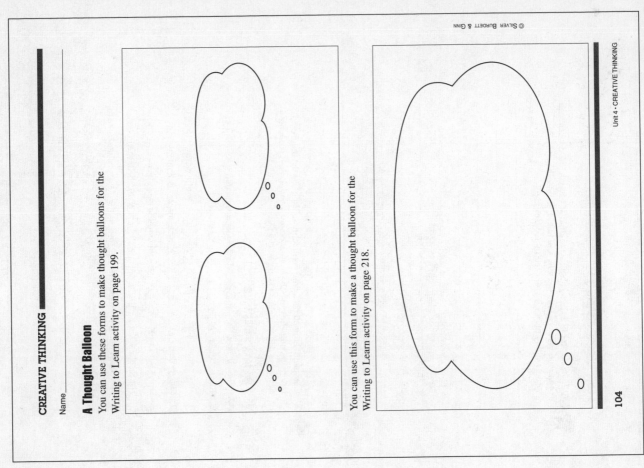

CREATIVE THINKING

Name

A Thought Balloon

You can use these forms to make thought balloons for the
Writing to Learn activity on page 199.

You can use this form to make a thought balloon for the
Writing to Learn activity on page 218.

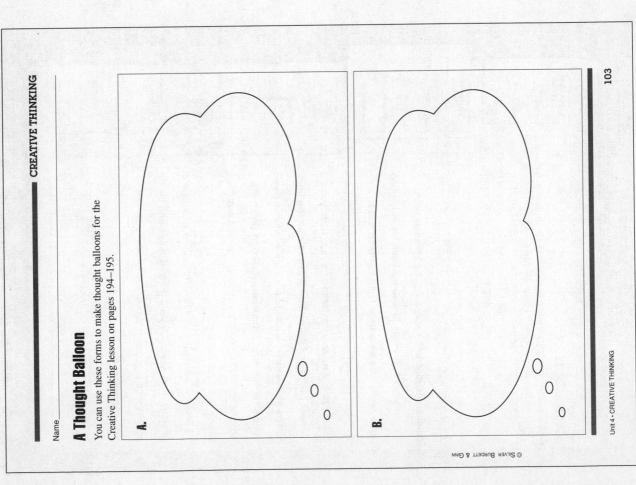

CREATIVE THINKING

Name

A Thought Balloon

You can use these forms to make thought balloons for the
Creative Thinking lesson on pages 194–195.

A.

B.

Name _____

Persuading

You have read a selection from "The Littlest Sculptor" by Joan T. Zeier about a very persuasive young artist. Pretend that you are the artist pictured below. You decide to paint a portrait of a famous person, but first you must persuade the person to sit for you. Who will it be? The President? A rock star? An actor? An athlete? On the back of this page, write a paragraph that will convince the person to allow you to do the painting.

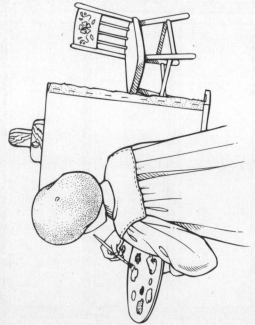

Writing Tips

◇ Use complete sentences to express your ideas. Use capital letters and punctuation carefully.

◇ Support your opinion with facts and reasons. List your reasons in order of importance.

◇ **Focus:** Remember to use the most persuasive words you can think of in your paragraph.

◇ You may wish to reread "The Littlest Sculptor" before you begin. Choose one thing that you like about the writer's way of writing, and try to use it in your own paragraph.

Name _____

T53

T54

Name _____

Strategy: An Opinion Ladder

Use this page if you choose an opinion ladder as a prewriting strategy for your persuasive letter.

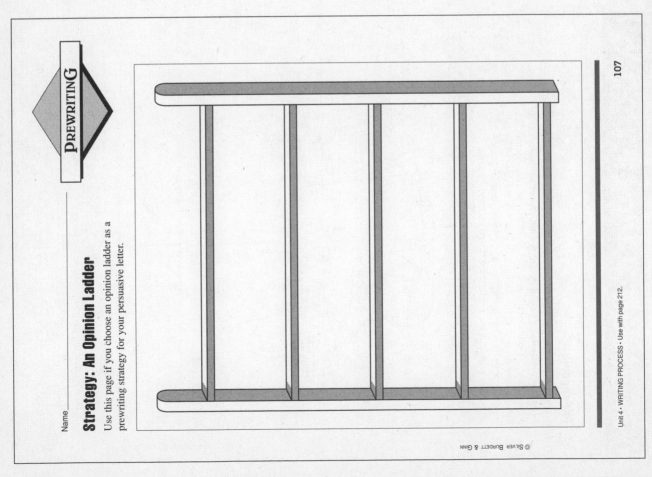

Unit 4 · WRITING PROCESS · Use with page 212.

107

Name _____

Strategy: A Thought Balloon

Use this page if you choose a thought balloon as a prewriting strategy for your persuasive letter.

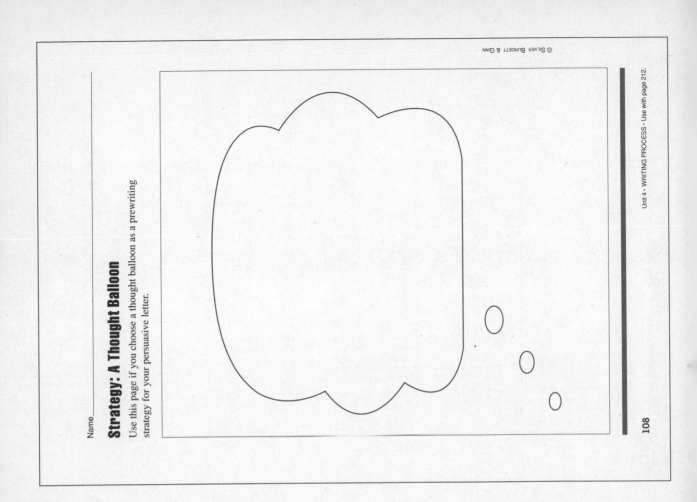

Unit 4 · WRITING PROCESS · Use with page 212.

108

REVISING PRACTICE

Name _____

cross out —— | add ∧ | move ⟲

A Persuasive Letter

Practice your revising on the persuasive letter below. Use the revising tips as a guide. Don't copy the letter. Use the revising marks to cross out, add, or move words and sentences.

Revising Tips

Check to see that the writer has

◇ written a persuasive letter.
◇ given reasons that will persuade the reader.
◇ used persuasive words.
◇ used pronouns instead of nouns to make the writing less repetitive.
◇ given an opinion and listed reasons to support it.
◇ listed the supporting reasons in the order of their importance.

Answers will vary. Possible answers follow.

Dear Fellow Students,

    I think our school colors should be blue and yellow. ~~Blue and yellow~~ **They are cheerful colors.** Blue and yellow can be found both inside and outside our school. Blue morning glories and yellow buttercups are growing all around the school grounds. Yellow shirts and sweaters can be found in most stores. The floor in the **main** hallway is light blue. The walls in the main hallway are light yellow. It would be easy for students to wear the school colors if ~~the school colors~~ **they** were blue and yellow. All students own a pair of blue jeans. ~~All students~~ could wear **them** ~~blue jeans~~ to school. We could even have some yellow T-shirts printed with Kaley Elementary in blue. **letters on school colors** We will be voting next week. I hope that you will vote for the colors blue and yellow.

Sincerely,

Nina Knowles

PROOFREADING PRACTICE

Name _____

capital letter ≡ | small letter / | indent paragraph ¶ | check spelling ◯

A Persuasive Letter

Practice your proofreading on the persuasive letter below. Use the proofreading tips as a guide. Don't copy the letter. Use the proofreading marks to make corrections.

Proofreading Tips

Check to see that the writer has

◇ spelled words correctly.
◇ indented paragraphs.
◇ used capital letters correctly.
◇ used correct marks at the end of sentences.

Dear Mayor Martin,

    I think we need a playground in our ~~neborhood~~ **neighborhood**. Our ~~neborhood~~ **neighborhood** has at least sixty children who would use the playground. Having a perfect place for the playground would be the **perfek** Empty lot on oak ~~Stret~~ **Street**. I heard on the news that the city received Approval for improvements. I think that a neighborhood playground would be an excellent improvement. It would add to the beauty of the neighborhood. It would make both the children and their parents very happy. I hope that you will consider building a neighborhood playground for the children. we would all be very grateful to the ~~sity~~ **city**.

Sincerely,

Tessie Carroll

SELF-EVALUATION

UNIT 4

Name _____

Writing a Persuasive Letter

Use this form as you do the Writing Process lesson beginning on page 210. Put a check next to each item you can answer yes to.

Revising

- [ ] **Purpose:** Did I write a persuasive letter?
- [ ] **Audience:** Will my reasons persuade the person I wrote to?
- [ ] **Focus:** Did I use persuasive words?
- [ ] **Grammar Check:** Have I replaced some nouns with pronouns to make my writing less repetitive?
- [ ] **Word Choice:** Have I used the best words?
- [ ] **Writing◆Business Letter:** Have I used all six parts of a proper business letter?

Proofreading

- [ ] Did I spell words correctly?
- [ ] Did I indent paragraphs?
- [ ] Did I use capital letters correctly?
- [ ] Did I use correct marks at the end of sentences?
- [ ] Did I use my best handwriting?

Publishing

- [ ] Have I shared my writing with readers or listeners?
- [ ] Has my audience shared reactions with me?
- [ ] Have I thought about what I especially liked in this piece of writing?
- [ ] Have I thought about what I would like to work on the next time?

Use the space on the other side to tell what you liked about your writing and to make notes of your plans for improvement.

SAVE
111

Name _____

What I liked about my writing: _____

My plans for improvement: _____

112

Writing a Persuasive Letter

Reader's Name _____

Writer's Name _____

Check Yes or No for each item. If you check No, explain or give a suggestion for improvement.

Revising

Yes No

☐ ☐ **Purpose:** Is the letter persuasive?

☐ ☐ **Audience:** Will the reasons in the letter persuade the person it is written to?

☐ ☐ **Focus:** Did the writer use persuasive words?

☐ ☐ **Grammar Check:** Has the writer replaced some nouns with pronouns to make the writing less repetitive?

☐ ☐ **Word Choice:** Has the writer used the best words?

☐ ☐ **Writing◆Business Letter:** Has the writer used all six parts of a proper business letter?

Proofreading

Yes No

☐ ☐ Are words spelled correctly?

☐ ☐ Are paragraphs indented?

☐ ☐ Are capital letters used correctly?

☐ ☐ Are there correct marks at the end of sentences?

☐ ☐ Is the handwriting neat and legible?

PEER EVALUATION

UNIT 4

Reader's Name _____

Writer's Name _____

Writing a Persuasive Letter

Use the questions below and on the other side of this page to help you review the writer's persuasive letter. Then give this form to the writer to read and save. Your comments can help the writer improve the persuasive letter.

A First Reaction

Here is what I thought in general about your persuasive letter:

_____

_____

_____

A Second Reaction

Now I have looked at your persuasive letter more closely. I have more specific comments about it.

Here is something you have done well as a writer:

_____

Here is an area that might be improved:

_____

Here is an idea for improvement:

_____

T58

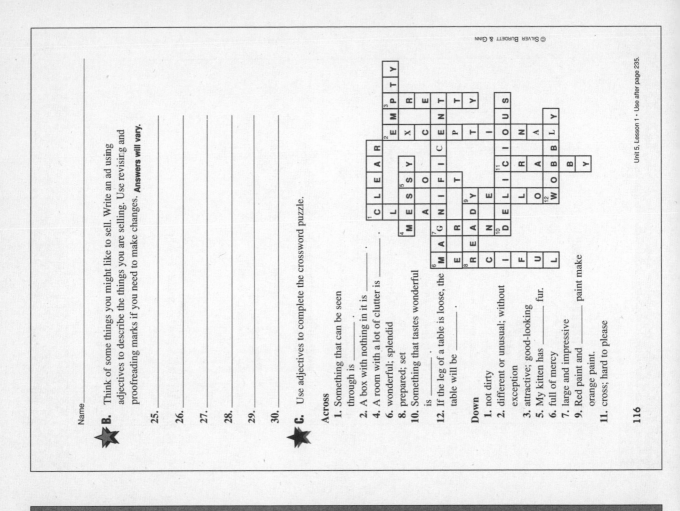

B.

Think of some things you might like to sell. Write an ad using adjectives to describe the things you are selling. Use revising and proofreading marks if you need to make changes. **Answers will vary.**

25. _____
26. _____
27. _____
28. _____
29. _____
30. _____

C.

Use adjectives to complete the crossword puzzle.

Across

1. Something that can be seen through is _____.
2. A box with nothing in it is _____.
4. A room with a lot of clutter is _____.
6. wonderful; splendid
8. prepared; set
10. Something that tastes wonderful is _____.
12. If the leg of a table is loose, the table will be _____.

Down

1. not dirty
2. different or unusual; without exception
3. attractive; good-looking
5. My kitten has _____ fur.
6. full of mercy
7. large and impressive
9. Red paint and _____ paint make orange paint.
11. cross; hard to please

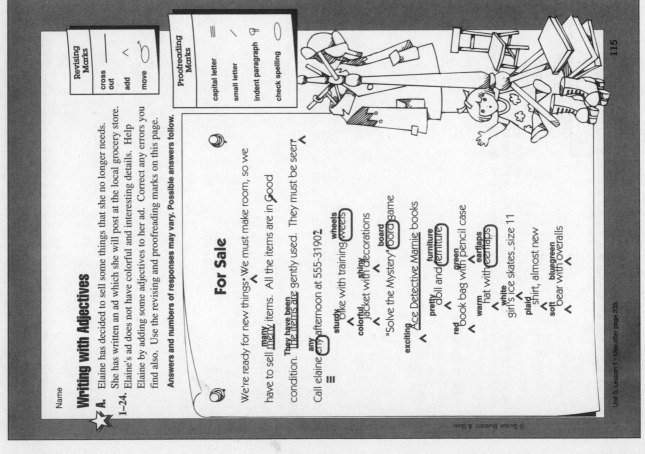

Writing with Adjectives

A. Elaine has decided to sell some things that she no longer needs. She has written an ad and which she will post at the local grocery store. Elaine's ad does not have colorful and interesting details. Help Elaine by adding some adjectives to her ad. Correct any errors you find also. Use the revising and proofreading marks on this page.

Answers and numbers of responses may vary. Possible answers follow.

1–24.

For Sale

We're ready for new things. We must make room, so we have to sell many items. All the items are in good condition. They have been gently used. They must be seen.

Call elaine any afternoon at 555-31902.

Revising Marks	
cross out	—
add	^
move	◌

Proofreading Marks	
capital letter	≡
small letter	/
indent paragraph	¶
check spelling	◯

Adjectives After Linking Verbs

★

A. The students in Mr. Perkins's class are writing travel brochures for their town. The brochures are supposed to attract visitors to the

1–28. town. Roland did his best, but he was having trouble coming up with good descriptive words. Can you help him? Add details to his paragraph by putting in a predicate adjective after each linking verb. Correct any errors you find also. Use the revising and proofreading marks on this page. **Answers will vary. Possible answers follow.**

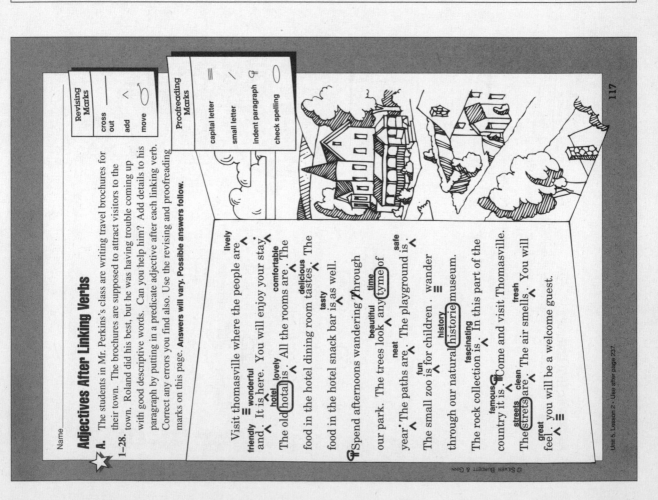

Revising Marks

cross out ———
add ∧
move ↶

Proofreading Marks

capital letter ≡
small letter /
indent paragraph ¶
check spelling ✓

friendly
Visit thomasville where the people are ∧.
≡ wonderful
lively
and ∧. It is here. You will enjoy your stay ∧.
hotel lovely comfortable
The old hotal is ∧. All the rooms are ∧. The
delicious
food in the hotel dining room tastes ∧. The
tasty
food in the hotel snack bar is as well.
¶ beautiful time
Spend afternoons wandering ∧ through
our park. The trees look any tyme of
neat safe
year. The paths are ∧. The playground is ∧.
fun
The small zoo is for children. wander
history fascinating
through our natural historie museum.
famous
The rock collection is ∧. In this part of the
country it is. ≡ Come and visit Thomasville. You will
streets clean fresh
The strets are. The air smells ∧. You will
great
feel ∧. you will be a welcome guest.
≡

★

B. How would you get people interested in visiting your town or area of the country? Write a paragraph for a travel brochure. Include some predicate adjectives. Use revising and proofreading marks if you need to make changes. **Answers will vary.**

_____
_____
_____
_____
_____
_____

★

C. Complete the comic alphabet by supplying a predicate adjective that begins with the letter of the alphabet. **Answers will vary. Possible answers follow.**

29. A is adorable.
30. B is **brave** .
31. C is **cuddly** .
32. D is drowsy.
33. E is exhausted.
34. F is **fast** .
35. G is **green** .
36. H is helpful.
37. I is important.
38. J is **jumpy** .
39. K is kind.
40. L is **lumpy** .
41. M is messy.

42. N is **nasty** .
43. O is out-of-date.
44. P is **peppy** .
45. Q is quick.
46. R is **radiant** .
47. S is **sad** .
48. T is **tasty** .
49. U is unclear.
50. V is vast.
51. W is **willful** .
52. X is X-rayed.
53. Y is **yellow** .
54. Z is zany.

Name _____

Adjectives That Compare

A. Tony wants to buy a radio he can wear while hiking in the woods.
1–23. To help him decide which radio to buy, he has written some notes about three radios he has seen. Help him by writing the correct form of each comparative adjective. Correct any other errors you find also. Use the revising and proofreading marks on this page.

Revising Marks	
cross out	———
add	∧
move	◯

Proofreading Marks	
capital letter	≡
small letter	/
indent paragraph	¶
check spelling	◯

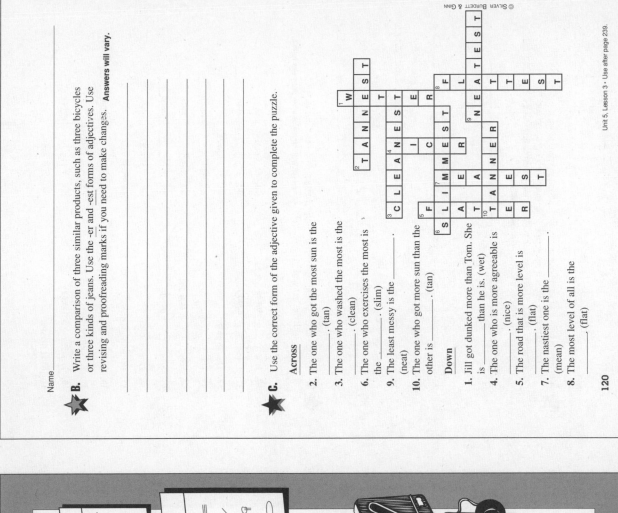

Comparison of three radios:

             lighter
the F–E is light than the R24.

                  lightest
The Xerophone radio is the light of all.
           has   *sound*
The R24 haz a clear sounde.

        clearer   *than*
the F–E and the Xerophone both have clear sounds then the R24.

                                   clearest
i think the Xerophone seems the clear of all.
     costlier
it is also costly than the R24.
               bigger
The R24 uses big batteries than the F–E.

                   biggest
The Xerophone uses the big batteries of all.

               fancier
The Xerophone is fancy than the R24.
                             radios
              fanciest
The F–E is the fancy of all three radeos.

Name _____

B. Write a comparison of three similar products, such as three bicycles or three kinds of jeans. Use the -er and -est forms of adjectives. Use revising and proofreading marks if you need to make changes. **Answers will vary.**

_____

_____

_____

_____

_____

_____

_____

C. Use the correct form of the adjective given to complete the puzzle.

Across

2. The one who got the most sun is the _____. (tan)

3. The one who washed the most is the _____. (clean)

6. The one who exercises the most is the _____. (slim)

9. The least messy is the _____. (neat)

10. The one who got more sun than the other is _____. (tan)

Down

1. Jill got dunked more than Tom. She is _____ than he is. (wet)

4. The one who is more agreeable is _____. (nice)

5. The road that is more level is _____. (flat)

7. The nastiest one is the _____. (mean)

8. The most level of all is the _____. (flat)

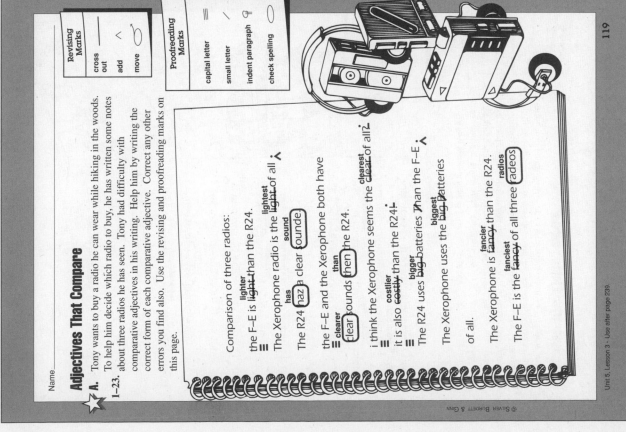

B.

Write a review of a movie or television show that you particularly liked. Use a variety of adjectives, including several that need more or most, to make comparisons. Use revising and proofreading marks if you need to make changes. **Answers will vary.**

_____

_____

_____

_____

_____

_____

_____

C.

Complete each of the following lines from different movie reviews. Remember to use the correct form of the adjective. **Answers will vary.** **Possible answers follow.**

26. The best of the three movies was The Shark because it was the __most suspenseful__ of all.

27. The Long Journey was __more interesting__ than the writer's first movie, Trails Westward.

28. The Fabulous Flight was the __best__ of all the science fiction films.

29. The Mystery at the Castle was __more thrilling__ than The Case of the Missing Letter.

30. The special effects in Planet Pranks were __better__ than the ones in Meteor Magic.

31. The costumes in Balloon Battles were the __worst__ I have seen in a long time.

Using more and most with Adjectives

A.

Tina wrote a movie review for her school newspaper. Tina had some trouble with comparative adjectives. Help her by supplying the correct form of the adjectives. Correct any other errors you find also. Use the revising and proofreading marks on this page.

1–25.

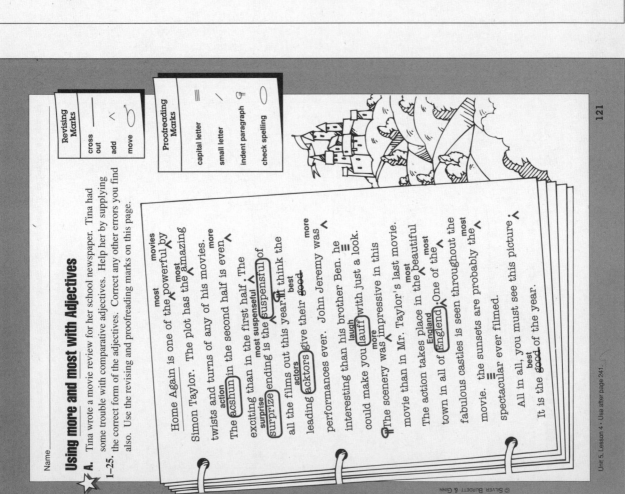

T61

Name _____

A Thought Balloon

You can use these forms to make thought balloons for the Creative Thinking lesson on pages 248–249.

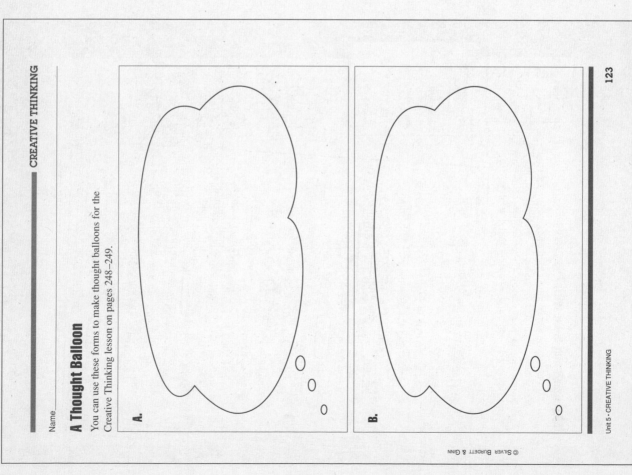

Name _____

A Thought Balloon

You can use this form to make a thought balloon for the Writing to Learn activity on page 255.

You can use this form to make a thought balloon for the Writing to Learn activity on page 272.

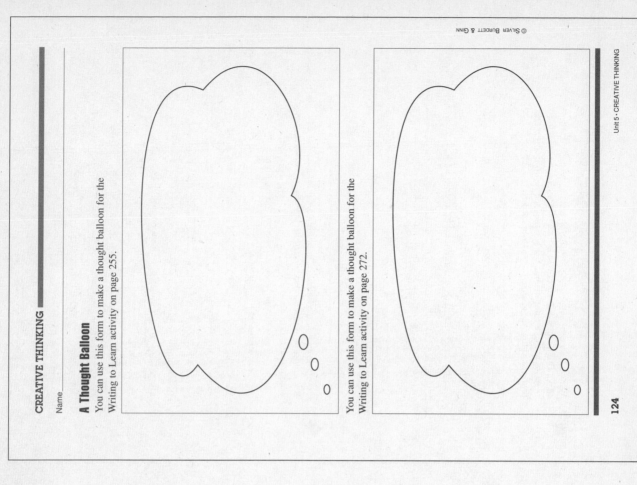

Story Starter

Name

Describing

You have read a selection from Zeely by Virginia Hamilton. Now imagine that you, Geeder, and Toeboy are in the picture below. You are hiking through the woods on the other side of Uncle Ross's farm. As you come to a clearing, you notice a shack. There are strange noises coming from inside. The door opens with a crash. On the back of this page, describe the character who walks out.

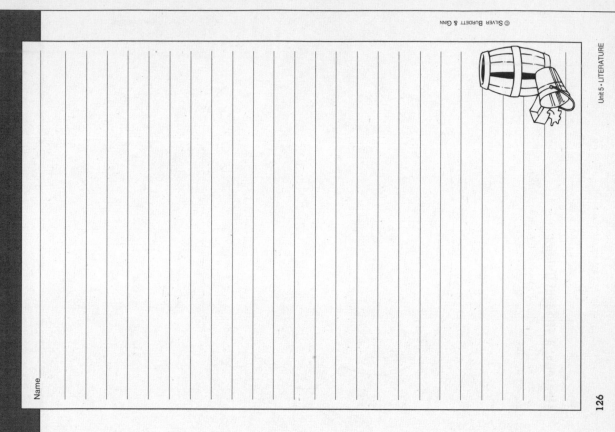

Writing Tips

◇ Use complete sentences to express your ideas. Use capital letters and punctuation carefully.

◇ Organize details by space order or order of importance to help the reader picture what you describe.

◇ **Focus:** Remember to use sensory words and other details to show what your character is like.

◇ You may wish to reread Zeely before you begin. Choose one thing that you like about the writer's way of writing, and try to use it in your description.

Unit 5 • LITERATURE • Use after the Reading-Writing Connection on pages 262–263.

Name

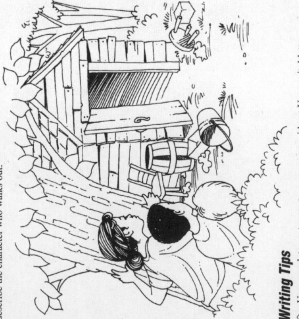

Unit 5 • LITERATURE

T64

Name _____

Strategy: A Character Map

Use this page to make a sketch if you choose a character map as a prewriting strategy for your character sketch.

Unit 5 • WRITING PROCESS • Use with page 266.

127

Name _____

Strategy: A Thought Balloon

Use this page if you choose a thought balloon as a prewriting strategy for your character sketch.

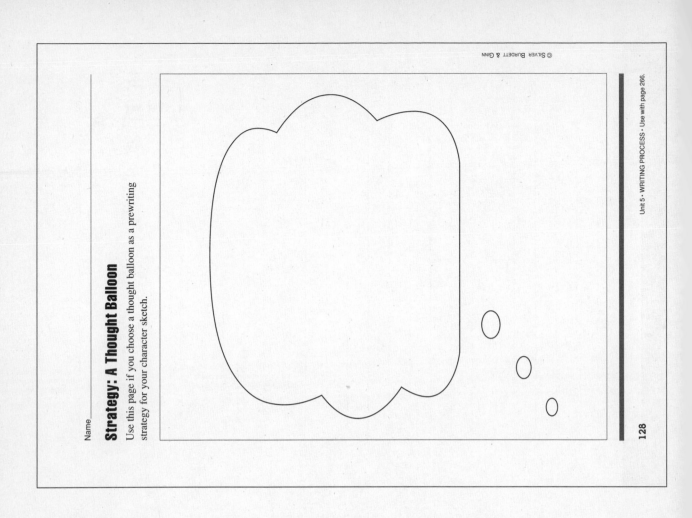

Unit 5 • WRITING PROCESS • Use with page 266.

128

PROOFREADING PRACTICE

Name _____

| ≡ capital letter | / small letter | ¶ indent paragraph | ◯ check spelling |

A Character Sketch

Practice your proofreading on the character sketch below. Use the proofreading tips as a guide. Don't copy the sketch. Use the proofreading marks to make corrections.

Proofreading Tips

Check to see that the writer has
◇ spelled words correctly.
◇ indented paragraphs.
◇ used capital letters correctly.
◇ used correct marks at the end of sentences.

◆ If you walk through Baker Landing School and listen, you can hear the sweet voice of Ann Prentiss. ms. Prentiss is our music teacher.
taught
She has tauht here for fifteen years. Her cheery face lights up the
halls. when she sings, everyone brightens up. She loves Music and
children. That is why she chose to be a music teacher.
introduce
Ms. Prentiss's job is to introduce music to all the students. She
teaches kindergarten through eighth grade. she brings her sturdy old
lesson
pitchpipe to each class. She begins each lessen with a song. Sleepy
children's ears perk up to listen. Her lively songs make everyone want
to join in.
believes   experience
Ms. Prentiss beleives that every child should xperience the joys of
singing. She is particularly wonderful with students who are not
naturally musical. I know because I am one. After she sings with the
students, Ms. Prentiss shares her knowledge with them. I'm so glad to
know this caring teacher!

Unit 5 • WRITING PROCESS • Use after page 270.

REVISING PRACTICE

Name _____

| — cross out | ∧ add | ◯↷ move |

A Character Sketch

Practice your revising on the character sketch below. Use the revising tips as a guide. Don't copy the sketch. Use the revising marks to cross out, add, or move words and sentences.

Revising Tips

Check to see that the writer has
◇ given a vivid description of someone.
◇ made the character sketch enjoyable to read.
◇ included details and sensory words to help the reader get to know the character.
◇ used adjectives to add specific details to the writing.
◇ used precise words for words such as good and cute.
◇ organized descriptive details clearly, using space order or order of importance.

Answers will vary.
Possible answers follow.

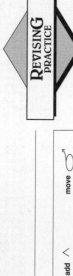

◆ Life is never dull when I'm with my sister Samantha. Sam is only five
years old. She still has all of her baby teeth. She has long golden braids
tiny
that go all the way down her back. Her eyes are dark. The freckles that dot
brown
pleasant
her face are brown, too. Her good smile makes you want to smile right
back.
endless
Sam has energy. No one in the family can keep up with her. She works
or plays busily from morning until night. Her voice chatters away all day.
adorable
The cute things she says tickle everyone.
soft
Sam makes me feel so special. She always asks me to braid her hair.
old   pink
She likes to wear my jeans and a T-shirt. She
picture
Sam likes to cuddle up with me while I read to her. Then she looks at a
I'm her favorite babysitter.
also likes to cuddle up with me while I do my homework. My sister Samantha is terrific.

Unit 5 • WRITING PROCESS • Use after page 269.

T65

SELF-EVALUATION

UNIT 5

Name _____

Writing a Character Sketch

Use this form as you do the Writing Process lesson beginning on page 264. Put a check next to each item you can answer yes to.

Revising

- [ ] **Purpose:** Did I write a vivid description of the person?
- [ ] **Audience:** Will my classmates enjoy my character sketch?
- [ ] **Focus:** Did I include details to show what this person is like?
- [ ] **Grammar Check:** Have I used adjectives to add specific details to my writing?
- [ ] **Word Choice:** Have I used precise words to make my meaning clear?
- [ ] **Writing◆Organizing Descriptive Details:** Have I used space order or order of importance to organize descriptive details in my character sketch?

Proofreading

- [ ] Did I spell words correctly?
- [ ] Did I indent paragraphs?
- [ ] Did I use capital letters correctly?
- [ ] Did I use correct marks at the end of sentences?
- [ ] Did I use my best handwriting?

Publishing

- [ ] Have I shared my writing with readers or listeners?
- [ ] Has my audience shared reactions with me?
- [ ] Have I thought about what I especially liked in this piece of writing?
- [ ] Have I thought about what I would like to work on the next time?

Use the space on the other side to tell what you liked about your writing and to make notes of your plans for improvement.

Name _____

What I liked about my writing: _____

My plans for improvement: _____

Writing a Character Sketch

Check Yes or No for each item. If you check No, explain or give a suggestion for improvement.

Revising

Yes No

☐ ☐ **Purpose:** Did the writer give a vivid description of a person?

☐ ☐ **Audience:** Did I enjoy the character sketch?

☐ ☐ **Focus:** Did the writer include details to show what the person is like?

☐ ☐ **Grammar Check:** Has the writer included adjectives to add specific details to the writing?

☐ ☐ **Word Choice:** Has the writer used precise words to make meanings clear?

☐ ☐ **Writing◆Organizing Descriptive Details:** Does the writer use space order or order of importance to organize descriptive details?

Proofreading

Yes No

☐ ☐ Are words spelled correctly?

☐ ☐ Are paragraphs indented?

☐ ☐ Are capital letters used correctly?

☐ ☐ Are there correct marks at the end of sentences?

☐ ☐ Is the handwriting neat and legible?

134

PEER EVALUATION   UNIT 5

Writing a Character Sketch

Use the questions below and on the other side of this page to help you review a classmate's character sketch. Then give this form to the writer to read and save. Your comments can help the classmate improve the character sketch.

A First Reaction

Here is what I thought in general about your character sketch:

A Second Reaction

Now I have looked at your character sketch more closely. I have more specific comments about it.

Here is something you have done well as a writer:

Here is an area that might be improved:

Here is an idea for improvement:

SAVE 133

Writing with Adverbs

A. Melissa started to write a bedtime story that she could tell her little sister. Read the story beginning and help Melissa add details to her writing. Add adverbs that describe how, when, or where the action occurs. Correct any errors you find also. Use the revising and proofreading marks on this page. **Answers and number of responses will vary. Possible answers follow.**

1–27.

An old man and woman worked on their small
    steadily

farm. They led a very quiet life. they had
    never

  visitors
  ~~visters~~. One morning a young boy appeared. he
    excitedly

spoke. He The
  slowly
had news from a nearby village. He spoke. The
    carefully

old man and woman listened. Then they
    friendly
questioned him. The boy said that a huge
    everywhere
~~frendly~~ giant had wandered into his village.

Day after day, the giant explored the villagers
    patiently   *always*
waited. What would the giant do? The giant had
    now
announced that he would stay. the giant had
    What would the villagers

wanted a new home. What would the villagers
do? Would they learn to live with the huge
    friendly giant? The old man and woman sat
    seriously
down. they thought about the situation. They
    later
thought about what they should say. They gave
their advice.

Revising Marks	
cross out	—
add	∧
move	◯

Proofreading Marks	
capital letter	≡
small letter	/
indent paragraph	¶
check spelling	◯

135

Name _____

B. Now write your own story beginning to go with the picture. Use adverbs to add details to your writing. If you need to show changes, use revising and proofreading marks. **Answers will vary.**

_____

_____

_____

_____

_____

_____

C. Read the story beginning below. Replace the adverb in each sentence with an adverb that has an opposite meaning. Reread the
28–38. story beginning to a friend. **Answers will vary. Possible answers follow.**

          completely
Jenny rushed to the school gym. She was ~~slightly~~ out of breath. The
          yesterday   *hurriedly*
tryouts for gymnastics were held ~~today~~. Her friends waited
      inside   *quickly*
~~impatiently~~. The girls lined up ~~outside~~. Jenny entered the gym ~~slowly~~. She
  carelessly   *backward*
began her tumbles ~~carefully~~. She tumbled ~~forward~~. Then she spun ~~slowly~~.
     badly   *sadly*   *excitedly*
She landed ~~well~~. Jenny ended her tryouts ~~happily~~. She ~~calmly~~ waited for
the second round of tryouts.

136

T68

Adverbs That Compare

A. Lee's mother was interested in buying a copier for her office. When
1-27. Lee heard a commercial for copiers, he wrote down the information
for his mother. Lee had trouble writing adverbs that compare. Help
him correct the form of each adverb he wrote. You may need to
change the word or add *more* or *most*. Correct any other errors you
find also. Use the revising and proofreading marks on this page.

	Revising Marks
cross out	—
add	∧
move	◯

	Proofreading Marks
capital letter	≡
small letter	/
indent paragraph	¶
check spelling	◯

Now is the perfect time to buy an office copier.

        best
The super x copies well of all machines
  available
available today. It works the smoothly of all
  brands   copies more
three leading brans. It copys quietly than Artful
    more
copier. It sorts carefully than Artful Copier? It
          more
can be used easily than copier king. It starts up
faster
fast than than Copier King, too. you can
believe   machines
beleive us when we say, "The Super X Copier
most   machines
copies clearly of all mashines." Buy one today
  more
and work quickly than ever. shop at Mini Mall
Machines. The salespeople there will gladly
help you.

B. Pretend you are a writer of commercials. You have been asked to
compare two bicycles. You want to show that Speed Racer is better
than Dirt Zoomer. Write your commercial below. Use adverbs to
compare how the bicycles go, stop, spin, brake, and last. If you need
to show changes, use revising and proofreading marks. **Answers will vary.**

_____

_____

_____

_____

_____

_____

_____

C. Read each question. Underline the adverb in parentheses ( ) that
correctly completes each sentence. Then answer the question by
circling the answer.

28. In stories, who acts (more cleverly, most cleverly)?   rabbit   ox   [fox]

29. Which month comes (earlier, earliest)?   [June]   August

30. Which breaks (more easily, most easily)?   [eggshell]   glass   gold ring

31. Which bends (more easily, most easily)?   [rubber]   steel

32. Which moves (more gracefully, most gracefully)?   penguin   [swan]

33. Which animal moves (more slowly, most slowly)?   snake   deer   [snail]

34. Which bird sings (more sweetly, most sweetly)?   crow   [canary]

35. Which animal acts (more playfully, most playfully)?   [dolphin]   zebra   shark

36. Which stands (taller, tallest)?   [giraffe]   elephant

37. Which winds move (more swiftly, most swiftly)?   hurricane   thunderstorm

T70

Name _____

Adverbs Before Adjectives and Other Adverbs

A. Rita received a mystery book as a gift from her Aunt Louisa. She wrote the following thank-you note to her aunt. Help Rita improve

1-24. the thank-you note. Add adverbs to make adjectives and other adverbs more exact. Correct any other errors you find also. Use the revising and proofreading marks on this page.
Answers and number of responses will vary. Possible answers follow.

Revising Marks	
cross out	———
add	∧
move	↻

Proofreading Marks	
capital letter	≡
small letter	/
indent paragraph	¶
check spelling	◯

14 Andrews drive
Portland, oregon 97208
June 20, 1992

Dear Aunt Louisa,
    truly   very
you are thoughtful. i was happy to recieve
                 quite   receive
the mystery book. It was beautifully wrapped?
    really   almost
It was a good present for me. I always read
           incredibly
mystery storys This was an exciting one. I
 unbelievably   totally
read it fast the ending baffled me. The
           unusually
author was clever. Thank you again for the
extremely   so
interesting book. It was kind of you to remember
                                    W
my birthday with such a wonderful gift.

                Love,
                Rita

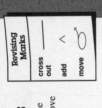

Name _____

B. Pretend this gift box is for you. Decide from whom the gift is and what it might be. Then write a thank-you note. Use adverbs to make the adjectives and adverbs in your writing more exact. If you need to show changes, use revising and proofreading marks. Answers will vary.

_____

_____

_____

_____

_____

_____

_____

C. Think of some gift ideas of your own to complete each sentence below. Also add an adverb on the appropriate blank in the sentences. Answers will vary.

25. The giant said, "Thank you for the _____ huge _____."

26. The tiger said, "Thank you for the _____ delicious _____."

27. The elephant said, "Thank you for the _____ enormous _____."

28. The ant said, "Thank you for the _____ tiny _____."

29. The princess said, "Thank you for the _____ delicate _____."

30. The dragon said, "Thank you for the _____ ferocious _____."

31. The frog said, "Thank you for the _____ cute _____."

32. The king said, "Thank you for the _____ serious _____."

140

Using Adverbs and Adjectives

A. Mrs. Hart asked her students to help her develop a questionnaire.

1-25. Each student wrote one question about schoolwork or homework. Read the questions. Correct errors in the use of adverbs and correct any other errors you find also. Use the revising and proofreading marks on this page.

Revising Marks	
cross out	——
add	∧
move	⟲

Proofreading Marks	
capital letter	≡
small letter	/
indent paragraph	¶
check spelling	○

Questionnaire

easily
Do you tire easy in school?   yes   no

neat
Is your handwriting neatly?   yes   no

eager   homework
Are you eagerly to do your homework?   yes   no

carefully
Do you work careful?   yes   no

usually
do you usual study at night?   yes   no

good
Are You a well worker?   yes   no

wonderful
Is your artwork wonderfully?   yes   no

rapidly
do you read rapid?   yes   no

slowly
Do you work slow?   yes   no

complete   thoroughly
Do you complet your work thorough?   yes   no

well
Do you do good in science?   yes   no

good
Are you a well math student?   yes   no

141

Name _____

B. Make up a questionnaire for your friends. Ask questions about sports or hobbies. The first one is started for you. Notice the answer choices are <u>sometimes</u> or <u>never</u>. Use adverbs and adjectives in your writing. If you need to make changes, use revising and proofreading marks. **Answers will vary.**

26. Can you throw a baseball _____ sometimes never
27. _____ sometimes never
28. _____ sometimes never
29. _____ sometimes never
30. _____ sometimes never
31. _____ sometimes never
32. _____ sometimes never
33. _____ sometimes never
34. _____ sometimes never
35. _____ sometimes never
36. _____ sometimes never

C. Complete this questionnaire about animals. Use <u>good</u> or <u>well</u> to complete sentences 37–42. Use <u>bad</u> or <u>badly</u> to complete sentences 43–46. Then answer the questions.

37. Is an ostrich a __good__ flier?   yes   no
38. Do leopards run __well__ ?   yes   no
39. Have you ever heard a monkey speak __well__ ?   yes   no
40. Is a mountain goat a __good__ climber?   yes   no
41. Do seals fish __well__ ?   yes   no
42. Are bears __good__ swimmers?   yes   no
43. Do hawks have __bad__ eyesight?   yes   no
44. Do female lions treat their young __badly__ ?   yes   no
45. Do camels have __bad__ tempers?   yes   no
46. Does a donkey ever behave __badly__ ?   yes   no

142

T71

Using Negative Words

A. Robert had the kind of day when everything seemed to go wrong. When he wrote about it in his diary, he used some double negatives.
1–26. Help Robert revise the diary page so that each sentence has only one negative word. Correct any other errors you find in the diary entry. Use the revising and proofreading marks on this page. **Some answers will vary.**

Revising Marks	
cross out	—
add	∧
move	◡

Proofreading Marks	
capital letter	≡
small letter	/
indent paragraph	¶
check spelling	○

Dear Diary,

You can't ~~never~~ imagine what **happened** today? I have ~~not~~ never forgotten so many things in one Day. This was the day of Our class trip. I didn't bring ~~no~~ lunch with me. none of my friends had ~~no~~ extra food. Luckily my teacher shared her lunch with me. Also, You know that I ~~never~~ go nowhere without my **mitt**. Well, today, of all days, I **left** it at home. I had to miss catching **practice**. Then, after School, I was **late** for glee club because nobody ~~never~~ told me that it was three o'clock instead of four o'clock. I hope **tomorrow** is a better day! it couldn't be ~~no~~ **worse**!

Robert

143

B. Now write your own diary entry. You might want to tell about a day when you forgot something or missed going somewhere. If you need to make changes, use revising and proofreading marks. **Answers will vary.**

C. Do a word search. Circle each negative word you find, except for the words no and not. You may look across or down. Then use each word to complete the following diary entry.
27–36.

```
U N O B O D Y S A Q
N O T H I N G J F R D
X N R N O W H E R E O
N E J Z T H W X Z I W
A C O U L D N ' T Y U
```

Dear Diary,

I **couldn't** _____ find my glasses. They were **nowhere** to be found. **Nobody** remembered **None** _____ of my friends had found them. There was **nothing** _____ to do but read without them. Then I felt something strange. I reached up and found them right on my head!

144

T72

Name _____

An Order Circle

You can use these forms to make order circles for the Critical Thinking lesson on pages 300–301.

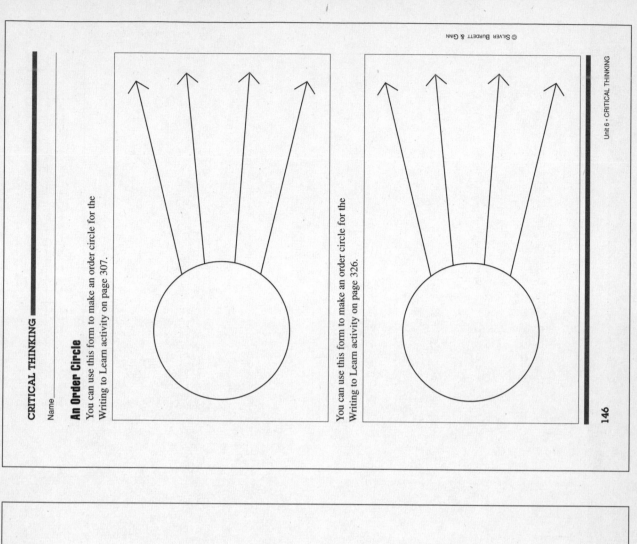

A.

B.

145

Name _____

An Order Circle

You can use this form to make an order circle for the Writing to Learn activity on page 307.

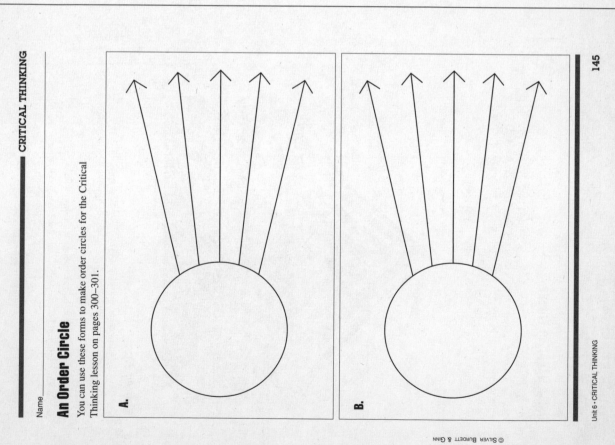

You can use this form to make an order circle for the Writing to Learn activity on page 326.

146

T73

Story Starter

Name _____

Researching

You have read a selection from *Volcano* by Patricia Lauber. Now imagine you are preparing to give a short talk about these eruptions. You will use the diagram below to explain what causes a volcano to erupt. On the back of this page, write what you will say in your talk. You may also use information from *Volcano* that is written in your own words.

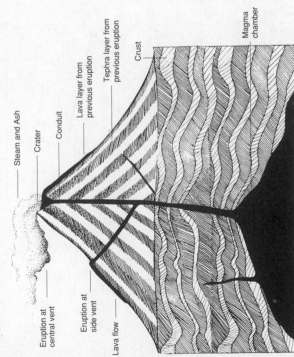

- Steam and Ash
- Crater
- Conduit
- Lava layer from previous eruption
- Tephra layer from previous eruption
- Crust
- Magma chamber
- Eruption at central vent
- Eruption at side vent
- Lava flow

Writing Tips

◇ Use complete sentences to express your ideas. Use capital letters and punctuation carefully.

◇ Organize your information into main ideas and supporting details.

◇ **Focus:** Choose a topic narrow enough for a short talk.

◇ When you reread *Volcano*, choose one thing that you like about the writer's way of writing, and try to use it in your report.

Name _____

Name _____

Strategy: An Order Circle

Use this page if you choose an order circle as a prewriting strategy for your research report.

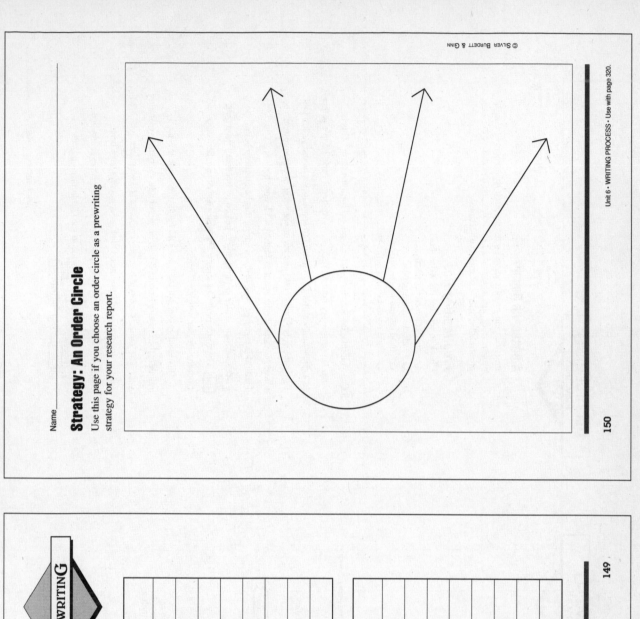

150

PREWRITING

Name _____

Strategy: Taking Notes

Use this page if you choose taking notes as a prewriting strategy for your research report. Use real note cards to take more notes.

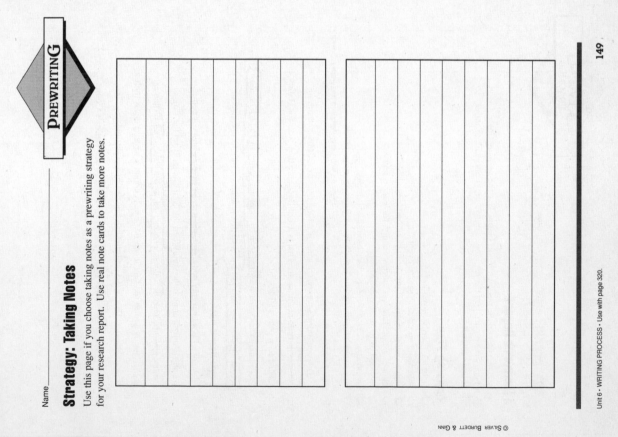

149

T75

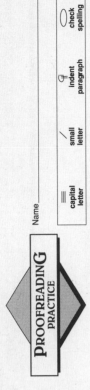

REVISING PRACTICE

cross out	add	move
——	∧	↶

A Research Report

Practice revising on the research report below. Use the revising tips. Don't copy the report. Use the revising marks to cross out, add, or move words and sentences.

Revising Tips

Check to see that the writer has

◇ told about an unusual natural event.
◇ made sure the report is interesting and understandable.
◇ chosen a topic that was narrow enough for a short report.
◇ avoided using double negatives.
◇ avoided overused words such as beautiful and said.
◇ organized information into a main idea with supporting details.

Answers will vary. Possible answers follow.

Do you think seventy-six years is a long time to wait for something?
Scientists
No scientists do not think so. That is about how long they wait for Halley's Comet to appear.

The majestic comet was first seen by Edmund Halley in 1682. The most
predicted
recent sighting was in 1986. He said that it would return in seventy-six years. He was right.

A comet is a heavenly body. A star is also a heavenly body. A comet travels in a path around the sun. When the comet is far from the sun, it cannot never be seen. It follows an orbit, just as the Earth does. When a comet gets nearer to the sun, it can be seen. A comet's ice and gases melt as
glowing
it nears the sun. That is the trail that can be seen in a nighttime sky. The
thrilling
comet's tail is a beautiful sight. I hope I'll be able to see Halley's Comet when it comes back!

© SILVER BURDETT & GINN

Name _____

PROOFREADING PRACTICE

capital letter	small letter	indent paragraph	check spelling
≡	/	⁋	⟳

A Research Report

Practice your proofreading on the research report below. Use the proofreading tips as a guide. Don't copy the report. Use the proofreading marks to make corrections.

Proofreading Tips

Check to see that the writer has

◇ spelled words correctly.
◇ indented paragraphs.
◇ used capital letters correctly.
◇ used correct marks at the end of sentences.

Can you imagine watching water shoot up from the earth? This is what happens every hour in Yellowstone national Park. People gather in a circle and wait for Old Faithful to spout its water and steam. Old Faithful ejects 5,000–7,000 gallons of hot water in one eruption. The tower of water shoots about as high as a 13-story building. Old Faithful is a geyser. A geyser is a spring that begins deep below the earth's surface. Water in the spring is heated by hot rocks deep in the earth. The water produces steam. The water and steam then shoot up from the geyser with great force.

This great geyser got the name Old Faithful because it is so reliable. the eruptions occur 20–30 times per day, every day, year after year. The shortest interval between eruptions is 33 minutes, while the longest interval is 148 minutes. Other great geysers have been inactive for months or even years. Old Faithful has never stopped.

people come from far and wide to see Old faithful. It is the
famous   world
most famis geyser in the word.

© SILVER BURDETT & GINN

Name _____

What I liked about my writing: _____

_____
_____
_____
_____
_____
_____
_____
_____
_____
_____

My plans for improvement: _____

_____
_____
_____
_____
_____

Name _____

SELF-EVALUATION

UNIT 6

Writing a Research Report

Use this form as you do the Writing Process lesson beginning on page 318. Put a check next to each item you can answer yes to.

Revising

- [ ] **Purpose:** Did I write a research report about an unusual natural event?
- [ ] **Audience:** Will my classmates find my report understandable and interesting?
- [ ] **Focus:** Is my topic narrow enough to be covered well in a short report?
- [ ] **Grammar Check:** Have I avoided double negatives?
- [ ] **Word Choice:** Have I avoided overusing certain words?
- [ ] **Writing◆An Outline:** Did I organize my information into main ideas and supporting details?

Proofreading

- [ ] Did I spell words correctly?
- [ ] Did I indent paragraphs?
- [ ] Did I use capital letters correctly?
- [ ] Did I use correct marks at the end of sentences?
- [ ] Did I use my best handwriting?

Publishing

- [ ] Have I shared my writing with readers or listeners?
- [ ] Has my audience shared reactions with me?
- [ ] Have I thought about what I especially liked in this piece of writing?
- [ ] Have I thought about what I would like to work on the next time?

Use the space on the other side to tell what you liked about your writing and to make notes of your plans for improvement.

Reader's Name _____

Writer's Name _____

Writing a Research Report

Check Yes or No for each item. If you check No, explain or give a suggestion for improvement.

Revising

Yes No

Purpose: Did the writer prepare a research report about an unusual natural event?

Audience: Did I find the report understandable and interesting?

Focus: Is the topic narrow enough to be covered well in a short report?

Grammar Check: Has the writer avoided double negatives?

Word Choice: Has the writer avoided overusing certain words?

Writing◆An Outline: Did the writer organize the information into main ideas and supporting details?

Proofreading

Yes No

Are words spelled correctly?

Are paragraphs indented?

Are capital letters used correctly?

Are there correct marks at the end of sentences?

Is the handwriting neat and legible?

156

PEER EVALUATION

UNIT 6

Reader's Name _____

Writer's Name _____

Writing a Research Report

Use the questions below and on the other side of this page to help you review a classmate's research report. Then give this form to the writer to read and save. Your comments can help the classmate improve the research report.

A First Reaction

Here is what I thought in general about your research report:

A Second Reaction

Now I have looked at your research report more closely. I have more specific comments about it.

Here is something you have done well as a writer:

Here is an area that might be improved:

Here is an idea for improvement:

SAVE 155

⭐ **B.** Marta needs several different posters to display in the neighborhood. Help her advertise for the carnival by creating a poster. Be sure to use prepositions correctly. Use revising and proofreading marks if you need to make changes. **Answers will vary.**

⭐ **C.** Discover the special event that will take place at the carnival. Read each sentence. If the letter P appears after a sentence, underline the preposition. If the letter O appears after a sentence, underline the object of the preposition. Write the first letter of each underlined word in the numbered spaces. The words that are formed name the special event.

27. Let's plan what we will have at the carnival. (P)
28. The clown is inside the tent. (P)
29. Should the magic show be in your room? (O)
30. No, it should be by the garage. (O)
31. I can climb up the ladder and hang this sign. (P)
32. The sign will look great in this tree. (P)
33. Place this game behind the tree. (O)
34. A better place might be somewhere around the garage. (P)
35. Don't put games near the road. (O)
36. At the carnival let's give prizes. (O)
37. The first person who walks over this line can get a prize. (P)
38. Let's have a refreshment stand near the picnic table. (P)
39. On the table we could have plates and napkins. (O)
40. Tickets should be sold at the entrance. (O)
41. Write the ticket prices on a sign. (O)
42. People will enjoy coming to our carnival! (P)

_a_ i r _g_ u i t a r c o n t e s t

Writing with Prepositions

⭐ **A.** Marta and her friends are putting on a backyard carnival. They are making posters to let people know about the event. Check the posters to see that prepositions have been used correctly. Correct any other errors you find also. Use the revising and proofreading marks on this page.

1-26.

Revising Marks

cross out —
add ∧
move ↻

Proofreading Marks

capital letter ≡
small letter /
indent paragraph ¶
check spelling ○

T80

Page 159

Name _____

Prepositional Phrases

A. Danny and his father are writing a travel brochure for Quiet Campgrounds. Danny's job is to write a section helping

1-21. visitors find their way around the park. Use the map to make sure he has described the different locations correctly. Check his use of prepositional phrases and add ones if necessary to make the meaning clear. Correct any other errors you find also. Use the revising and proofreading marks on this page. **Answers will vary. Possible answers follow.**

Revising Marks	
cross out	———
add	∧
move	○

Proofreading Marks	
capital letter	≡
small letter	/
indent paragraph	¶
check spelling	○

Finding Your Way Around Quiet Campgrounds

through a covered bridge

As you enter Quiet Campgrounds you will drive under the bridge. The river flows east over mirror Lake. A rushing river can be seen. Below the surface by the lake about lake are natural springs. The campers' lodge is. You can learn about the Above Beside many campground activities for the lodge. Boats can be rented at the lodge you will find a large sun deck. The nature trails begin over near the lodge there. Campsites are located along the Old settlement Trail. Camping at supplies and Food can be found for Pioneer's Trading Post. Nightly entertainment takes place on the deck. If you need help getting around Have the park, Free maps can be found on the lodge. Have an enjoyable stay at quiet Campgrounds.

159

Page 160

Name _____

B. Think of a place you have visited, such as a park or a playground. Write a description of how to get around this place. Be sure to include prepositional phrases. If you need to make changes, use revising and proofreading marks. **Answers will vary.**

_____

_____

_____

_____

_____

_____

_____

_____

_____

C. Find your campsite at Quiet Campgrounds. Underline the prepositional phrase in each sentence. Then trace a path through the campground as directed by each sentence. Circle your campsite.

22. Begin at Settlement Trail.
23. Walk across the wooden bridge.
24. Follow the path by the lake.
25. Walk around the large stone.
26. Go to the tall lamppost.
27. Walk through the tall grass.
28. Climb up the stone steps.
29. Your campsite is by the wildflowers.

160

Prepositions and Adverbs

★ **A.**

1-25. Chen has been working on an article for the newspaper about a monkey that has escaped from the zoo. But Chen's computer has a virus. It has printed many adverbs, but in each case a prepositional phrase would give more information. Help Chen revise the article. Change all the adverbs to prepositional phrases. Correct any other errors you find also. Use the revising and proofreading marks on this page. **Answers will vary. Possible answers follow.**

Revising Marks	
cross out	—
add	∧
move	↺

Proofreading Marks	
capital letter	≡
small letter	/
indent paragraph	¶
check spelling	○

Merrille the Monkey Is on the Loose

Merrille the Monkey (escaped) from the city zoo
yesterday. The escape was Discovered this morning
~~for~~ at feeding time. "all the Monkeys were in the
monkey house except Merrille," exclaimed mr. allen,
the zoo keeper. merrille was last seen inside. *the monkey house*
Witnesses saw the monkey running around. "The *the jungle gym*
monkey climbed up," said one eyewitness. "When *the ladder*
I (tried) to get him, he ran down, i chased him *the ladder again*
around, but he ran faster than I could." The *the park*
monkey was seen running inside. Then he quickly *a snack bar*
ran out. Another observer saw the monkey hiding *the door*
underneath. The monkey waved and jumped over. *some rose bushes* *the flowers*
Merrille was (las) seen racing along. If you have *Park Road* *last*
any Information about merrille, please call the zoo.

★ **B.** Write a newspaper article about another animal that escaped from a zoo. Use some of the following words in your article: along, around, below, down, in, inside, near, off, out, outside, under, up. Use these words as prepositions or as adverbs. If you need to show changes, use revising and proofreading marks. **Answers will vary.**

★ **C.** To learn where Merrille was hiding, follow these directions. Read each sentence. After each sentence write whether the underlined word is a preposition or an adverb. Circle the numbers of the sentences with adverbs. Shade the boxes having those numbers to find out where Merrille was found.

26. Merrille does not like to stay <u>inside</u>. — **adverb**
27. She will most likely be found <u>outside</u>. — **adverb**
28. A police officer saw a monkey hanging <u>in</u> a tree. — **preposition**
29. The tree was <u>near</u> the lake. — **preposition**
30. The monkey jumped <u>down</u> and ran. — **adverb**
31. Merrille hid <u>in</u> a hollow log. — **preposition**
32. The officer reached her hand <u>inside</u>. — **adverb**
33. The monkey quickly scrambled <u>out</u>. — **adverb**
34. The people standing <u>around</u> began laughing. — **adverb**

34	26	30	32	28	26	27	30	33	29	33	26	34	31	33	34	26
27	31	24	32	25	33	29	31	30	29	34	31	27	24	31	27	28
30	33	32	30	31	33	28	29	34	31	34	30	32	29	29	33	24
33	24	32	24	27	31	24	26	34	24	34	27	29	24	30	31	
27	33	26	24	34	27	31	24	27	32	24	29	32	24	29	34	28

T82

Name _____

Using Prepositional Phrases

A. Virginia wrote a letter to her friend, Linda. She told Linda about her trip to the circus. Help Virginia correct her letter. Check to see that she has used prepositional phrases correctly. Correct any other errors you find also. Show the changes that need to be made by using the revising and proofreading marks on this page.

1-24.

Revising Marks	
cross out	—
add	∧
move	᷃

Proofreading Marks	
capital letter	≡
small letter	/
indent paragraph	¶
check spelling	◯

Dear Linda ⋏

   Mom and Dad took ̲J̲i̲l̲l̲ and I̶ to the circus

   yesterday. To ̲w̲e̲ the circus was very ⟨exiting⟩. ∧

   We sat b̶e̶t̶w̶e̶e̶n̶ all the ⟨peopel⟩ in the bleachers.

   Jill liked the clown-and-dog show best. To

   s̶h̶e̶ it was the funniest show of all. We saw two

   clowns with ⟨my⟩ faces painted on t̶h̶e̶y̶. The dogs

   pranced a̶m̶o̶n̶g̶ two clowns. ̲t̲h̲e̲ one with the tall

   hat made the dogs jump with h̶e̶. Then the clowns

   the little dog house for t̶h̶e̶y̶. The dogs ran inside

   the house and it ̲f̲ell down. For ̲d̲ad and I̶ this was

   the ⟨funnest⟩ part. I hope we can go the ̲C̲ircus

   together some time soon. Seeing it together would

   be a lot of fun for you and I̶.

            Your friend ⋏

            Virginia

163

Name _____

B. Write a letter to a friend. Tell about something exciting you have seen or experienced. Use some of the following object pronouns in your letter: me, you, him, her, it, us, them. Also use the prepositions between and among. If you need to show changes, use revising and proofreading marks. **Answers will vary.**

_____

_____

_____

_____

_____

_____

C. Circle the preposition or object pronoun that correctly completes the sentence. Complete the crossword puzzle by printing each word in the proper place on the puzzle.

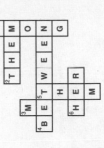

Across

2. The lion tamer wore boots with stars all over (they, ⟨them⟩).

4. We saw her standing (⟨between⟩, among) two lions.

6. The lion tamer told the lions to stand by (she, ⟨her⟩).

Down

1. She stood (⟨among⟩, between) all the lions as they jumped through the ring.

3. This was the most exciting part to (I, ⟨me⟩).

5. The lion tamer lit a ring of fire near the lions and hung it before (they, ⟨them⟩).

164

Name

Answering "What If?"

You can use these forms to make "what-if" charts for the
Creative Thinking lesson on pages 354–355.

A.

B.

Name

Answering "What If?"

You can use these forms to make "what-if" charts for the
Writing to Learn activity on page 359.

You can use this form to make a "what-if" chart for the
Writing to Learn activity on page 376.

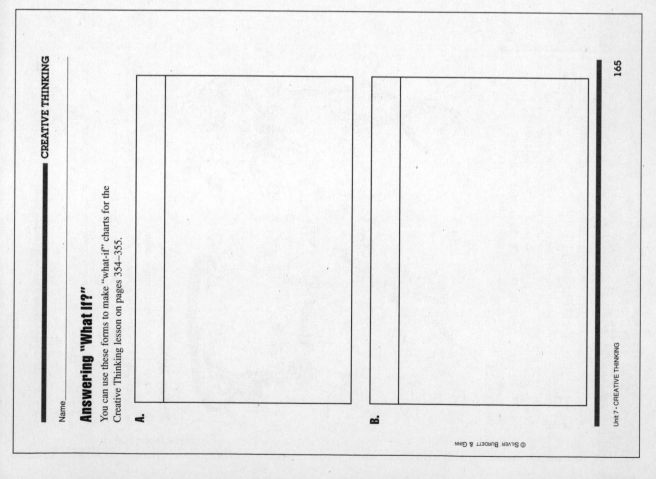

T84

Story Starter

Name

Creating

You have read poems by six different writers in which ordinary objects come to life and act like people. If you were an object, what would you be and what would you do? "Be" one of the objects below or think up one of your own. Then on the back of this page, write a poem to tell about yourself.

Writing Tips

◊ Use capital letters and punctuation carefully.

◊ Use repetition of words or phrases to bring sound to your poem.

◊ **Focus:** Remember to use personification to give life to the object you are writing about.

◊ You may wish to reread the poems before you begin. Which is your favorite? Choose one thing that you like about the poem, and try to use it in your poem.

Name

Name _____

Strategy: Answering "What If?"

Use this page if you choose a "what-if" chart as a prewriting strategy for your poem.

PREWRITING

Name _____

Strategy: Playing a Role

Use this page to take notes if you choose playing a role as a prewriting strategy for your poem.

REVISING PRACTICE

Name _____

cross out —— add ∧ move ↶

A Poem

Practice revising on the poem below. Use the revising tips. Don't copy the poem. Use the revising marks to cross out, add, or move words and sentences.

Revising Tips

Check to see that the writer has

◇ written a poem that expresses a fresh image or idea.
◇ made the poem enjoyable to the reader.
◇ used personification to help give life to the object.
◇ used prepositions or prepositional phrases to clarify the relationship between one thing and another.
◇ used poetic words.
◇ used some repetition of words or phrases to bring sound to the poetry. **Answers will vary. Possible answers follow.**

The Rainbow

lovely   spreads
The ~~beautiful~~ rainbow ~~rises~~
across the blue-gray sky
brilliant
a coat of many colors.

Gently she lends her bright tones
and soft pastels
to the pale, white clouds.

                    for all
She sings out a melody to hear.
dances through the sky
She ~~moves~~
bringing beauty for a moment,
just a moment or two.
whispers
Then she ~~says~~ goodbye and
slowly wanders away.

171

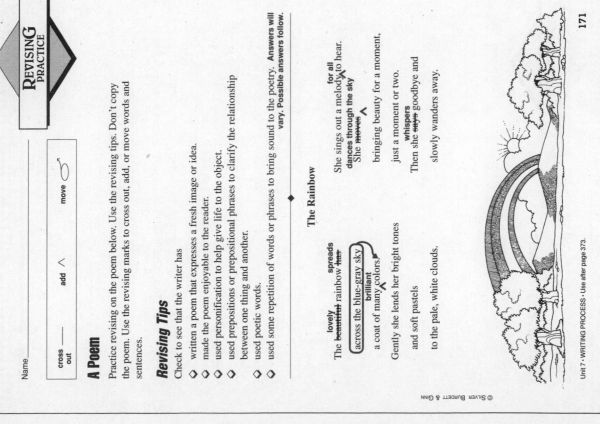

PROOFREADING PRACTICE

Name _____

≡ capital letter   / small letter   ¶ indent paragraph   ◯ check spelling

A Poem

Practice your proofreading on the poem below. Use the proofreading tips as a guide. Don't copy the poem. Use the proofreading marks to make corrections.

Proofreading Tips

Check to see that the writer has

◇ spelled words correctly.
◇ used capital letters correctly.
◇ used correct marks at the end of sentences.

The Oak Tree

How wise you must be, you old oak tree,
but why do you never speak to me?
                                leaves
Your rich green ~~leave~~ shade me,
and your gentle Shade cools me.
                          quietly
How quietly you stand there.
                        carefully
You never say a word.
You always listen carfully
like a good old friend.

as I sit under your branches,
I think about Many things.

You seem to hear my thoughts
and offer your wise, silent counsel.
                         you're
Why do you Never speak, oak tree?
Is it that your waiting for someone to listen,
A special friend and admirer?
i'm here!

172

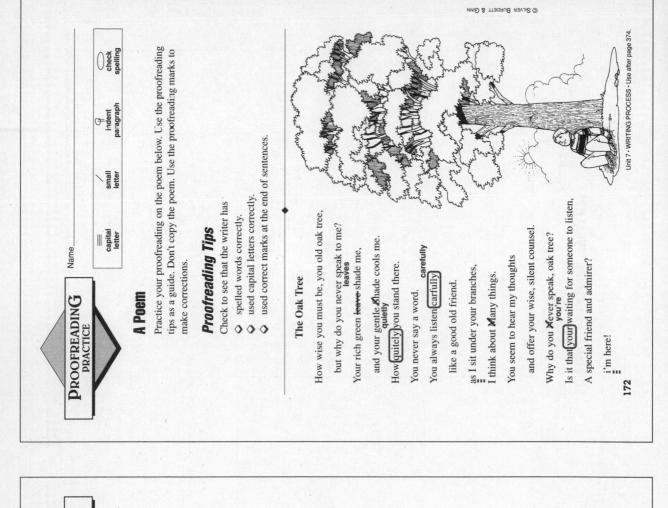

Name _____

SELF-EVALUATION
UNIT 7

Writing a Poem

Use this form as you do the Writing Process lesson beginning on page 368. Put a check next to each item you can answer yes to.

Revising

☐ **Purpose:** Did I write a poem that expresses a fresh image or idea?

☐ **Audience:** Will my friend enjoy the poem I wrote for him or her?

☐ **Focus:** Did I use personification? Did I show an object behaving like a person?

☐ **Grammar Check:** Have I used prepositions or prepositional phrases to clarify relationships?

☐ **Word Choice:** Have I used poetic words?

☐ **Writing◆Repetition in Poetry:** Have I used repetition to bring sound to my poem?

Proofreading

☐ Did I spell words correctly?

☐ Did I use capital letters correctly?

☐ Did I use correct marks at the end of sentences?

☐ Did I use my best handwriting?

Publishing

☐ Have I shared my writing with readers or listeners?

☐ Has my audience shared reactions with me?

☐ Have I thought about what I especially liked in this piece of writing?

☐ Have I thought about what I would like to work on the next time?

Use the space on the other side to tell what you liked about your writing and to make notes of your plans for improvement.

SAVE
173

Name _____

What I liked about my writing: _____
_____
_____
_____
_____
_____

My plans for improvement: _____
_____
_____
_____
_____
_____

174

Reader's Name _____

Writer's Name _____

Writing a Poem

Check Yes or No for each item. If you check No, explain or give a suggestion for improvement.

Revising

Yes No

☐ ☐ **Purpose:** Does the poem express a fresh image or idea?

☐ ☐ **Audience:** Will the friend it is written for enjoy it?

☐ ☐ **Focus:** Did the writer use personification? Did the writer show an object behaving like a person?

☐ ☐ **Grammar Check:** Has the writer used prepositions or prepositional phrases to clarify relationships?

☐ ☐ **Word Choice:** Has the writer used poetic words?

☐ ☐ **Writing◆Repetition in Poetry:** Has the writer used repetition to bring sound to the poem?

Proofreading

Yes No

☐ ☐ Are words spelled correctly?

☐ ☐ Are capital letters used correctly?

☐ ☐ Are there correct marks at the end of sentences?

☐ ☐ Is the handwriting neat and legible?

◆176

PEER EVALUATION

UNIT 7

Reader's Name _____

Writer's Name _____

Writing a Poem

Use the questions below and on the other side of this page to help you review a classmate's poem. Then give this form to the writer to read and save. Your comments can help the classmate improve the poem.

A First Reaction

Here is what I thought in general about your poem:

_____

_____

_____

_____

A Second Reaction

Now I have looked at your poem more closely. I have more specific comments about it.

Here is something you have done well as a writer:

_____

_____

Here is an area that might be improved:

_____

_____

Here is an idea for improvement:

_____

_____

SAVE ◆175

Left page (177)

Name _____

Reviewing the Parts of Speech

A. Six students wrote a story together. When the story was complete,
1–25. they looked it over and decided to make some changes. The story needs more adjectives and adverbs to better describe things. Some of the verbs need to be changed to add more action and excitement. More pronouns are needed in place of nouns. Some prepositions are missing or need to be replaced. Help the children improve their story. Correct any other errors you find. Use the revising and proofreading marks on this page.

Answers and number of responses will vary. Possible answers follow.

Revising Marks
cross out —
add ∧
move ◯

Proofreading Marks
capital letter ≡
small letter /
indent paragraph ¶
check spelling ◯

> warm   in August children   fun
> It was a summer day. Some kids were looking for something to do.
>   They   build   thirsty
> This title decided to set up a lemonade stand, with the money they
> earned   build   of lemonade
> made, they hoped to make a clubhouse. The children had a lot of
>   quickly   closed
> customers that afternoon. They sold twelve pitchers. At the end
>   building
> of the day they closed the lemonade stand and counted the money.
> They had earned $12.64! This Money could go toward building
> their dream clubhouse!
>   supplies   building
> The children started making a list of things they would need for
>   writing
> the clubhouse, then the children started listing the cost of
>   realized   much
> the materials. They knew they would need to sell more lemonade
> to build the clubhouse. The $12.64 would get them started.
> decided   was
> They decided that when the clubhouse were built, they would
> name it the Lemonade Locker Room. They also decided to give out
>   customers
> free lemonade every Saturday to thank their people for
> the clubhouse.

Unit 8, Lesson 1 • Use after page 389.

© SILVER BURDETT & GINN

177

Right page (178)

Name _____

B. Write a story of your own. Choose one of the sentences below as a beginning, and work with a partner to complete the story. Remember to use a variety of parts of speech. If you need to make changes, use revising and proofreading marks. **Answers will vary.**

It was a rainy, gloomy night.
The crowd could not wait for the game to begin.
The trip to the zoo was filled with surprises.

_____

_____

_____

_____

_____

C. Find the names of six parts of speech hidden in the puzzle. Then complete the sentences below the puzzle.

```
A B N O U N Q V W E
A D J E C T I V E V L
D V A S D F G H R I K
P E O N Y U R T B X J
P R E P O S I T I O N
A B L P R O N O U N K
```

They are young skiers. Tony races down steep, snowy slopes. Cindy avoids them and skis carefully on smaller mountains.

26. The pronoun in the first sentence above is ___They___ .

27. The verbs in the sentences are ___are___ , ___races___ , ___avoids___ , and ___skis___ .

28. The words skiers, Tony, slopes, Cindy, and mountains are ___nouns___ , not verbs, in the sentences.

29. The adverb in the third sentence is ___carefully___ .

30. The adjectives in the sentences are ___young___ , ___steep___ , ___snowy___ , and ___smaller___ .

178   Unit 8, Lesson 1 • Use after page 389.

© SILVER BURDETT & GINN

Name _____

Compound Subjects

A. The Sloan family has decided to do some spring cleaning. They have made a list of what needs to be done. At first they gave only one person each chore. Then they decided that the work would go faster if two or three people worked together. Help the Sloans revise their list by using compound subjects. Correct any errors you find also. Use the revising and proofreading marks on this page.
Answers will vary. Possible answers follow.

1–26.

Workers: Mom, Dad, Mary, Jenny, Tad, Billy, and Mark

Mom ∧ will wash the windows   **and Mark**
Dad ∧ will scour the oven.   **and Mary**
Billy ∧ will prepare lunch.   **, Billy, and Dad**
Jenny ∧ will dust the furniture.   **Tad and**
Mark ∧ will wax the floors.   **Mary and**
Tad ∧ will polish the silverware?   **and Mark**
Mary ∧ will prepare the grill for the cookout.   **and Jenny**
Tad ∧ will clean up from dinner.   **Dad, and Jenny**
Billy ∧ will scrub the sinks.   **Mark and**
Mary ∧ will empty the trash.   **will**
Dad ∧ will clean up from lunch.   **and Billy**
Jenny ∧ will wash the curtains.   **Mom and**
Dad ∧ will sweep the porch.   **and Tad**
Mom ∧ will straighten the closets.   **and Jenny**
Dad ∧ will grill the meat.   **and Tad**
Mary ∧ will make the salad.
The whole family will go to the movie.   **movie**

Revising Marks	
cross out	—
add	∧
move	◯

Proofreading Marks	
capital letter	≡
small letter	/
indent paragraph	¶
check spelling	◯

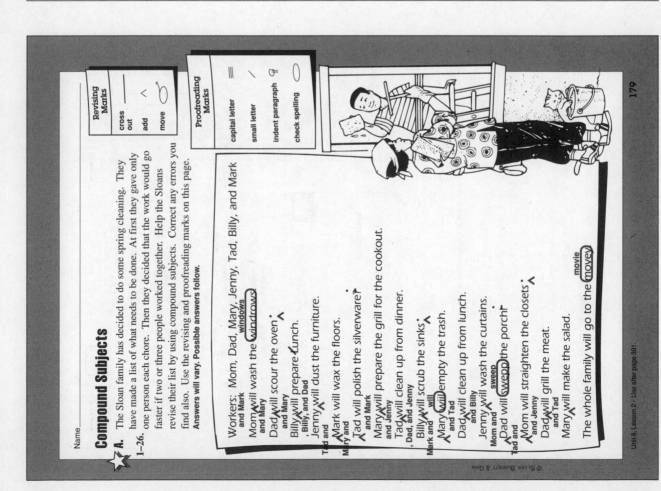

Name _____

B. What things might you and the members of your family do to help around the house? Make a list of chores that you could do together. Use compound subjects to assign more than one person to each task. Use revising and proofreading marks if you need to make changes. **Answers will vary.**

C. Read the following list. Find the sentences that have compound subjects. Circle the first letter in each of those sentences. Use these letters to discover a special message.

27. Lists and notes help you remember things.
28. Some people list activities for each day.
29. Anna and Luis use lists all the time.
30. People make lists for certain jobs.
31. Names and numbers can be listed in a special book.
32. Good friends and family members might be in the book.
33. I have a list of all my favorite authors.
34. Uncle Bill and Aunt Marie keep their address book up to date.
35. A friend or a relative will get a birthday card.
36. I have a list of all my favorite songs.
37. Gan and Chim make lists of their favorite games.
38. My friend makes lists of all his grades.
39. Even my little brother and sister like to make lists.
40. Important days and dates can be listed.
41. Dad never goes shopping without a list.
42. Susie, Taro, and Winona make lists of their favorite foods.
43. Food and drinks for a party should be written on a list.
44. I made a list of important phone numbers.
45. Uncle Pete and Aunt Jean make guest lists.
46. Names and numbers are not the only things you can put on lists.

L A N G U A G E   I S   F U N !

T90

Page 181

Name _____

Using Subjects and Verbs That Agree

A. The students in Mrs. Kramer's class gave a chili dinner for their parents in the school cafeteria last week. Now they are making a bulletin board display with pictures and captions. Help the class check their captions to be sure the subjects and verbs agree. Correct any other errors you find also. Use the revising and proofreading marks on this page.

1–24.

Revising Marks
cross out —
add ∧
move ⟳

Proofreading Marks
capital letter ≡
small letter /
indent paragraph ¶
check spelling ○

Andrew and manuel decorate decorates the cafeteria.

Cindy and Her helper place places flowers on each table.

The kramers and Tony toss tos salads.

Chili salid, and bread taste all tastes great.

Kristy and mr. Hall have has fun Dancing.

Steve, patty, and Jose play plays some music.

the Parents and our teacher are is busy talking.

Tracy and Amy clear clears the tables.

Page 182

Name _____

B. Think about a dinner your class might prepare for families and friends. What kind of food would you like to serve? Who would help, and what jobs would they have? Make up captions for pictures of your class dinner. Make sure subjects and verbs agree. Use revising and proofreading marks if you need to make changes. **Answers will vary.**

_____

_____

_____

_____

C. Some more bulletin board captions are written in the code shown below. Decode and write the captions. Correct each caption so that the subject and verb agree. Then tell what event the captions describe. At the bottom, use the code to write your own caption. Be sure that your subject and verb agree. Have a classmate decode your caption.

1–A	2–B	3–C	4–D	5–E	6–F	7–G
8–H	9–I	10–J	11–K	12–L	13–M	14–N
15–O	16–P	17–Q	18–R	19–S	20–T	21–U
22–V	23–W	24–X	25–Y	26–Z		

25. 2 9 12 12 19 13 9 20 8 1 14 4 16 1 20 19 12 15 1 14
13 1 11 5 19 2 1 19 11 5 20 19. **make**
Bill Smith and Pat Sloan makes baskets.

26. 20 8 5 3 8 5 5 18 12 5 1 4 5 18 19 1 14 4 20 8 5 2 1 14 4
5 14 20 5 18 20 1 9 14 19 20 8 5 3 18 15 23 4. **entertain**
The cheerleaders and the band entertains the crowd.

27. 20 8 5 6 1 14 19 1 14 4 20 8 5 3 15 1 3 8 3 8 5 5 18 19
6 15 18 20 8 5 20 5 1 13. **cheer**
The fans and the coach cheers for the team.

28. The captions describe a ___ basketball game ___ .

29. _____ Answers will vary.

Compound Predicates

Name _____

A. Ben's friend Cam just won the state championship for running the
100-yard dash. Ben wrote a note to Cam to congratulate her. Read
1–22. Ben's note to see if any changes need to be made. Look for ways to
avoid repeating the same subject by using compound predicates.
Correct any errors you find also. Use the revising and proofreading
marks on this page.
Answers and number of responses may vary. Possible answers follow.

Revising Marks	
cross out	—
add	∧
move	◯

Proofreading Marks	
capital letter	≡
small letter	/
indent paragraph	¶
check spelling	◯

dear Cam,

I think it is grate that you won the state championship
for the 100-yard dash. You ran far every day. Your
worked vary hard.

A good runner must concentrate. A good runner must
stay in good fisical shape. You have done your homework
welll

I am thinking about joining the track team at school.
Being on the trak team would help me stay fit. Being on
the track team would let me meet friends. Maybe You
can give me some tips. Maybe you can tell me how to
prepare myself. I know i should run. I know I should
work out every day. What else do I need to do?

Congratulate you. I want to tell you how proud I am to
have you as a friend. Keep up the good work!

your friend,
Ben

183

Name _____

B. Ben has another friend, Marco, who has just won the school spelling
bee. Help Ben write a note that congratulates Marco on his victory.
Use some compound predicates in your sentences. Use revising and
proofreading marks if you need to make changes. **Answers will vary.**

_____

_____

_____

C. The pairs of verbs below are antonyms. Unscramble and write the
verbs. Then use each pair to complete the sentences below with
compound predicates. Select three antonym pairs to use as
compound predicates in your own sentences.

ndfuo	**found, lost**
keat	**take, give**
veals	**leaves, arrives**
dselco	**closed, opened**
ardetst	**started, finished**

23. I _____ **started** _____ my homework at three o'clock and
_____ **finished** _____ at four o'clock.

24. Who _____ **closed** _____ this window tightly and _____ **opened** _____ that
door so wide?

25. Cindy _____ **leaves** _____ New York in the morning and
_____ **arrives** _____ in Texas in the afternoon.

26. I _____ **found** _____ my misplaced notebook and _____ **lost** _____
my new pen.

27. I will _____ **take** _____ a pear and _____ **give** _____ it to a friend.

28. **Answers will vary.**

29. _____

30. _____

184

Name _____

Compound Sentences

A. Kevin is entering a contest that he read about on the back of an
1–31. oatmeal box. He wrote a letter telling what he made from the
oatmeal box. The winner will be awarded an all-expenses-paid trip
to an amusement park. Kevin needs help revising his letter so it
reads more smoothly. Help Kevin combine simple sentences into
compound sentences. Place a comma before each conjunction you
use. Correct any errors you find also. Use the revising and
proofreading marks on this page.
Answers and number of responses may vary. Possible answers follow.

Revising Marks	
cross out	—
add	⋀
move	↺

Proofreading Marks	
capital letter	≡
small letter	/
indent paragraph	¶
check spelling	○

My brother and I eat Toasty Oats for breakfast every
morning, and We like it better than any other cereal. Tim
likes his toasty oats with sugar, but I like mine plain.
Yesterday we read about your oatmeal box contest, and We
decided to enter. I wanted to make a toy from the empty
box, but My brother wanted to make something else. He is
still deciding what to make.

The toy I made was a Rocket. First you cover the
outside of the box with tin foil. Next you must make
a cone-shaped cover for the top of the box. Tag-board
is best for this, but Construction paper will also work.
after you shape the cone, cut it to fit the top. You can
paste the cone on the top, or You may prefer to tape it.
Decorate the box with an american flag and carefully
cut a door in the side.

When you play with the rocket, you can place
Action figures inside. An oatmeal box makes a
great rocket, and oatmeal makes a great breakfast.

Name _____

B. Think of something you could make out of an oatmeal box or out
of a cereal box. Write the directions on how to make the item. Use
compound sentences to combine related ideas. If you need to make
changes, use revising and proofreading marks. Answers will vary.

_____

_____

_____

_____

_____

_____

C. Kevin won the oatmeal box contest! His family and friends are
throwing a big party for him. Use a pencil to trace the path
containing only compound sentences. Circle the place where the
party is being held.

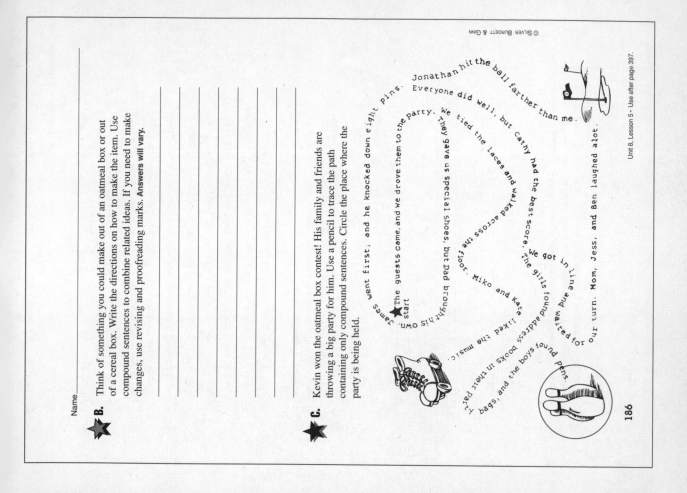

James went first, and he knocked down eight pins.
The guests came, and we drove them to the party.
We tied the laces and walked across the floor.
They gave us special shoes, but Dad brought his own.
Miko and Kate liked the music.
We got in line and waited for our turn.
Mom, Jess, and Ben laughed a lot.
The girls found address books in their bags, and the boys found pens.
Jonathan hit the ball farther than me.
Everyone did well, but Cathy had the best score.

T93

T94

Name _____

Avoiding Run-on Sentences

A. Steve is a tour guide at an eighteenth-century village. He wrote a script to use for his tours. When he read it, he found some run-on sentences. Help Steve correct the run-on sentences in his script. Correct any other errors you find also. Use the revising and proofreading marks on this page.
Answers will vary. Possible answers follow.

1–26.

Revising Marks	
cross out	—
add	∧
move	⟳

Proofreading Marks	
capital letter	≡
small letter	/
indent paragraph	¶
check spelling	◯

This tour will help you take a step back in time.
Your host today are dressed in typical (typical) eighteenth-century clothing (clothing). The men then wore trousers, shirts, suspenders, and hats the women wore long cotten (cotton) dresses, aprons, and bonnets.
First we will visit the town inn we will see that the inn (inn) was a hotel for travelers. It was also an important meeting place (place) for the townspeople, but (but) All town meetings were held in the inn people (people) weddings (weddings) took place there. Quite often the inn was the only place in town for travelers to stay.
Now let us walk down this path to the farmhouse. These people worked hard here were always plenty of chores to go around women (Women), and men (Men) tended the livestock and the feilds (fields) children often helped by gathering berrys (berries) or feeding the chickens?

hosts

187

Name _____

B. Write the beginning of a tour guide's script for an interesting place you have visited. Be sure to avoid run-on sentences. Use revising and proofreading marks if you need to make changes. **Answers will vary.**

_____
_____
_____
_____
_____
_____

C. Read the following tour guide's script. Look for run-on sentences. Use revising and proofreading marks to separate the run-on sentences into simpler sentences. Then use the first letter of each sentence to find the message below.

27–35.

I will guide you on a walking tour of a park with marine animals live dolphins and whales swim in water shows I see that the seal and otter show is about to begin. Kids sometimes take part in this show. Everyone will have a chance to feed the dolphins try to walk faster so that we will be able to see the sharks on the left is a special exhibit of beautiful seashells. Under the bridge you will see a place to have lunch and rest just for ten minutes, and then we will begin the second half of the tour. Some people like the second half of the tour better than the first half.

The special message is __I__ __l i k e__ __t o u r s__ !

188

Name

An Observation Chart

You can use this form to make an observation chart for the Writing to Learn activity on page 411.

You can use these forms to make observation charts for the Writing to Learn activity on page 428.

Name

An Observation Chart

You can use these forms to make observation charts for the Critical Thinking lesson on pages 406–407.

A.

B.

Name _____

Story Starter

Name _____

Classifying

You have read "Two of a Kind" by Ron Hirschi. Imagine that while on a camping trip last fall, you took lots of photographs of the different plants, trees, and animals that you saw. Two of your favorite photos are below. On the back of this page, write about how two things in the photos are alike.

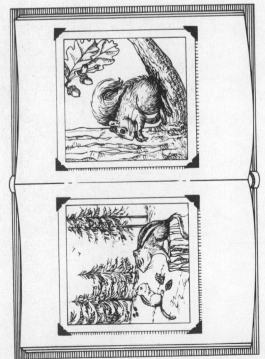

Writing Tips

◇ Use complete sentences to express your ideas. Use capital letters and punctuation carefully.

◇ Show how things are alike in a paragraph of comparison.

◇ **Focus:** Remember to classify the information in your paragraph according to likenesses. You should leave out information about differences.

◇ You may wish to reread "Two of a Kind" before you begin. Choose one thing that you like about the writer's way of writing, and try to use it in your own writing.

Unit 8 • LITERATURE • Use after the Reading-Writing Connection on pages 418—419.

Name _____

Strategy: An Observation Chart

Use this page if you choose an observation chart as a prewriting strategy for your article that compares.

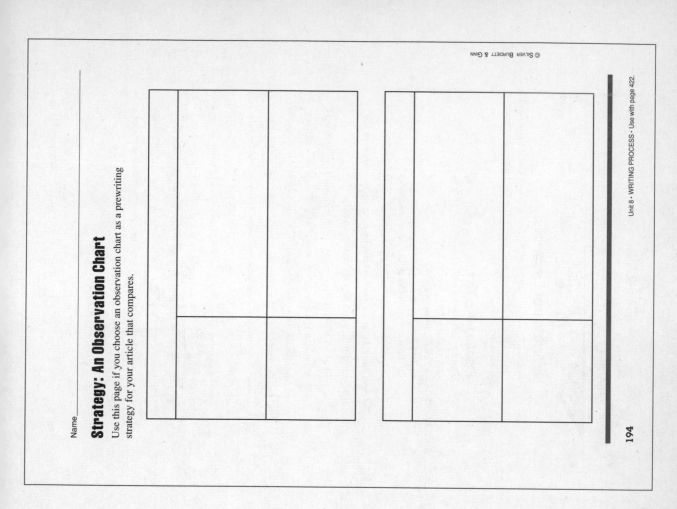

Name _____

Strategy: Sketch and Label

Use this page if you choose sketch and label as a prewriting strategy for your article that compares.

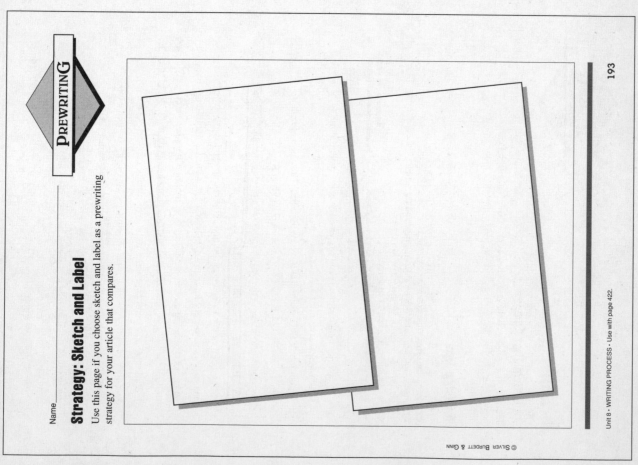

T97

Name _____

PROOFREADING PRACTICE

capital letter	small letter	indent paragraph	check spelling

An Article That Compares

Practice your proofreading on the article below. Use the proofreading tips as a guide. Don't copy the article. Use the proofreading marks to make corrections.

Proofreading Tips

Check to see that the writer has
◇ spelled words correctly.
◇ indented paragraphs.
◇ used capital letters correctly.
◇ used correct marks at the end of sentences.

¶Have you ever seen a moth or butterfly up close You may think they are very different, but they are very much alike.

First of all, butterflies and moths are both insects. Like all Insects they have three body parts. both butterflies and moths have two sets of wings that work as a single unit. They have larger front wings and
scales
smaller hind wings. The wings are covered with flat skates it is these scales that give them their beautiful colors. Most adult moths and butterflies eat nectar, which they take from flowers. they may transfer
flower
pollen from one flour to another. Both butterflies and moths belong to
group
a special groop of insects called Lepidoptera.

¶Butterflies and moths grow in much the same way. They both begin
eggs   their
life as tiny eggs. The egs hatch into caterpillars. As caterpillars, they eat constantly and shed there skin. Then they enter a stage of change when they become adult butterflies and moths.

196

Name _____

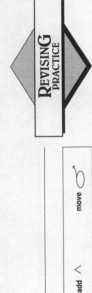

REVISING PRACTICE

cross out	move
add	

An Article That Compares

Practice your revising on the article below. Use the revising tips. Don't copy the article. Use the revising marks to cross out, add, or move words and sentences.

Revising Tips

Check to see that the writer has
◇ written an article that compares two things.
◇ made sure the reader will be able to understand the article.
◇ clearly described the likenesses of two things.
◇ used subjects and verbs that agree.
◇ used precise words for words such as give and good.

Answers will vary. Possible answers follow.

usually
People don't think of soccer and basketball as being similar sports.
many
However, these two sports are alike in ways.
are
Both soccer and basketball is played using a ball. The object of both games is to place a ball into a net. In basketball the net is under a hoop. In both sports players move the ball up and down a playing area. In soccer the
is
net is the goal at the end of the field.

Some of the same terminology are used in the two sports. In basketball and soccer a player shoots for a goal. In both sports the ball is dribbled up and down the playing area. Basketball and soccer have players known as forwards and centers. Each sport has different uniforms, though.

Basketball and soccer have some of the same penalties as well. When one of the teams in basketball makes an error, the opposing team gets a free
allowed
throw. In soccer the opposing team is given a free kick. Another similar
proper   In soccer there
penalty involves good handling of the ball. In basketball there is a penalty for moving the ball with the feet. There is a penalty for moving the ball with the hands.

195

T98

SELF-EVALUATION

UNIT 8

Writing an Article That Compares

Use this form as you do the Writing Process lesson beginning on page 420. Put a check next to each item you can answer yes to.

Revising

☐ **Purpose:** Did I write an article that compares two things?

☐ **Audience:** Will my classmates understand my article?

☐ **Focus:** Did I clearly describe likenesses?

☐ **Grammar Check:** Did I use adjectives to add specific details to my writing?

☐ **Word Choice:** Have I used precise words?

☐ **Writing◆Comparison Paragraphs:** Did I begin paragraphs with a topic sentence?

Proofreading

☐ Did I spell words correctly?

☐ Did I indent paragraphs?

☐ Did I use capital letters correctly?

☐ Did I use correct marks at the end of sentences?

☐ Did I use my best handwriting?

Publishing

☐ Have I shared my writing with readers or listeners?

☐ Has my audience shared reactions with me?

☐ Have I thought about what I especially liked in this piece of writing?

☐ Have I thought about what I would like to work on the next time?

Use the space on the other side to tell what you liked about your writing and to make notes of your plans for improvement.

What I liked about my writing:

_____

_____

_____

_____

_____

_____

_____

My plans for improvement:

_____

_____

_____

_____

_____

_____

_____

Reader's Name _____

Writer's Name _____

Writing an Article That Compares

Check Yes or No for each item. If you check No, explain or give a suggestion for improvement.

Revising

Yes   No

☐   ☐   **Purpose:** Does the article compare two things? _____

☐   ☐   **Audience:** Did I understand the article? _____

☐   ☐   **Focus:** Did the writer clearly describe likenesses? _____

☐   ☐   **Grammar Check:** Has the writer included adjectives to add specific details to the writing? _____

☐   ☐   **Word Choice:** Has the writer used precise words? _____

☐   ☐   **Writing◆Comparison Paragraphs:** Did the writer begin paragraphs with a topic sentence? _____

Proofreading

Yes   No

☐   ☐   Are words spelled correctly? _____

☐   ☐   Are paragraphs indented? _____

☐   ☐   Are capital letters used correctly? _____

☐   ☐   Are there correct marks at the end of sentences? _____

☐   ☐   Is the handwriting neat and legible? _____

200

PEER EVALUATION

UNIT 8

Reader's Name _____

Writer's Name _____

Writing an Article That Compares

Use the questions below and on the other side of this page to help you review a classmate's article that compares. Then give this form to the writer to read and save. Your comments can help the classmate improve the article that compares.

A First Reaction

Here is what I thought in general about your article that compares:

_____

_____

_____

_____

_____

A Second Reaction

Now I have looked at your article that compares more closely. I have more specific comments about it.

Here is something you have done well as a writer:

_____

_____

Here is an area that might be improved:

_____

_____

Here is an idea for improvement:

_____

_____

SAVE 199

T100

My WRITING FOLDER

Name _____

By _____

My Writer's Journal